The Catholic
Theological Union
LIBRARY
Chicago, Ill.

Tell el-Hesi
Modern military trenching and Muslim cemetery in Field I, Strata I-II

Lawrence E. Toombs

Tell el-Hesi, located in southern Israel at the juncture of the Negev Desert and the foothills of the Judean Mountains, provides an excellent opportunity for the archaeological study of the impact of a variety of physical environments on the peoples who inhabited a single site. The site has been occupied at various times from the Early Bronze Age through to the military trenching of 1948. Level one revealed the modern military trenching. Level two contained a Muslim cemetery that the author has dated to the period 1600-1800 A.D. This work analyzes the military trenching and provides the first statistical analysis of an entire cemetery in this geographic region. Using a computer code to analyze numerous attributes describing the burial cysts, skeletal data, and grave goods, the author has developed a typology of burials and drawn conclusions about the community which they represent.

More than eighty photographs of individual burials and burial goods in addition to tables, plans, and section drawings illustrate the text.

The methodology employed in this work makes it a valuable source of information for archaeologists investigating burials in any cultural context. The broader audience of anthropologists interested in burial customs will also find the book useful.

Lawrence Toombs teaches Near Eastern Studies at Wilfrid Laurier University.

WITHDRAWN

Tell el-Hesi

Modern military trenching
and
Muslim cemetery in Field I,
Strata I-II

The Joint Archaeological Expedition
to Tell el-Hesi

Volume Two

AMERICAN SCHOOLS OF ORIENTAL RESEARCH
EXCAVATION REPORTS

edited by
Eric M. Meyers

EXCAVATION REPORTS

Tell el-Hesi

Modern military trenching
and
Muslim cemetery in Field I,
Strata I-II

by
Lawrence E. Toombs

WWAROHTIW

Tell el Hesi

Modern military trenching
and
Muslim cemetery in Field I,
Strata I-II

The Joint Archaeological Expedition
to Tell el-Hesi

Volume Two

by

Lawrence E. Toombs

edited by

Kevin G. O'Connell, S.J.

Wilfrid Laurier University Press

The Catholic
Theological Union
LIBRARY
Chicago, Ill.

Canadian Cataloguing in Publication Data

Toombs, Lawrence E., 1919-
  Tell el-Hesi

Bibliography: p.
ISBN 0-88920-134-X

1. Tel-Hasi Site (Israel). 2. Cemeteries—
Israel. 3. Intrenchments. 4. Excavations
(Archeology)—Israel. I. Title.

DS110.T4T66 1985   933   C85-090024-7

Copyright © 1985

WILFRID LAURIER UNIVERSITY PRESS
Waterloo, Ontario, Canada N2L 3C5

85 86 87 88 4 3 2 1

*No part of this book may be stored in a retrieval
system, translated or reproduced in any form, by
print, photoprint, microfilm, microfiche, or any other
means, without written permission from the publisher.*

Contents

Tables

Figures

Plates

xv

Pocket Inserts

Preface

The presence of Strata I and II, the modern military trenching and the Muslim cemetery, forced the Joint Expedition to an important archaeological decision. Both strata belong to the modern period and fall into the rather vaguely defined category of "historical archaeology." Strata of this kind are frequently disregarded, or are treated very summarily, in the excavation and reporting of Near Eastern sites. In 1970 the Joint Expedition decided to excavate these strata with the same care and to report them in the same detail as the more ancient levels of the mound. This decision launched what may fairly be called a pioneering effort in the archaeology of the Palestine area. It necessitated the development of new excavation techniques and new methods of recording and computer analysis; new, that is, insofar as the treatment of this type of cemetery at a site in Israel is concerned.

The author undertook to publish these strata, not because of special qualifications, but because of the challenge of correlating and interpreting so wide ranging a body of data. The aim has been fourfold: to present in an organized form all the data on Strata I and II gathered by the expedition; to analyze this data so as to winnow the significant from the merely casual; to offer cultural conclusions, suggestions, and speculations on the basis of the analysis; and to compare the results in a preliminary way with the data from other sites and with the published work of anthropologists and travellers. The result is a report of unusual fullness, marred, no doubt, by numerous sins both of omission and of commission.

The author would not have been able even to begin this formidable task without the help of a great many people. The list of acknowledgements, if given in full, would be a long one indeed, and the absence of a name or office from this brief listing does not mean that the contribution has been forgotten or is unappreciated.

Everyone who worked on the dig between 1970 and 1975 contributed substantially to these pages. Special thanks, however, ought to be given to the expedition's anthropologist, Dr. Jeffrey Schwartz, for his work in developing the field techniques of excavation and the coded field forms for the recording of the burials; to Drs. W. J. Bennett, Jr. and D. Glenn Rose for their constructive criticisms of the manuscript at various stages of its preparation; and to the anthropologists, photographers, artists, and draftsmen whose work is incorporated here.

I am grateful also for the help of my colleagues in the scientific disciplines at Wilfrid Laurier University, and in particular to Dr. Rick Elliot for his guidance in mathematical questions, to Dr. John Kominar for his advice in chemical matters, and to Ms. Sandra Woolfrey and Mr. Robert Trotter for their work on the computer programs involved in the examination of the data.

The General Editor of the Hesi Series, Dr. Kevin G. O'Connell, S.J., has been indefatigable in ferreting out inconsistencies, infelicities, and errors in the manuscript, and has made many helpful substantive contributions to its pages. Thanks are also due to the Israeli archaeological community, especially to Dr. Ephraim Stern, for unfailing willingness to share findings and vast knowledge of Israeli sites with a visiting colleague.

A major source of support for the Hesi expedition during the four seasons on which this volume is based has been the financial contributions from the academic institutions comprising the Hesi consortium for one or more seasons. In addition to Oberlin College, which has been a member of the consortium from the first season to the present, the following institutions were members of the consortium for the seasons indicated: Ashland Theological Seminary (1973), CHERS: Consortium for Higher Education—Religious Studies (1975), College of the Holy Cross (1975), General

Theological Seminary (1973), Hartford Seminary Foundation (1970, 1971), Seabury-Western Theological Seminary (1973, 1975), Smith College (1975), The Protestant Episcopal Theological Seminary in Virginia (1975), Trinity Lutheran Seminary (1975), and Wilfrid Laurier University (1973, 1975). Several of those institutions also made financial and other contributions to the work of the Joint Expedition either in addition to their consortium payments or for seasons during which they were not consortium members. In particular, Wilfrid Laurier University generously provided staff time, equipment, and archival facilities for the expedition's photographic work, made its computers available for analysis of data, and provided generous support for the author's research as a member of its faculty. The encouragement of the administration of Wilfrid Laurier University and its policy of support for faculty research are acknowledged with gratitude.

Other institutions also providing support to the Joint Expedition for one or more of its first four seasons include Christian Theological Seminary, Golden Gate Baptist Theological Seminary, Harvard Semitic Museum, Phillips University, and Weston School of Theology.

Further major support was received by way of grants from The Smithsonian Institution (1970-73), the National Endowment for the Humanities (1973-76), and the Canada Council (1971). The latter grant made possible the development of the computer code discussed in Chapter 7.

Both staff and volunteers served at Hesi at great personal expense, and their shared spirit of generosity and dedication to a common task did much to make a difficult and often tedious operation exciting and attractive. The countless hours of contributed services in and out of the field, the travel costs paid by so many participants, and the hefty volunteer fees since 1973 together constituted the largest contribution to the total Hesi budget. Without that contribution, none of the work reported on in this volume could have been brought to successful conclusion. In addition, various contributions were received from private donors each season.

Last of all, my sincerest thanks go to my wife, Carolyn, for her faithful work on the manuscript and for the amazing equanimity with which she lived for four years almost literally in a Bedouin cemetery.

This book has been published with the help of a grant from the Social Science Federation of Canada, using funds provided by the Social Sciences and Humanities Research Council of Canada. The Joint Expedition to Tell el-Hesi has also provided support for the publication of this volume.

Abbreviations

A	articulated (skeleton)	lt	left
Aeg	Aegean	m	meter(s)
Ar.	artifacts, objects	m²	square meter(s)
Arab	Arabic	Mal.	malacological (samples), shell (including snails)
Ass	Assyrian		
Bot.	botanical (remains)	MB	Middle Bronze
bs	body sherd	MB 1	Middle Bronze 1
Byz	Byzantine	MB 2	Middle Bronze 2
C	to be coded	MB 2A	Middle Bronze 2A
ca.	circa, about	MB 2B	Middle Bronze 2B
Chal	Chalcolithic	MC	material culture
cm	centimeter(s)	MCR	material culture registry
Cyp	Cypriot	mm	millimeter(s)
D	(1) disarticulated (bones); (2) to be drawn	mort.	mortaria
		mos.	months
Dispo.	disposition	Myc	Mycenaean
E	East	N	North
EB	Early Bronze	na	not available
EB 1	Early Bronze 1	NA	neutron activation
EB 2	Early Bronze 2	NE	Northeast
EB 3	Early Bronze 3	no(s).	number(s)
EB 3A	Early Bronze 3A	nr	not recorded
EB 3B	Early Bronze 3B	NR	not registered
EB 4	Early Bronze 4	ns	not saved
EW	East-West	NS	North-South
ext	exterior	NW	Northwest
Fig(s).	Figure(s)	OR	object registry
freq	frequency	Osteo.	osteological (samples), human and animal bones
Geol.	geological (samples), stone		
Hell	Hellenistic	Ot	other
H 70 (etc.)	Hesi 1970 (etc.)	PA	articulated partial (skeleton)
i.d.	insufficient data	Pers	Persian
imp	import	Phil	Philistine
int	interior	Pl(s).	Plate(s)
I_1, I_2	Iron 1, Iron 2 (field forms only)	PR	pottery registry
km	kilometer(s)	R	to be registered
LB	Late Bronze	Rom	Roman
LB 1	Late Bronze 1	rt	right
LB 2	Late Bronze 2	S	South
LB 2A	Late Bronze 2A	SE	Southeast
LB 2B	Late Bronze 2B	Spec.	specialist('s/s/s')
		SW	Southwest

ua	unassigned	us	unstratified
ud,UD	undetermined	viz.	namely
UK	unknown	Vt	vertical
ur	unregistered	W	West
UR	unrecorded, unreported	yrs.	years

CHAPTER 1

General Introduction

The geographical location of Tell el-Hesi, its agricultural, commercial, and military importance, and the principal topographical features of the site will be fully described in Volume 4 of the Tell el-Hesi publications (Koucky, forthcoming, *passim*). The contour map of the site, reproduced here as Pl. 1, summarizes the data directly relevant to the present volume, including the position of the excavated fields and the numbering system of the areas in Fields I-III.

Volume 4 will also contain an analysis of the sequence of occupation on the site as it was known at the end of the 1975 season (Toombs, forthcoming). The present report deals only with Strata I and II of this sequence. In order to indicate the stratigraphic context of these strata, a chart showing the site's history of occupation is given in Table 1.

In the terminology employed by the Joint Expedition a field is a system of contiguous areas

Table 1.   Summary of the occupational history of Tell el-Hesi (as known at the end of the 1975 season). The strata dealt with in this volume appear at the bottom of the chart.

Period	Date	Location	Stratum or Phase Number
Chalcolithic	Ca. 3200 B.C.	Field III, Area 5	
EB I and II		No clear evidence	
EB III	27th-24th cent. B.C.	Fields IV, V, VI, and VII	
EB IV and MB		No clear evidence	
LB I		No clear evidence	
LB II		Ceramic abundant in fills	
Iron I		A few Philistine sherds in Field I. Other forms abundant.	
Iron IIA		Ceramic abundant in fills	
Iron IIB		Ceramic in fills	
Iron IIC	9th-7th cent. B.C.	Field I, Areas 41-71	Stratum VIIc-a
		Ash Layer	
	6th cent. B.C.	Field I, Areas 41-71	Stratum VI
Persian	540-332 B.C.	Field I, and succession of walls in Field III	Stratum Vd-a
Hellenistic	332-37 B.C.	Field I only	Stratum IVc-a
Late Arabic	?	Field I only	Stratum III
Late Arabic	1400-1800 A.D.	Fields I, V, and VI. Muslim cemetery.	Stratum II
Modern	After 1948 A.D.	Fields I, V, VI, and VII. Military trenching.	Stratum I

1

whose layout is designed for the systematic investigation of a particular sector of the site. Areas, the units which compose a field, are usually 5m × 5m squares, separated from one another by balks 1m wide. The size of an area is flexible, however, and may vary in accordance with the purpose which it serves in the strategy of the field. Within the areas the locus forms a still smaller unit. The term is applied to any feature (soil layer, surface, wall, installation, etc.) which was excavated as a unit and for which the area supervisor filled out a separate report sheet. Fields are designated by Roman numerals, areas by Arabic numerals, and loci by Arabic numbers of three digits. A particular locus is, therefore, fully identified by a series of three numbers, separated by periods. Thus, I.22.075 indicates Locus 75 in Area 22 of Field I.

Of the seven fields opened by the Joint Expedition four contained material relevant to Strata I and II. Stratum I, the modern military trenching, occurs in Fields I, V, VI, and VII. Stratum II, the Muslim cemetery, is found in Fields I, V, and VI.

A brief description of each of these fields will show their extent and relative importance for the two strata under discussion. The terminology used for the various topographical features of the site has been worked out by F. L. Koucky and is shown in Fig. 1.

The field of greatest significance for both strata is clearly Field I. It comprises all the work done by the expedition on the mound proper, also referred to as the upper city or acropolis. The field consists of fifteen areas, oriented north-south and east-west. The northern line of four areas (1, 2, 3, 4) parallels the southern edge of Bliss's excavation in the northeast quadrant of the acropolis (Pl. 1-H). The eastern line parallels the eastern edge of the mound, where it falls away steeply to the Wadi Hesi (Areas 1, 11, 21, 31, 41, 51, 61, 71). The last two areas in this line (61, 71) extend beyond the relatively flat summit of the acropolis down the southern slope of the mound. Strata I-II are absent from these two areas.

In Field I, therefore, the upper two strata were

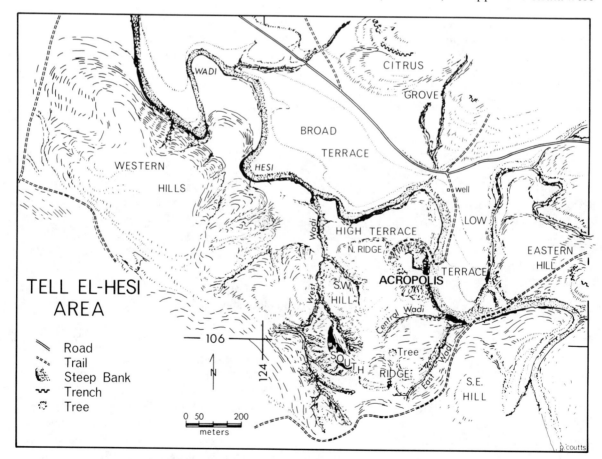

Fig. 1.   Map of the topography of Tell el-Hesi, giving the nomenclature used for the various physical features of the site. Drawn by P. Coutts from an original by F. L. Koucky.

investigated in whole or in part in thirteen areas (1, 2, 3, 4, 11, 12, 13, 21, 22, 31, 32, 41, 51). The position and numbering of these areas is shown on Pl. 1. Stratum I has been cleared in all thirteen areas, but in Areas 4 and 13 the excavation of Stratum II was not completed. Thus the full sequence of both strata is available from eleven areas or, when the internal balks are removed, over a horizontal extent of 354m².

The lower city is defined by the north ridge, the southwest hill, the south ridge, the east wadi, the Wadi Hesi, and the eastern and northern slopes of the acropolis (see Fig. 1). The southern limit of the lower city, the southern ridge, is formed by three prominent sand dunes, their tops consolidated by occupational remains (Pl. 1-D). The presence of shallow depressions on all three dunes shows that Stratum I trenching is found on the high ground of the southern ridge as well as on the acropolis. Fields V, VI, and VII were probes into the Early

Bronze Age remains on the south ridge. They were opened in order to provide information upon which large-scale excavation of the Early Bronze settlement of the lower city could be based.

Field V, on the central hillock, began as an area 7m × 2m, but, as the unexpected depth of occupation became clear, it was contracted to a deep probe 2m × 1m. Field VI, on the eastern dune, was a 2m-wide probe down the southern slope. Field VII was a probe only 0.50m wide on the southern slope of the western dune. In Fields V and VI graves of Stratum II were encountered, but the limited exposure in Field VII provided no material from either Stratum I or Stratum II. More extensive excavations of the cemeteries in Fields V and VI, begun in 1979 and 1977, are beyond the scope of the present study. They will be published in full by Dr. J. Kenneth Eakins in a subsequent volume of the Hesi series.

PART I: STRATUM I

The Military Trenching

CHAPTER 2

Stratum I: The Military Trenching

General Structure of the Trenching

When the Joint Expedition to Tell el-Hesi began its work in 1970 evidence of partially filled trenches was visible on the surface in the form of an interconnected system of shallow depressions with gently sloping sides and slightly concave bottoms (Pls. 2, 3). Since the trenches were almost filled with wind-blown earth and other debris, the system had clearly been out of use for several years at least. Side supports of corrugated iron are still present in the comparable trench system at nearby Lahav, and are a common feature of military trenches still in use in Israel. Such supports are absent from the Hesi trenches, although they would have been a desirable installation in view of the loose earth of the site. Either the trenches were hastily constructed, or the supports were removed after the system fell into disuse.

The general configuration of the trenches can be seen in Fig. 2, adapted from a drawing by F. L. Koucky in which he had superimposed the grid of excavated squares on an aerial photograph of the site taken in 1949. The trench system consists of two loops. The northernmost loop flanks the cut made by F. J. Bliss in the northeast corner of the acropolis during his 1891-92 excavations (Bliss, 1894). It has two clearly defined firing points on its western side, overlooking the lower city. Two less distinct positions appear at the northwest and northeast angles of the loop. Along the east side, adjacent to Bliss's cut, the photograph suggests only one firing point, near the center of the vertical face of the cut. The northern loop of trenching lies entirely outside the excavated areas.

The southern loop cuts every excavated area except Areas 1 and 32. It has one large firing posi-tion on the north, overlooking the south edge of Bliss's cut; another on the east side, commanding the center of the steep drop-off into the Wadi Hesi; and a third near the wadi face at the south-east angle of the mound. These firing points are built well out from the main loop of trenching, to which they are connected by crawl trenches. On the south and west of the southern loop the firing points are not well defined. There is a suggestion of one in the center of the south side, and of another at the southwest corner of the summit.

The northern and southern loops are united by a single trench, running almost east-west through Areas 3 and 4. A subsidiary trench extends southward from the northern loop, and a similar, though shorter, trench extends westward from the southern loop, with a circular pit at its western extremity. The two subsidiary trenches virtually enclose a roughly oval area, protected to the west by an isolated firing point. The central location of this oval area and its accessibility to all parts of the trench system indicate that it was the command post of the defenses on the summit of the mound.

In contrast to the regular occurrence of natural strong points in the mountainous regions of Israel, the coastal plain and northern Negev afford defensive positions only along the wadi systems and on the artificial mounds of ancient cities (Lorch, 1961, 231-32). The trench system on Tell el-Hesi takes advantage of the high ground to provide a field of fire covering the relatively flat surrounding terrain in all directions. The principal dead ground is to the south, where the southern ridge forms a partial barrier. To cover this area isolated pits, probably observation posts rather than set defensive positions, were sited along the southern edge of the ridge.

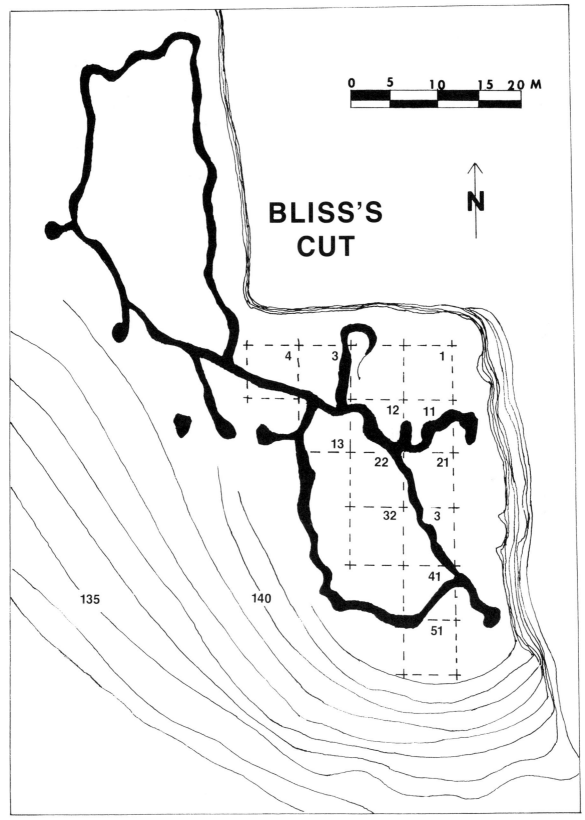

Fig. 2.   The military trenching on the summit of Tell el-Hesi (Field I). The drawing is adapted from an original made by F. L. Koucky from an aerial photograph on which the grid of excavated squares was superimposed.

History of the Defense System

Local reports tell of fighting in the Hesi area during the British advance from Egypt in October and November 1917. The main Turkish defenses, manned by about 180,000 troops, lay along a line from Gaza to Beersheva. On October 31, Beersheva fell, and after a week of heavy fighting Gaza capitulated. The Turks established their next line of defense along the Nahal Sorek, well north of the Hesi region. Within the first few days after the fall of Beersheva the tide of battle must have rolled past Tell el-Hesi. The 1917 fighting was, therefore, probably part of a Turkish rearguard action, rather than the defense of a fortified position, and left no permanent marks on the site. This conclusion is supported by the fact that aerial photographs taken prior to 1948 give no indication of a trench system on the tell. The trenches excavated by the Joint Expedition must have originated during Israel's 1947-49 War of Independence (see Fig. 3).

along the coastal road. Bypassing Kfar Darom and Nirim, where initial attacks failed, the Egyptian forces advanced quickly to Yad Mordecai. After a fierce battle lasting six days, the settlement fell, and the road to Tel Aviv, 40km to the north, lay open to the Egyptians. The main obstacle to further advance was the demolished bridge at Ashdod, blown up by sappers of the Jewish Givati Brigade. Checked by this barrier, the Egyptians dug in around Ashdod. Subsequently, heavy fighting took place along the coastal highway, but the Egyptians made no further northward advance.

While the Egyptian troops were moving up the coastal road, a parallel column advanced from Rafa through Beersheva, Hebron, and Bethlehem to the southern outskirts of Jerusalem. The forces on the coastal road were linked to those on the Beersheva-Bethlehem line by a force of about 15,000 well-equipped troops, holding a chain of fortified positions from Majdal on the coast to Bet Gubrin. The principal strong points were the

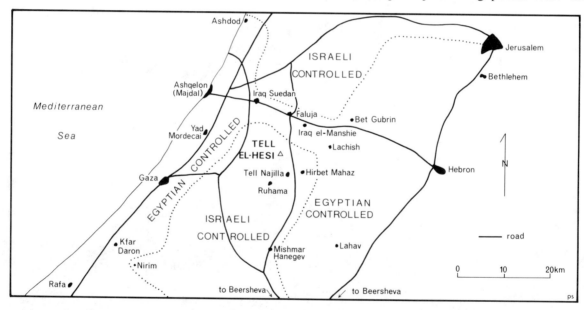

Fig. 3. Map showing the military situation in the Tell el-Hesi region after the "Battles of Hirbet Mahaz." The spelling of proper names here and in the text follows the usage of Lorch, 1961. Original by L. E. Toombs.

The preliminary reports (see Bibliography) reflect uncertainty as to the origin of the trenching, describing it variously as Turkish, Egyptian, Israeli, or some combination of the three. The evidence of the aerial photographs and the accounts of military historians, however, indicate clearly that the trenching was dug by the Israelis in 1948.

In May 1948 an Egyptian army moved out of bases at El-Arish and Rafa and marched north

police post at Iraq Suedan, which earned the ominous nickname "the Monster on the Hill," Faluja, and Iraq el-Manshie, near Tell Gat, where the present city of Kiryat Gat is located. The command center of this line was at Faluja. The Faluja line formed an "isolation belt" controlling the roads leading north from the Negev and cutting off the Jewish forces operating south of the line from their supply bases to the north. An airlift of arms and equipment from Akir to a newly-constructed air strip at Ruhama (Operation *Avak*) provided a temporary solution to the problem. The more permanent resolution was, of course, to pierce the isolation belt by direct assault and thus open an overland route to the north. To accomplish this Operation Ten Plagues, later known as Operation *Yoav*, was planned.

The projection of Operation *Yoav* and the existence of the vital air transport base at Ruhama brought Tell el-Hesi into the strategic picture. The ruins at Hirbet Mahaz and its neighboring tells were not occupied by either side. However, if the Egyptians seized them, they could bring the Ruhama air base under artillery fire. Moreover, it was important to the Israeli forces to strengthen the northeast angle of their territory, opposite the Egyptian fortifications at Iraq el-Manshie. The prominent mound of Tell el-Hesi, and its satellites, particularly Tell Quneitira (Keshet), adjacent to the north-south road, were vital to both sides.

Early in October 1948 the Israeli Yiftach Brigade occupied Hirbet Mahaz and its neighboring tells. This action drew an immediate Egyptian counterattack, and a battle boiled up along the north-south road. The Egyptians launched seven attacks, and the key point at Hirbet Mahaz changed hands twice. During the fighting the Israeli headquarters was at Tel Najilla (Tell en-Nagila), about 5km south of Tell el-Hesi. The command post was strafed by eight Spitfires of the Egyptian air force. When the "Battles of Hirbet Mahaz," which Lorch describes as "among the most bitter local engagements of the entire war" (Lorch, 1961, 408), died down, the Hirbet and its surrounding tells were firmly in Israeli hands. The action secured the Ruhama airfield, and effectively denied the road from Faluja to Beersheva to the Egyptians.

When Operation *Yoav* developed, the forces in the Negev were not employed against the isolation belt. They were too few in numbers and too difficult to supply. The main attack, therefore, came from the north. After an unsuccessful assault on Iraq el-Manshie, the Israelis concentrated on breaking the isolation belt west of Iraq Suedan. The success of the operation opened an interior road, parallel to the coastal highway, and ended the isolation of the Negev. At about the same time, the Bet Gubrin end of the isolation belt was breached, and the "belt" became a pocket in which the Egyptian forces at Iraq Suedan, Faluja,

and Iraq el-Manshie were surrounded and sealed off. The pocket shrank still further with the capture of Iraq Suedan on November 9, but the Egyptian troops continued to hold Faluja and Iraq el-Manshie until the end of hostilities.

The trench system on Tell el-Hesi was most probably established at the beginning of the "Battles of Hirbet Mahaz," and figured directly in the fighting during that action. This accounts for the relatively hasty construction of the trenches. During Operation *Yoav* and later fighting, it was securely within Israeli-held positions and functioned as an observation and support position in the front against Faluja and Iraq el-Manshie.

The Trenching as Excavated

Pl. 4, based on the daily top plans of the area supervisors, illustrates the system of trenches as found in the excavated areas. The widths shown on the drawing are those given for the bottom of the trench. The drawing agrees well with the reconstruction based on the 1949 aerial photograph (Fig. 2). Most of the discrepancies are the result of the difficulty of distinguishing, both on the aerial photograph and in the excavation process, between the mounds of earth thrown out when the trench was dug and the trench proper. In order to illustrate the variety of cross-sectional shapes taken by the trenching, three sections through the trenches are given as insets in Pl. 4.

A detailed description of each locus associated with the trenching would be repetitious in the extreme, and would be of relatively little value, since the contents of the trench fill are largely a matter of accident. A general treatment, applicable to the trench system as a whole, will, therefore, be given first. This will be followed by a discussion of the trenches area by area. Here the loci assigned in each area to the trench system will be listed with a brief description. This will be followed by a note on the distinctive features of the trenching in the area under consideration. For points not mentioned in the text, it may be assumed that the trenching in the area conforms to the general description.

General Features of the Trenching

Dimensions

The width of the trenches at the bottom varied between 0.35m and 0.70m. One or both sides of the trench usually sloped gently inwards toward the bottom, so that the width of the top of the trench was between 0.65m and 1.25m. Measured from the present ground surface the trenches were 0.80m to 1.15m deep. The preserved depth of the trenches was thus below the chest level of the average man. The earthen parapets, formed by the throw-out from the trench, would certainly have eroded down over the years, rendering the effective depth less at the time of excavation than when the trenches were in use. Moreover, sand bags may have been used to give the trenches greater depth. Even allowing for these factors, the trenches were both narrow and shallow. This suggests that most of the trenching in the excavated areas functioned as a communications network, connecting the various firing points, and that anyone passing through it did so at a crawl or in a stooped position.

Varieties of Cross-section

The account of the dimensions, given above, indicates the profile of a normal trench section. A typical example of this configuration appears in Section A-A¹ (Pl. 4). In a few parts of the system, however, notably in Areas 11 and 41, the bottom of the trench had the normal shape, but the upper part sloped outward rapidly to a width at the top of up to 2.50m (sections B-B¹ and C-C¹, Pl. 4). This phenomenon may have been the accidental result of erosion, but was more likely provision for a rifleman or light machine gunner, firing from the prone position. The preserved flooring of the trenches was tramped earth. A good deal of decayed wood and some partially decomposed wooden slats were found in the trenches. These may have been the remains of wooden duckboards, laid over the earthen floor to minimize the effects of mud. It is less likely that they were used as side supports for the trench.

The military trenching cut deeply into earlier stratigraphy. It penetrated below the level of the graves of infants and children, and its bottom is at or just above the level of the deepest adult burials. Section C-C¹ (Pl. 4) was cut in the midst of a veritable nest of graves and is below the base of all but the deepest. The trenches thus virtually destroyed the Stratum II cemetery along the course of the system. The trench section shown in B-B¹ cut through Strata II, III, and IV, and into Va levels. The trenching, therefore, constituted a major intrusion, complicating the excavation of Strata II, III, IV, and Va.

Varieties of Trench Use

Two specialized sections of the trench system have already been identified: the crawl trenches used for communication, and the widened sections employed as firing positions. In Areas 11 and 13, and perhaps also in Areas 41 and 51 (see below, p. 13), bay-like projections jutted out from the main trench. No sections through these projections are available. They may have been lay-bys to allow soldiers to pass one another in the trench. The high incidence of ash in the bays, however, raises the possibility that they were used as cooking and eating areas. Unfortunately, none of the principal firing points shown in Fig. 2 lay within the excavated areas.

Nature and Contents of the Primary Fill

Sections A-A¹, B-B¹, and C-C¹ (Pl. 4) all show the same profile of soil layers within the trenching. A shallow layer of packed earth overlay the original floor of the trench. Above this were several layers of finely sorted, water-deposited material, displaying layering caused by successive flooding and drying. Several of the area supervisors reported evidence that the trenches were redug at least twice. This evidence included both irregularities in the deposition of the water-laid layers, which did not directly overlie one another, and the manner in which adjacent soil layers were cut. The evidence was slight and somewhat ambiguous, since a widening of the trench would inevitably have destroyed the earlier excavation.

The water-laid layers and the packed earth below may be identified as primary fill, because they appear to have been deposited before the decay of the trench system began. Most of the artifacts from the primary fill layers are useless for dating purposes. Almost every trench locus contained sherds from all occupational periods represented on the site, usually broken into small fragments. Lithic specimens were common. Bones, both animal and human, occurred frequently. The human bones were undoubtedly washed in from the graves cut by the trench. Among the animal bones there was a very high incidence of sheep/goat. Some of these bones may possibly represent the diet of the soldiers using the trench, but this cannot be demonstrated. Other objects of less frequent occurrence are an occasional bead, a few pieces of badly corroded iron, some ceramic loom weights of uncertain date, one or two pieces of worked bone, ceramic oven fragments, and a few projectile points. All these probably predated the trench system and were present in it as accidental ingredients. A more significant element of the primary fill was the fine ash and larger pieces of charcoal reported from virtually every locus, indicating that a good deal of cooking was done in the trench system and that the debris of the fires was distributed throughout the water-laid layers.

Nature and Contents of the Secondary Fill

The deposit overlying the water-laid layers was in the main finely sorted earth, laid down by the action of the wind. It contained only a few pebbles. Scattered through it were ceramic fragments and miscellaneous modern garbage, thrown in while the filling process was going on. The secondary fill contained also a large amount of decayed and decaying vegetable matter, including pieces of wood and the roots of shrubs and of one small tree. Very rarely was there evidence of puddling due to water collecting in the partially filled trench.

The color of the primary and secondary fill was remarkably uniform. The Munsel color identification was 10YR 6/3 ("pale brown"), the color of the pervasive loess of the Hesi region. The surface soil was loess with a sparse growth of grass and shrubs.

The Trenching by Area (see Pl. 4)

Area 1

Area 1 had no Stratum I trenching.

Area 2

Loci involved are:
Locus 2.002—both the primary and the secondary fill within the trench.
Locus 2.003—the original flooring of the trench, 0.02m in thickness.
These loci represent part of the crawl trench leading from the northern section of the loop to the firing point near the center of the south face of Bliss's cut (see Fig. 2). Area 2 proper contained only the eastern side of the trench, the remainder of which was excavated as Loci 3.038 and 3.096.

Area 3

The loci involved are:
Locus 3.002—a probe to define the edges of the trench.

Locus 3.003—the primary and secondary fill of the trench. The area supervisor reported evidence that the earth from the excavation of the trench was thrown up to form a parapet 0.50-0.60m wide on the north side of the trench.
Locus 3.038—the continuation of Loci 2.002/3 in Area 3 proper.
Locus 3.096—the continuation of Loci 2.002/3 in the balk between Areas 2 and 3. This locus, which involved both primary and secondary fill, contained three artifacts of possible chronological interest: a paper wrapper for army rations, a cartridge case (undated), and the seal from a yogurt preparation with the trade name "*Zivdah*," a brand name introduced about 1966. The seal was found immediately above the primary fill. It is uncertain whether the object blew or was thrown into the trench after it went out of use, or whether it was associated with the last use of the trench system.

Area 4

Area 4 contained part of the northern section of the loop of trenching. This section probably functioned as a communication trench. Section A-A[1], drawn by the area supervisor, Y. Lehavi (1971), is taken through Loci 4.002/3.
The loci involved are:
Locus 4.002—a probe dug to locate the edges of the trench.
Locus 4.003—the primary and secondary fill of the trench. The debris of this locus contained food and sardine cans, aluminum foil, and a Philip Morris cigarette package. The locus cut in half a Hellenistic ceramic oven, many fragments of which were found in the trench fill.

Area 11

The loci involved are:
Locus 11.002—the secondary fill in the trench.
Locus 11.003—the primary fill. The locus was water-laid silt, deposited on an ash-filled layer which, in turn, overlay a compact earth surface. The ash layer included an unusually large amount of hardwood charcoal. In the center of the area the trench widened on both sides to form a rectangular bay, tentatively identified above as a lay-by, which may have doubled as a cooking area. The large amount of charcoal in the locus tends to support the latter part of the hypothesis.
The trenching in Area 11 was part of a branch trench running eastward from the main loop to a firing point near the wadi face.

Area 12

Only one locus is involved. Locus 12.010 included the entire contents of the trench. The area supervisor noted that the bottom of the trench contained water-deposited layers, while the higher fill was of about the same consistency but included numerous pebbles. The fill contained a cartridge case, an unidentified iron fragment, and several pieces of leather. The upper part of the fill had a great deal of decayed and partially decayed vegetable matter, and the stump and roots of a small tree. The incidence of ash was again high, and numerous pieces of charcoal appeared.

The trenching in Area 12 was a portion of the eastern side of the loop. In the center of the square it was somewhat wider than normal (0.95m), perhaps to accommodate a rifleman.

Area 13

The loci involved are:

Loci 13.010, 13.011, and 13.012—probes to identify the limits of the trench.

Locus 13.017—the primary and secondary fill of the trench.

Locus 13.019—a probe made during the excavation of Locus 13.017, when the limits of the trench became uncertain.

The primary fill consisted of layers of water-deposited sediment in which were numerous thin ash pockets. In this layer several cartridge cases and a few fragments of paper along with several cigarette butts were found. The secondary fill was mostly loess, but included a good deal of finely sorted brick debris. The area supervisor concluded that the trench had been widened during its period of use, but did not give the evidence on which the conclusion was based.

The field sheets and top plans of Area 13 show that the grave of a child (Locus 13.007) was cut into the trench. This observation, if accurate, indicates that the burial was made after the trench had been filled in and leads to the conclusion that a few burials took place in the Hesi cemetery after 1949.

The trenching in Area 13 was on the west side of the loop where the subsidiary trench leading to the presumed command post began. Excavation revealed a lay-by, extending southward off the trench, but not shown in Fig. 2. These features suggest that the segment of trenching in Area 13 came in for a good deal of use, and the contents of the fill bear out that assumption.

Area 21

The loci involved are:

Locus 21.002—the primary and secondary fill of the trench. The only distinctive artifact of the locus was a badly decayed orange peel! Numerous ash layers were found, concentrated in the wider central part of the locus. Also in this widened section, at the point marked x in Pl. 4, a group of stones was arranged in a benchlike way against the east side of the trench. It probably functioned as a step to allow easier observation to the east. The presence of this step was evidence that the trench system anticipated attack from the east, an expectation which agrees with the tactical situation of the "Battles of Hirbet Mahaz." The widened central part of the locus would have provided a firing position for a rifleman or light machine gunner near the center of the east side of the loop.

Locus 21.004—the original floor of the trench and the earth immediately below it.

Locus 21.102—the secondary fill in the trench where it crossed the balk between Areas 21 and 31.

Locus 21.103—the primary fill beneath locus 21.102.

Area 22

The loci involved are:

Locus 22.046—primary and secondary fill from the tiny segment of trench in the northeast corner of the area.

Locus 22.053—primary and secondary fill in the trench in the balk between Areas 22 and 12. The locus cut through the burial of a child (Locus 22.127), removing everything but the skull.

Locus 22.132—further clearing of trench in balk between Areas 22 and 12.

Locus 22.195—clearing of trench in balk between Areas 22 and 21.

Area 31

The loci involved are: 31.002, 31.003, 31.004, 31.006, 31.008, 31.010, 31.012, 31.041. The large number of loci assigned to the trenching was the result of sectioning along the length of the trench from north to south. Loci 31.002 and 31.003 represented secondary fill, and the other loci were probes into primary fill. The fill and its contents corresponded to the descriptions given for other areas. In Locus 31.010 a rectangular sheet of tin (0.16m × 0.25m) was uncovered at the point marked y in Pl. 4. It is not clear whether this was an accidental deposit in the trench, or whether it once formed part of a side support or roofing for the trench.

The trenching in Area 31 was part of the east side of the loop. Its width indicates that it served mainly for communication.

Area 32

There was no Stratum I trenching in Area 32.

Area 41

The loci involved are:
Locus 41.006—secondary fill in the northeast corner of the area.
Locus 41.011—primary fill underlying Locus 41.006. This locus ran directly over and partially destroyed Burial 41.104.
Locus 41.098—secondary trench fill in the southeast quadrant of the area.
Locus 41.131—primary fill below Locus 41.098.
Area 41 contained two segments of the eastern side of the loop of trenching. Fig. 2 shows the junction of these two segments within Area 41, but excavation revealed that they met outside the area to the east, where a communication trench branched off to a firing point near the wadi face (compare Fig. 2 and Pl. 4). The reason for the discrepancy between the two drawings is the large amount of throw-out at this point, which gave a confused impression of the actual course of the trench.

The southern part of the loop angled through the southeast quadrant of Area 41. Several cartridge cases, dated 1956 and 1957, were found in its primary fill (Locus 41.131), along with pieces of tinfoil and plastic bags.

Section B-B¹ lay along the main east balk section, where the trenching of Loci 41.098/131 entered the balk (Pl. 4). Section C-C¹ shows where the same segment of trenching entered the south balk (Pl. 4).

Just to the east of trench-section C-C¹ a peculiar installation appeared at the point marked z on the plan (Pl. 4). It was a shallow pit or trench filled with loose earth. Its eastern limits were outside the excavated area. The installation was covered with wooden slats, placed close together and in a good state of preservation. A layer of rough field stones lay on the slatting. The full extent and shape of the installation is uncertain, and the excavated portion had no direct connection with the

main trench. Indeed, the layering in the section indicates that the pit/trench (Locus 51.105) was earlier than the main trench (Loci 41.131/51.120, Pl. 4), and was covered by throw-out from it. The good state of preservation of the wood indicates that the pit was of recent origin. Its function is unknown, and guesses range from part of an earlier trench system to an army latrine.

Area 51

The loci involved are:
Locus 51.005—secondary trench fill in a probe in the northwest corner of the area.
Locus 51.006—throw-out from the trench on the north side.
Locus 51.009—secondary fill in the trench. This locus yielded a miscellaneous collection of modern artifacts: a cigarette filter, the lid of a tin can, a piece of photographic film, and two cartridge cases, one of which was dated 1957. It also contained charcoal flecks and thorn branches.
Locus 51.010—primary fill in the trench, containing several cartridge cases, one of them dated 1959.
Locus 51.021—primary fill in the trench, continuing Locus 51.010 near the north balk.
Locus 51.062—same as Locus 51.021. The locus contained aluminum foil and several cartridge cases.
Locus 51.104—secondary fill in the trench where it passed through the north balk; continues Locus 51.021 through the balk.
Locus 51.105—see description under Area 41, above.
Locus 51.120—primary fill in the trench below Locus 51.104; continues Loci 51.021/062 through the balk.
The trench in Area 51 belonged to the eastern end of the south section of the loop. The turn to the north came just at the balk between Areas 41 and 51 (Fig. 2 and Pl. 4). This section of the trench served mainly for communication.

Period of Use of the Trench System

The origin of the trench system during the Israeli War of Independence (1948) seems secure. How long the trenches were kept open is less certain. The "Zivdah" cap is suspect evidence, because it occurs so high in the fill and because, when the writer visited the site in 1969, the trenches were filled to the same level as when excavation began, and bushes and one small tree were growing in them. The military command in the region said that the trenches were used after 1949 for troop training, but was unsure when they ceased to be used for that purpose. The most convincing evidence for the end of use for the trench system is the cartridge cases. Old cases would be cleaned out while the trench was in use, so that the cartridge cases should in the main represent the last period of use for the trenches. All the datable casings reported were from 1956-59. It is safe to conclude, therefore, that the trench system went out of use during or soon after 1959.

PART II: STRATUM II

The Muslim Cemetery

CHAPTER 3

Archaeological Context

Muslim cemeteries are frequently found on the summits of Palestinian tells, where the close-packed graves must be dealt with before the excavators can safely penetrate the more ancient levels below. Such a cemetery is often associated with the shrine of a Muslim holy man (*weli*), which stands either adjacent to or within the limits of the cemetery. The shrine is not infrequently located near a large tree. Six examples, all situated on or near the Coastal Plain, may be regarded as typical of these cemeteries.

Tel Gat

Tel Gat (Tell Gath or Tell esh-Sheikh Aḥmed el-ʿAreini), about 9km northeast of Tell el-Hesi, displays so many parallels to the Hesi cemetery that the excavator's brief description is worth quoting in full.

> Even before the beginning of excavations it was known that the ruined *wely* (the tomb of *Sheykh ʾAhmed el-ʿAreyny* at the south-eastern end of the *tell*) was surrounded by a small Moslem cemetery, the date of which was not clear. It was not, at any rate, in use recently, since the cemetery of the neighboring village, *ʾIraq el-Manshiyye*, is situated to the west of the settlement, south of the Bet-Govrin−Ascalon highway. However, to the archaeologists' surprise it became evident, immediately upon the beginning of excavations in Area A, that the entire area is densely covered with graves; and with the deepening of excavations it was discovered that the graves penetrated deep into the ground; frequently three or four superimposed burials were found one on top of the other, the later disturbing the earlier inhumations. As a result, the clearing and cleaning of the graves in the area (to a depth of 3 m. or more under the surface of the ground) continued for almost the entire first season of excavations (see pl. I:1).

> This cemetery, that served the people in the vicinity for an extended period, was dated to the VIIth-XVth centuries C.E., to the extent that it was possible to do so with the help of the scanty remains in the graves, mainly small glass perfume bottles and some jewellery made of glass and bronze (see pl. I:2). In all about 100 individual graves were uncovered and investigated. (Yeivin, 1961, 3-4.)

The first plate referred to in the above quotation shows a skeleton resting on the earth floor of a stone-lined grave. It lies on its right side with its knees slightly flexed and its eyes directed to the south. The head is in the west of the grave. These are precisely the characteristics of the Hesi burials of Stratum II. The grave illustrated by Yeivin is, however, more sharply rectangular in outline, and is of more careful construction than those found at Tell el-Hesi. The second plate gives a typical collection of artifacts from the graves of the cemetery, including bracelets and rings, earrings, beads, and metal disks, as well as a group of small glass bottles.

The long chronological range allowed by the excavator is probably due to the presence in the same cemetery of glass vessels of comparatively early form and glass bracelets of relatively modern appearance. It is worthy of note that no glass bottles were found in the Hesi burials. This fact, on its face value, would tend to place the Hesi cemetery toward the end of the range suggested by Yeivin.

Tel Nagila

At Tel Nagila (Najilla), 7.5km southwest of Tell el-Hesi, a large tamarisk, similar to the tree which dominates the south ridge at Hesi, stands near the remains of a rectangular structure, as yet unexcavated. This building is probably the ruins of a large *weli*. The excavators do not report the presence of a cemetery at Nagila, but M. V. Guérin reports that at the time of his visit to the site the summit was occupied by "un vaste cimetière musulman" (Guérin, 1888, 295). In the flat central part of the tell are the remains of a huge rectangular building, identified as a *khan* or caravanserai and dated to the twelfth to fifteenth centuries A.D. (Amiran and Eitan, 1965, 113-17). On Guérin's evidence the *khan* was an inconspicuous ruin, but the cemetery was still in use in his day. Unfortunately, he does not tell us whether or not the graves of the cemetery overlay the ruins of the *khan*. The cemetery clearly postdated the *khan*, however, and must have been established between the sixteenth and the mid-nineteenth centuries, and probably between 1700 and 1800.

Tel Gezer

The magnificent mound of Gezer on the edge of the northern Shephelah lies just under 30km northwest of Tell el-Hesi. Volume 1 of the Gezer reports indicates the presence of a Muslim cemetery and an associated *weli* on the western peak of the tell (Dever, Lance, and Wright, 1970, 1). When published, the results of the excavations in Gezer, Field VI, in which the cemetery is located, should provide another important link in the chain of evidence under consideration.

Tel Zeror

Tel Zeror, 10km from the Mediterranean east of Hadera, consists of two peaks separated by a narrow valley (Ohata, 1967, Pl. 3). The northeastern peak is the site of an extensive Muslim cemetery. The larger southwestern peak contains the remains of an Arab village, dated on the basis of green and yellow glazed pottery found in association with a stone-paved courtyard to the Middle Arab Period, 1200-1400 A.D. (Ohata, 1966, 19, 22-23, 32-33).

The graves of the cemetery were found at a depth of up to 1.50m below the present surface. They cut deeply into earlier remains. Some interments were simple earth burials; others were stone-lined; others were both stone-lined and stone-covered. Later graves frequently cut into and partially destroyed earlier burials. None of the graves had stone bottoms. All the skeletons "lie on the side at full length, the skull pointing always to the east or to the west and the face turned southward, namely towards Mecca." "The graves contained almost no accompanying additional articles with the dead except for a few accessories for women, iron or bronze bracelets, rings with stone inset, beads, etc." (Ohata, 1966, 3).

The two capped and lined graves shown in Ohata, 1966, Pl. X, could have been found in the Hesi cemetery. The plate indicates also that the graves must have been at the bottoms of shafts, since in both cases the capstones of the grave are well below the tops of Hellenistic walls. Volume 2 of the Tel Zeror report illustrates one of these burials after the stone covering was removed. The skeletal position, except for the bent left arm, is typical of that found in the Hesi cemetery (Ohata, 1967, Pl. XII).

The excavator made the logical assumption that the cemetery and the buildings on the southwestern peak were contemporary, since the cemetery of the recent village of Khirbet et-Tell Dhurur lay elsewhere on the site. This gives the cemetery a chronological range from the thirteenth to the fifteenth century A.D.

Tel Mevorakh

At Tel Mevorakh, some 11km north of Tel Zeror, an expedition under the direction of Ephraim Stern uncovered a cemetery consisting of about forty-two graves, covering almost the entire surface of the site (Stern, 1978, 4-9). Three principal types of graves were identified: Type A, simple earth graves; Type B, rectangular graves lined and covered with robbed building stones; Type D, burials of infants in pottery jars. Type C consists of a single burial, that of an adult under a stone cairn.

Graves of Types A and B were at the bottom of deep shafts, which penetrated into and partially destroyed the Persian Period remains. All the graves were oriented east-west and the skeletons faced south. Graves were often superimposed on or dug into one another. The objects included with the burials consisted of bracelets, earrings, and pendants of bronze, iron, and glass, and beads of semi-precious stones and glass.

One grave of Type A was dated on the basis of a twelfth-century-A.D. coin and three glass plaques to the Crusader Period. The excavator suggested that the stone-built cists date to the late twelfth and thirteenth centuries A.D., and the simple earth graves to "the nineteenth century onwards" (Stern, 1978, 9). No direct dating evidence was available for the simple earth burials, however, and "it is difficult to determine whether the different burial types have any chronological significance" (Stern, 1978, 9). The Type A and Type B burials may in fact have been contemporary, as they proved to be at Hesi. The report also suggested that the cemetery may have belonged to the Crusader occupants of Caesarea. If this is indeed the case, the orientation of the bodies indicates that they were Muslims (servants of the Crusaders?) rather than Christians.

Caesarea Maritima

The dunes south of the Crusader castle at Caesarea Maritima, about 5km southwest of Tel Mevorakh, were used as a burial ground over a long period of time. The cemetery had three principal phases: a pre-Crusader, a Crusader, and a post-Crusader period of use (Toombs, 1978, 228-29). In the first and third phases the graves were mostly capped and lined with building stones purloined from the Byzantine remains. The bodies were extended on the right side with the head to the west and the face toward Mecca.

The dating of the cemetery awaits further study of the burials, but the Caesarea cemetery may well contain both the earliest and the latest burials of the type under consideration. The pre-Crusader examples may go back to near the beginning of the Islamic period, and the latest graves in the loose sand near the top of the dunes may belong to the Muslim settlement established in 1879 and abandoned in 1948.

Conclusions

The foregoing discussion provides an archaeological context into which the cemetery at Tell el-Hesi may be placed. It indicates the existence of many such cemeteries whose locations are unknown to the present inhabitants of the region. Stern (1978, 8) mentions similar, but unpublished, cemeteries at 'Atlit, Beer-Sheba, and Tel Sera'. These cemeteries conform to a common pattern of burial practices which was highly conservative, and hence extremely long-lived.

The dates given for the cemeteries, always tentative and subject to doubt, range from the seventh to the nineteenth, or even the twentieth centuries. The comparatively hard evidence of Tel Zeror points to the thirteenth to fifteenth cen-

turies. The Nagila and Caesarea cemeteries seem certainly to go into the nineteenth century. The combined weight of the evidence strongly suggests a set of burial customs which remained virtually unchanged from the beginning of the Muslim period.

The cemetery at Tell el-Hesi (Stratum II) is the most extensive representative of this type of burial ground yet excavated in Israel. It offers a unique opportunity for the study of the burial practices which gave these cemeteries their distinctive characteristics.

The Hesi Cemetery as Excavated by
F. J. Bliss

On the advice of Sir Flinders Petrie, Bliss began his work at Tell el-Hesi by excavating in the northern part of the lower city (Bliss, 1891a, 282-83). Here he found no trace of a Muslim cemetery. Such burials as there were belonged to the "Phoenician Period" (Late Bronze Age) and included one earth burial and several burials in jars.

When Bliss turned his attention to the acropolis, removing most of its northeast quadrant (Pl. 1-H), he at once encountered numerous graves. His description of these burials is cursory in the extreme (Bliss, 1894, 122-23) and is quoted almost verbatim from his earlier report to the Palestine Exploration Fund (Bliss, 1891a, 284). He distinguished two types of burials: those covered with stone slabs and those both covered and lined with stones. He made no mention of simple earth burials nor, beyond the vague word "many," did he offer any estimate of grave frequency. Details of grave orientation, body position, age, and sex are absent, and no indication of patterns of graves within the cemetery is given.

Bliss's interest, indeed, centered on one grave "in perfect condition—a space hollowed out in the shape of a coffin, with slabs placed across the top. It contained a skeleton, the skull being toward the east [sic] and bracelets made of glass, such as are worn today" (Bliss, 1894, 122). In addition to the glass bracelets, Bliss mentioned bracelets of twisted brass, anklets, beads, and agates "precisely such as may be bought in any Arab market." Thin glass was also found, but whether the glass fragments were parts of bottles, such as those found at Tel Gat, is not indicated. Pipe bowls "of a somewhat different shape than those in use today" were apparently associated with the cemetery.

The nature of the artifacts inclined Bliss to the opinion that the burials were very recent, but the fact that his workmen knew nothing of the existence of the cemetery and made no objection to digging it up forced him to allow it a little greater antiquity. His final conclusion was, "The cemetery is undoubtedly Arab, and may not be more than a century or two old" (Bliss, 1891a, 284; revised in Bliss, 1894, 123, to "two or three centuries"). Bliss's opinion, then, places the cemetery within the seventeenth or eighteenth century.

A medal of the time of 'Abd-al-Hamid (whether the Sultan in question is 'Abd-al-Hamid I [1773-89] or 'Abd-al-Hamid II [1877-1909] is not stated) came from the upper levels of Bliss's excavation, but was not specifically related to a burial. It is, therefore, not directly relevant to the date of the cemetery (Bliss, 1894, 122-23).

In spite of the brevity of Bliss's reporting, it is beyond doubt that Stratum II in Field I is a southward continuation of the cemetery uncovered by Bliss on the summit of the mound.

CHAPTER 4

The Cemetery in General

Location of Stratum II Burials

As already indicated (p. 2), graves of Stratum II occur only in Fields I, V, and VI; that is, they are found only on the acropolis and on the summits of the central and eastern dunes of the south ridge (Pl. 1-A and 1-D). No graves were uncovered in Field IV on the north ridge (Pl. 1-G), in Field II on the low ground north of the central and eastern dunes (Pl. 1), or on the upper portion of the southern slope of the acropolis (Field I, Areas 61 and 71; Pl. 1).

A cemetery, consisting of more than forty graves, was uncovered in the eastern end of Field III (Areas 1, 2, 3, 5, 13, 14, 15, 16; Pl. 1). These burials have been analyzed by M. D. Coogan (Coogan, 1975, 37-46) and dated to the end of the Persian Period (Stratum Va; Table 1). Four lines of evidence support this dating and exclude the Field III cemetery from Stratum II. The typical orientation of the skeletons and their characteristic eye direction were the reverse of those normally found in Stratum II burials. The bones were less well preserved, more fragile, and hence probably older than those of Stratum II. The practice of burying pottery with the dead was fairly common in Field III, but with three exceptions it was unknown in Stratum II. The artifacts and pottery agree with a Persian, rather than a Late Arab, date. Particularly persuasive evidence is a small seal, found among the bones of one of the skeletons, and bearing the inscriptions "Montu, Lord of Heaven" and "Amon-Re, Lord of the Two Lands"—an artifact obviously out of place in a Muslim context.

During the period of the Stratum II cemetery, the area of the lower city with its rich soil and easy accessibility was probably under cultivation. The acropolis and the south ridge, where cultivation was more difficult and where the elevation added to the solemnity and religious symbolism of the site, were used as a burial ground. The western dune was not employed for this purpose, however, because the ridged nature of its summit offered practically no level ground.

Catalogues and Indices

Pocket Insert 1 shows the distribution of burials in Field I, Fig. 6 in Field V, and Fig. 7 in Field VI. The full designation of a grave is given by field, area, and locus number. For example, I.22.077 is Burial Locus 77 in Area 22 of Field I. To avoid cluttering the plan (Pocket Insert 1) with numbers, individual graves are identified by locus number only, since the reader can determine from the plan itself the field and area to which the grave belongs. For burials located in the balks between the areas, however, it is also necessary to indicate on the plan the area from which the grave number was assigned. Thus, 11.211 indicates Locus 211 in the Area 11 sequence of locus numbers in Field I. On the sections (Pocket Inserts 2, 3, and 4) both area and locus numbers are given for each grave.

Grave numbering in Field V differs slightly from that in Field I. The Field V probe was divided into 1m × 1m plots, each of which was given a letter designation, as shown in Fig. 6. The field has fourteen such plots, lettered "a" to "q" ("i," "1," and "o" being omitted to avoid confusion). The full descriptive number of a grave in Field V is the field number, the plot number, and the locus number. Thus, V.P-1a.006 refers to Locus 6 in Plot 1a of Field V. On the plan (Fig. 6) individual graves are identified by locus number, followed by plot designation: for example, 6a indicates Locus 6 in Plot 1a, and 6b indicates Locus 6 in Plot 1b.

Field VI (Fig. 7) is treated in this report as a single plot, 1a, and the loci are numbered serially beginning with .001.

The numbering system of the various fields has been described in detail because it is the means by which the reader may pass from the plans and sections to the descriptive material contained in the text and indices. The Index of Burials (Appendix 1) is arranged sequentially according to the full numerical designations of the graves (I.1.007, I.1.010, V.P-1a.006, VI.P-1a.001, etc.). These appear in Column 1 of the index. Column 2 gives the grave type to which the burial belongs (e.g., I.C.8.a.). Thus it is possible to move readily from the Index of Burials to the Typological Catalogue (Appendix 2), where more detailed information is provided. The third column gives the page or pages in the text on which the burial is discussed, and Column 4 indicates the plate or plates where the grave, skeleton, or associated artifacts are illustrated.

The Typological Catalogue classifies the graves under four headings: typed graves, secondary burials, burial pits, and graves where the data are insufficient to allow a classification to be made. The first category is organized serially by type number, and gives a full description of grave and skeletal data in ten columns for each entry. The remaining three categories are arranged in order of grave numbers.

Artifacts associated with the burials may be located in two ways. Column 5 of the Typological Catalogue lists the objects from each grave by their object registry numbers. The Index of Artifacts (Appendix 3), like the Index of Burials, is arranged serially by the full burial number. It gives in five columns the burial type, the object registry numbers, a brief prose description of the artifacts, and the text and plate references where discussion and illustration of the artifacts may be found.

The fact that so many burials, particularly in Field I, were superimposed on one another made it necessary to illustrate their vertical relationships. This is done directly on the sections for those very few graves which touch the balks, and the second column of the Typological Catalogue gives the vertical relationships of each grave indexed. The plans (Pocket Insert 1, Figs. 6 and 7) presented a more serious problem. The initial idea of printing the bottom level of each grave on the plan was abandoned, because it filled the drawing with a bewildering array of virtually meaningless numbers, and the levels were relegated to the third column of the Typological Catalogue. A more directly visual device for indicating the vertical relationships of the graves was adopted for the plan, based on the type of line used to outline the burial. Single graves are defined by a solid line. Where graves are superimposed on one another the uppermost in the series is outlined by a solid line, the second by a broken line, the third by a broken line with dots, and the fourth by a dotted line. Four is the maximum number of superimposed graves found in the cemetery. It should be stressed that this system is only a rough indication of the relative chronology of the burials. The lowest grave in a series is not necessarily the earliest. Many cases occur where a later grave was dug through an earlier, destroying only a part of the skeleton, but leaving the later burial at a lower level than the earlier.

Pls. 6 and 7 illustrate the phenomenon of intersecting burials. Pl. 6 shows Burial I.41.085A, which cut through and almost totally destroyed Burial I.41.085B. The leg bones of I.41.085B can be seen south of the main skeleton, but the latter's pelvic area and upper limbs are missing. After the loose earth was cleared away, it became clear that the missing parts of I.41.085A had been removed when the grave of a child (I.41.089) was dug cleanly through the middle of the earlier burial. Pl. 7 shows the two skeletons exposed together.

Grave Frequencies (Field I)

The figure in Pocket Insert 1 graphically illustrates the intense concentration of Stratum II burials in Field I. The thirteen areas involved contained a total of 400 burials, classified as follows: 287 typed burials, 23 secondary burials, 5 burial pits, 85 burials with insufficient data. Of this total, 380 graves are located in the ten areas where the cemetery has been completely excavated (275 typed burials, 23 secondary burials, 5 burial pits, and 77 burials with insufficient data). The distribution of graves by area is shown in Table 2. The figures given in the table do not represent the total number of burials in this portion of the cemetery, but only the number of graves which survived in a sufficiently good state of preservation to be identified as burials.

Table 2. Grave frequencies (Field I). The upper registers show the number of graves per area in the eastern row of squares. The lower registers show the corresponding data for the row to the west.

Area	1	11	21	31	41	51
Number of Graves	24	30	32	29	79	43

Area	2	12	22	32
Number of Graves	23	29	43	48

The upper two rows in Table 2 give the distribution of graves in the eastern line of squares nearest to the Wadi Hesi. The lower rows give the distribution in the line immediately to the west. The concentration of graves in the eastern line increased to the south, reaching its maximum in Area 41 and diminishing in Area 51, where the southern slope of the acropolis begins. The proximity of this slope restricted the number of burials in the southern half of Area 51, and erosion may have carried away some of the graves.

Area 31 was an anomaly in that it contained significantly fewer than the expected number of graves. There are two reasons for this phenomenon. The military trenching of Stratum I ran through the area from north to south, cutting a swath through the burials in the center of the area (see Pls. 3 and 4). Moreover, at some time in the history of the cemetery Area 31 was partially cleared to make way for new burials, and the disinterred bones were deposited in two burial pits, I.31.036 and I.31.051. The former was a deep pit whose top was cut off by the military trench. It contained a mass of disarticulated bones, including fifteen skulls. The second pit was a more elaborate construction with a stone lining and a crude arched roof. It contained the disarticulated remains of seven to nine individuals. These pits were clearly a form of secondary burial. The practices of secondary burial employed by the users of the cemetery are discussed in Chapter 6. At the present stage it is sufficient to note that we must reckon with at least twenty-two additional burials originally present in Area 31.

The grave frequency in the western line of areas also increased to the south. Areas 2 and 12 had a concentration almost identical to that of their eastern counterparts (Areas 1 and 11). In Area 22 the concentration substantially exceeded that of

Area 21 to the east. For the reasons given above, the comparative frequencies in Areas 31 and 32 are misleading. The evidence thus indicates, but does not prove, that grave frequency is greatest in the southern portion of the field and somewhat back from the eastern and southern slopes. Unfortunately, this conjecture cannot be confirmed or denied, because Areas 42 and 52 of the western line were not excavated.

The distribution figures suggest either that the southern portion of the cemetery was earlier in date and was used over a longer period than the northern part, or that it was preferred as a place of burial to the area further north and, consequently, received more burials over the same period of time. The presence of the *weli* in Field VI may be the reason for the popularity of the southern part of the cemetery (see below, pp. 30-32).

Ground Plan of the Cemetery (Field I)

The long-continued use of the cemetery and the consequent intersecting and overlapping of the graves have obscured the original ground plan, if in fact any systematic arrangement of the graves existed. The general plan (Pocket Insert 1) shows no evidence of regular burial plots, nor of permanent walkways or roads through the cemetery. Surface markers, such as plot dividers and grave stones, had disappeared before the Petrie-Bliss excavations in the 1890s, when the mound was under cultivation. Therefore, any attempt to reconstruct the original layout of the cemetery must inevitably contain a large element of conjecture.

Grave Clusters

Although the burials shown on the general plan (Pocket Insert 1) were crowded together in an apparently haphazard fashion, there is some indication of the clustering of graves. Single graves occurred frequently, but, in most cases, the graves appeared in clusters, sometimes separated by a narrow space between neighboring groups. This phenomenon could be the result of chance, but it might also have been caused by an attempt to keep related individuals together. Ten such clusters were selected for study (see Table 3) on the basis of the following criterion: the group must consist of at least three *articulated* burials, for each of which age data were available. Graves are listed in the clusters from upper to lower. UR means "unrecorded."

Table 3. Grave Clusters

Cluster 1		*Cluster 6*	
I.11.062	sex UR, 0-3 yrs.	I.41.018	sex UR, 18 mos.-3 yrs.
I.11.127	sex UR, 4-8 yrs.	I.41.026	sex UR, 18 mos.-3 yrs.
I.11.172	male, over 24 yrs.	I.41.115	sex UR, 18 mos.-3 yrs.
		I.41.120	sex UR, over 17 yrs.
Cluster 2			
I.21.005A	sex UR, 2 yrs.	*Cluster 7*	
I.21.005B	sex UR, 3 yrs.	I.41.028	sex UR, 18 mos.-3 yrs.
I.21.005C	sex UR, 4 yrs.	I.41.121	male, over 65 yrs.
I.21.022	sex UR, 0-3 yrs.	I.51.136A	sex UR, 0-3 yrs.
I.21.015	sex UR, over 24 yrs.	I.51.135B	sex UR, 17-24 yrs.
I.21.036	sex UR, over 17 yrs.		
		Cluster 8	
Cluster 3		I.41.042	sex UR, 18 mos.-3 yrs.
I.21.027	sex UR, over 17 yrs.	I.41.089	sex UR, 3-4 yrs.
I.21.063	sex UR, 12-17 yrs.	I.41.085A	female, 17-24 yrs.
I.21.072A	sex UR, 0-3 yrs.		
I.21.072B	female, over 24 yrs.	*Cluster 9*	
		I.41.204	sex UR, 6-18 mos.
Cluster 4		I.41.217A	male, over 24 yrs.
I.22.016	sex UR, 0-6 mos.	I.41.217B	sex UR, about 30 yrs.
I.22.015	female, 17-24 yrs.		
I.22.034	female, over 17 yrs.	*Cluster 10*	
I.22.103	female, over 24 yrs.	I.51.024	sex UR, 4-6 yrs.
		I.51.037	sex UR, 6-18 mos.
Cluster 5		I.51.038	sex UR, 0-6 mos.
I.41.013	sex UR, 3-4 yrs.	I.51.039	sex UR, over 17 yrs.
I.41.012	sex UR, 18 mos.-3 yrs.	I.51.041	sex UR, 3-8 yrs.
I.41.043	sex UR, 18 mos.-3 yrs.	I.51.043	sex UR, over 24 yrs.
I.41.049	female, over 24 yrs.		

Each cluster contains one or more adults and one or more infants or children, but this fact cannot be taken as evidence that family groups were buried together. The tabulation makes it plain that the age data available for the adults are not sufficiently precise to permit any conclusion as to whether or not the clusters represent single families. If the members of more extended families were buried together, almost any combination of adult ages would be possible.

The most significant result of the tabulation is to show that the *present* grave clusters are the result of chance, not deliberate design. The small number of clusters which satisfy the criterion employed argues strongly for this conclusion. The relative depth of adult and infant burials is even more persuasive. In almost every case intact skeletons of infants or children overlie articulated skeletons of adults. It is highly unlikely that parents would uniformly die before their infant offspring. Hence, the age/depth relationship of burials within the clusters cannot be explained on the hypothesis of family burials.

The depth of the burials appears from the tabulation to be a function of the age (or size) of the deceased. Adult interments would destroy earlier child burials beneath them, while later child burials would remain above the level of earlier adult graves, thus producing the arrangement of graves actually found in the clusters. More evidence will be presented in support of this conclusion on pp. 36-37.

Paired Burials

Another line of approach to the question of whether or not the cemetery reflects family relationships is to examine the burials which, during the excavation, the area supervisors recognized as closely related to one another. These fall into three categories, which will be examined separately.

Groups Composed of Infants or Children

Seven groups fall under this category.

(1) I.12.018A and B. The articulated skeletons of two infants, aged six to eighteen months

and eighteen months to three years, lay in a simple earth grave. The body of the older child was directly on top of the younger. They were probably buried at the same time.

(2) I.21.005A, B, and C (Pl. 8). The burial contained two infants of about two and three years and a child of four years in what appears to be a common grave. As the photograph shows, the bodies were separated from one another by low walls of earth, but the grave was covered as a unit with flat stone slabs and was partially lined with stone. It is highly probable that the occupants of this grave died and were buried at the same time.

In Pl. 8, and in general in all photographs of skeletons, the reader may notice an awkwardness in the placing of meter sticks and, in some cases, in the positioning of grave numbers. This is not the fault of the area supervisors or the field photographers. It results from the author's decision to illustrate the orientation of the skeletons in the cemetery by using the convention that west is at the left of the photograph. Turning the pictures to achieve this orientation frequently alters the point of view from that of the photographer in the field.

(3) I.22.065A and B (Pl. 9). A single grave, capped with small stones but not stone-lined, contained the bodies of two infants, aged six to eighteen months and six months or younger. The bodies lay side by side. In a rather pathetic gesture, the head of the younger rested on the right arm of the elder. This grave represents a clear case of the burial of two infants at the same time.

(4) I.32.012A and B (Pl. 10). This burial contained the skeletons of two infants, aged six months or younger and eighteen months to three years. The grave was capped as a unit with flat stones. The skeleton of the elder infant lay extended on the back; that of the younger rested in an extended position on the chest and abdomen of the elder, embraced in the child's arms. Although the skeleton of the newborn infant was badly crushed, while that of the elder was intact, the interments probably took place at the same time.

(5) I.32.019A and B. Two infants, both aged between eighteen months and three years, shared a common grave under a covering of small field stones. The bodies rested one upon the other.

(6) I.32.032A and B. Two infants, aged six months or younger and six to eighteen months, lay side by side in a common grave, covered by six stone slabs.

(7) I.41.209, 212, 213. This burial contained the remains of three infants buried together in a

simple earth grave. The bodies were placed directly on top of one another with the youngest, an infant of six months or younger, uppermost. The other two occupants of the grave were aged eighteen months to three years. The position of the bodies was such that the infants lay in one another's arms.

Conclusions

(1) The incidence of multiple burials of infants obviously indicates a high infant mortality rate in the community which used the cemetery. It also suggests that the community was exposed to epidemics which, on occasion, brought death to a number of children almost simultaneously.

(2) The distribution of the multiple infant burials did not result from the mass disposal of plague victims, however. The maximum number of bodies in a burial was three, and the multiple interments were found throughout the cemetery. Therefore, the infants found in any one burial probably belonged to the same family. The placing of the younger infants in the arms of the elder would have been an apt expression of familial affection.

(3) The multiple infant burials thus provide the first strong evidence that family relationships influenced the configuration of the cemetery. The evidence is blunted by the likelihood that the infant deaths took place at the same time, when the bodies would naturally have been buried together anyway.

(4) The community which used the cemetery followed two burial customs in the multiple interment of infants and children, apparently with about equal frequency. The bodies were placed either side by side or one above the other. In both cases the younger child was occasionally laid in the arms of the elder.

Groups Composed of Adults

Five such groups occur in the cemetery.

(1) I.12.019A and B (Pl. 11). This grouping consisted of two graves side by side. The earlier burial (I.12.019B) was that of an adult male, over twenty-four years of age, in an unlined and uncovered grave. South of this burial was the skeleton of an adult female, also over twenty-four years old. The man was somewhat older than the woman. The burial of the female was capped and lined with stones, but the stone lining was missing on the north side of the cist (see Pl. 11). The body of the female disturbed and partially overlapped

that of the male. The propinquity of the burials may be the result of chance, but the presence of the stone lining on the south side of the female burial only, and not between the skeletons, suggests a deliberate attempt to bring the later burial into relationship with the earlier. The deceased persons may even have been husband and wife.

(2) I.32.024A and B (Pl. 12). These graves are the most interesting of the adult pairs. I.32.024A, shown on the north in Pl. 12, was the earlier of the two burials, since I.32.024B removed its right leg and part of its pelvis. The body in I.32.024A was that of an adult female over twenty-four years of age. The later burial was that of an adult male somewhat more advanced in years. The second burial could not have taken place at the same time as the first. Sufficient time must have elapsed between the burials for the body of the female to have been reduced to a skeleton. Three features of the grave argue against the pairing of the bodies as the result of chance. The grave is capped as a unit with flat field stones. The heads of the skeletons are separated by a group of stones. A flat stone slab has been placed upright between the feet. The apparently deliberate attempt to bring the bodies together in the cemetery after the passage of some years suggests that the individuals had a close, perhaps a family, relationship in life.

(3) I.32.046 and I.32.056 (Pls. 13, 14, and 15). The cemetery contained many examples of bodies buried one directly above the other. Most of these have been left for later consideration, because there is no way of telling whether the pairing resulted from design or accident. The present case is less ambiguous. The skeletons were those of two adult females. The lower burial was a woman twenty-five to thirty years of age (Pl. 14); the upper a woman aged seventeen to twenty-four years (Pl. 13). The two bodies were separated only by a thin layer of earth, and the later burial badly crushed the skeleton of the earlier interment. The feature of the grave indicative of deliberate design is that the capstones originally covering the lower burial were removed and reused to cover the joint grave (Pl. 15). To this may be added the fact that the lower skeleton was disturbed but not removed. If family relationship dictated the intimacy of the burials, the two women were probably sisters.

(4) I.41.081 and I.41.106 (Pl. 16). This grave pair has been included because it illustrates the ambiguities involved in the study of multiple burials. The lower of the two graves contained the body of an adult female twenty-one to twenty-five years old. The upper held the body of an adult male of the same age range. The graves were not directly superimposed, but the later grave was slightly south of the earlier. The situation is complicated by the fact that the burials virtually destroyed a still earlier interment (I.41.105). The feature suggesting that the burials belong in the present category is that the two graves were capped as a unit with a covering of stone slabs. The slabs originally covering I.41.106 were evidently removed when Burial I.41.081 was made, and were then replaced, covering both bodies.

(5) I.41.217A and B (Pl. 17). The characteristics of this paired burial resemble those of (3) above. The skeletons of two adults rested one above the other, separated by a thin layer of earth. The upper (later) burial was an adult male over twenty-four years of age; the lower was an adult about thirty years old whose sex was not determined. The joint grave was capped as a unit. Pl. 17 illustrates the cist after both skeletons had been removed, showing it in relation to the west balk of I.41. The capstones of the upper burial are in place on a lip of earth left by the gravediggers to support them. At a lower level is the corresponding lip on which the stones rested when in use with the earlier grave. The joint capping of burials, seen in four of the five grave pairs described, is not conclusive evidence that the burials are related to one another. It may result from a desire to economize on stone.

Three other burials, paired by the area supervisors, should be mentioned for the sake of completeness. I.11.026A and B was the burial of an adult female with the disarticulated bones of a secondary burial in the shaft of the grave. I.11.027A and B was the obviously secondary burial of parts of the same individual in two adjacent pits. I.21.017A, B, and C was another case of secondary burial in which the skeleton of a child of undetermined sex was cut into and disturbed by two pits, each containing the disarticulated bones of an adult. The phenomena of secondary burials in the cemetery will be discussed fully in Chapter 6.

Conclusions

(1) In none of the cases considered did the two burials take place at the same time. They were separated by a sufficient period to allow the body in the earlier burial to decay completely.

(2) The phenomena of the burials strongly suggest, but do not conclusively prove, that the double burials were made by design and did not result from the accidents of burial in a crowded cemetery.

(3) The first two conclusions can best be explained on the assumption that the individuals involved in the paired burials were related to one another in some way, most probably by blood ties. This assumption receives support from an Arabic expression traditionally associated with burial rites, "*Nidfin Hasan 'ala akhou*" or "*'ala immou*" ("Let us bury Hasan upon his brother," or "upon his mother," or upon any close relative). In the light of the preposition "upon" in this formula, it is not surprising that the body of the deceased was laid in the same grave as, and directly above, the body of the designated relative. The identity of the relative with whom the deceased will be associated in death may be a subject for negotiation at an early stage in the preparation for the funeral. The problem of where to bury a certain woman, who was over a hundred years old and had long outlived her husband and most of her children, was settled in favor of burial with her father's family, rather than with that of her husband (oral communication to the author). Ashkenazi noted that many semi-nomadic tribes bury their dead in family tombs (Ashkenazi, 1938, 112).

(4) In order for the burial tradition described in (3) to be carried out effectively, it must have been possible to recognize the approximate position of a particular grave after the lapse of several years. This implies some form of grave marker. Excavation at Hesi has revealed no trace of built sepulchres of the type common in the cemeteries of cities and large towns, nor have any inscribed headstones been recovered. This may be considered negative evidence for the use of a simpler form of grave marker.

Writing about the burial customs of the Arabs in the land of Moab, Jaussen mentioned the practice of marking the grave with two worked stones, one at each end of the burial. These served not only to indicate the position of the grave, but also to invoke the presence of two guardian spirits (Jaussen, 1908, 98). Elsewhere he included the placing of simple stone markers at the ends of graves among the burial customs in the Nablus district (Jaussen, 1927, 340). Ashkenazi, dealing with the customs of the semi-nomads of northern Palestine, stated that the graves were marked by a small

heap of rocks. The cemetery, she said, resembled a field of scattered stones (Ashkenazi, 1938, 113). Such simple stone markers were probably used in the Hesi cemetery, although no trace of them survives. They were probably removed *en masse* when the site was restored to agricultural use.

Groups Composed of Adults and Infants or Children

This category consists of four burials only.

(1) I.21.026A and B. This unusually well-made grave is both covered and lined with stone slabs. This type of burial usually contains a single skeleton, but in this case two individuals occupied the grave, the one an infant and the other an adult of undetermined sex. The bodies lay side by side, separated by a thin wall of earth. There is no way of telling whether the bodies were buried separately or at the same time, although the fact that the same stone line encloses both bodies favors the latter alternative.

(2) I.21.072A and B. This simple earth grave contained the body of an adult female and the disarticulated remains of an infant resting almost directly on the adult skeleton. The burials could be explained as a primary and a secondary burial in unusually close association with one another or equally well as a joint burial, perhaps of a mother and her newborn infant in the same grave.

(3) I.22.134A and B. An infant and an adult of undetermined sex were buried in a stone-covered grave. The capstones covered both burials, but a stone lining enclosed the skeleton of the infant. It did not extend around the adult burial. It is not clear whether the bodies were buried separately or at the same time.

(4) I.51.136A and B. In this simple earth grave the principal burial was that of an adult female between seventeen and twenty-four years of age. On top of this skeleton lay the disarticulated bones of an infant. The burial may be interpreted either as a secondary interment in the grave shaft of the primary burial or as the remains of a mother and child in a common grave.

Conclusions

The conclusions that may be drawn from the third group of burials are tenuous because of the ease with which this group may be confused with secondary burials.

(1) The details of burials (2) and (4) suggest the burial of mothers who died in childbirth with their

stillborn infants. The case would be strengthened if the adults in these graves were female. Unfortunately, for neither burial could the sex of the adult be established.

(2) If the group represents mother-and-child burials, the influence of family relationships on the structure of the cemetery is reinforced. Since, however, the deaths would have occurred simultaneously, the burial of mother and child together would be expected, and the presence of such burials is not as strong evidence for the family nature of the cemetery as is that provided by the paired burial of adults.

Horizontal Arrangement of Graves

In Areas 1 and 2, where the grave frequency was low, dubious traces of a systematic arrangement of graves could be discerned. The burials appeared to have been laid out in roughly parallel rows, running in a general north-south direction. A similar pattern showed up among the sparse graves in Area 51.

Graves Containing Articulated Skeletons of Adults

In order to test this hypothesis, the centers of the graves containing the articulated skeletons of adults were plotted on a 1:200 grid, on the assumption that maximum care would have been taken in the placing of an adult in the cemetery and that articulated burials were likely to be in their original position, whereas disarticulated remains had almost certainly been moved. The result of this experiment is shown in Fig. 4.

No absolutely clear pattern emerges from the plot. Symmetrical north-south or east-west rows appear to be impossible. The only discernible pattern, which takes into account a large number of burials, appears to be roughly parallel rows running north-northwest to south-southeast. Six such lines have been placed on the plot. They work out best in Areas 22 and 32, but many exceptions occur, and another plotter might well locate the lines of maximum concentration in different places.

Capped and Lined Graves

A second plan was obtained by plotting the graves which were either capped or lined with stones (Fig. 5). The rationale for choosing those graves, which included infants and children as well as adults, is that graves in which cappers or liners remained in place were likely to have been undisturbed. On this plot meaningful lines are difficult to determine, but when the lines located on Fig. 4 were superimposed on Fig. 5, the better-built graves, i.e., those with both cappers and liners (marked "x" on Fig. 5), were concentrated along the lines, and most of the exceptions were capped but unlined graves (marked on Fig. 5 by dots).

Areas 3, 4, and 13 had too few burials to give valid information, and Areas 4 and 13 have no counterparts to the south, so that the extension of grave rows from these areas cannot be determined, and the areas are of little value in determining grave arrangement.

Line "a" probably inclined more to the east than the plot shows. Since most of the graves in the line are on the extreme eastern edge of the areas, their centers cannot be located with accuracy. Moreover, the line may actually have been skewed to the west because of its proximity to the steep edge of the wadi. There was probably an additional line of graves between lines "a" and "b" (marked "b'" on Fig. 5). The skewing of line "a" and the fact that the military trenches of Stratum I destroyed many graves in the presumed line make its presence a strong possibility.

Conclusions

The presence of regular grave rows, inclined from north-northeast to south-southwest, is suggested by Figs. 4 and 5. The suggestion receives support from the fact that this is precisely the predominant eye direction of the skeletons in the cemetery (see Chapter 8) and is the direction from Tell el-Hesi toward the Holy City of Mecca. Moreover, the axes of the graves are almost uniformly somewhere between due east-west and southeast-northwest. Graves arranged in rows as described above would be nearly at right angles to the axis of the row.

If the cemetery originally had a pattern of regular rows, the arrangement has been badly disturbed by numerous interments outside of and across the rows. In the light of the conclusions drawn from the study of paired burials, it is probable that the disruption of the original ground plan was caused in part by the traditional desire to keep family groups together, which eventually resulted in the overcrowding of the family plots. A second reason for the present disorder of the cemetery could be the loss of the precise position of graves and grave rows, as the cemetery remained in long-continued use.

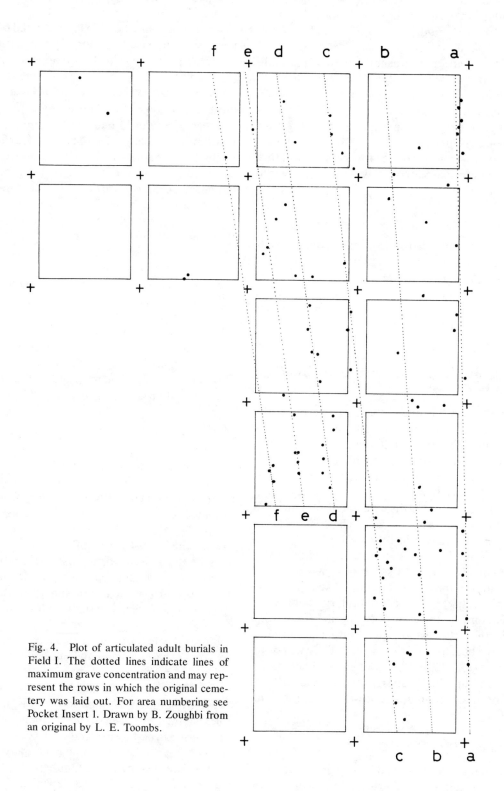

Fig. 4. Plot of articulated adult burials in Field I. The dotted lines indicate lines of maximum grave concentration and may represent the rows in which the original cemetery was laid out. For area numbering see Pocket Insert 1. Drawn by B. Zoughbi from an original by L. E. Toombs.

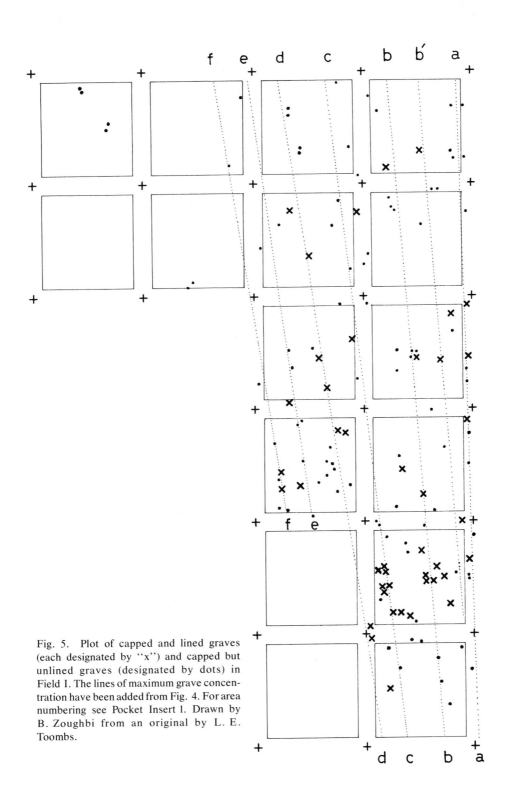

Fig. 5. Plot of capped and lined graves (each designated by ''x'') and capped but unlined graves (designated by dots) in Field I. The lines of maximum grave concentration have been added from Fig. 4. For area numbering see Pocket Insert 1. Drawn by B. Zoughbi from an original by L. E. Toombs.

The Cemetery in Fields V and VI

General Description

In both Fields V and VI the horizontal exposure was too small and the graves excavated too few to add any information on the layout of the cemetery. In Field V, the central dune of the south ridge, only a few graves were visible on the surface, but the 1975 probe revealed that the burials were numerous from just below the surface to a depth of about 2.00m. Both adult and child burials were found, and the characteristics of the graves were the same as those in Field I. Six burials were recorded in Field V (Fig. 6). Five of these were

building has collapsed nearly to its foundations. It was not excavated, but its surviving remains were surveyed and drawn (Fig. 8).

The *weli* is a trapezoidal building. Its south and east walls are 5.50m long, its north wall 5.30m, and its west wall 5.00m. The walls are 0.60m thick. The material of the building, at least in its foundation and lower walls, is limestone blocks finished to a smooth surface and laid in regular courses. The entrance is on the north side. The remains of two niches, a little over 0.50m wide and about 0.30m deep, are symmetrically placed in the east wall. The grave of the holy man was not excavated, but it was probably in the center of the

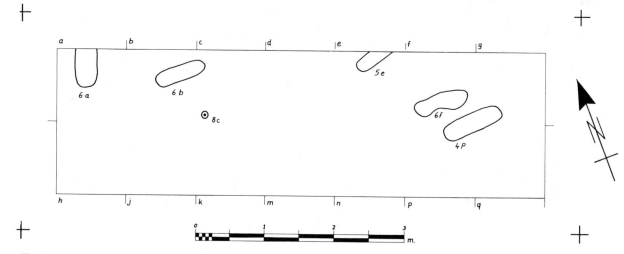

Fig. 6.   General plan of the Stratum II cemetery in Field V. Drawn by B. Zoughbi from an original by L. E. Toombs.

typed burials and one was a burial pit. The situation in Field VI was similar to that in Field V, except that on the eastern dune many grave cappers were exposed on the surface. To judge by these stones, the grave frequency was even higher in Field VI than in Field I. From the small probe made in the field in 1975, five graves were recorded (Fig. 7). Four were typed burials, and one had insufficient data for classification. The more extensive burials excavated in both fields in 1977 and 1979 will be discussed in a subsequent volume.

The Weli

The most striking, and to the excavators the most welcome, feature of Fields V and VI is the presence on the northern slope of the south ridge of a tall tamarisk. It is the only large tree on the site, and its broad branches sheltered the camp canteen and played host to many afternoon gatherings. Five meters east of the tree are the ruins of a small *weli*, the tomb of a Muslim holy man. The

floor space, oriented east-west, and covered by a sepulchre built above ground level. A reconstruction of the *weli* is given in Fig. 9.

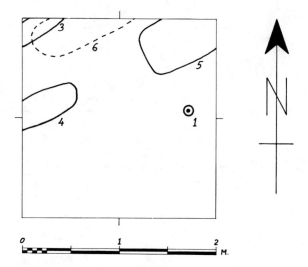

Fig. 7.   General plan of the Stratum II cemetery in Field VI. Drawn by B. Zoughbi from an original by L. E. Toombs.

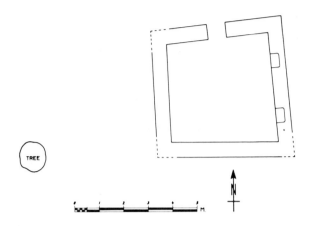

Fig. 8. Ground plan of the *weli* in Field VI in relation to the nearby tamarisk. Drawn by B. Zoughbi.

Fig. 9. Isometric reconstruction of the *weli* seen from the north. Drawn by B. Zoughbi.

Muslim *weli*s have been studied by T. Canaan (Canaan, 1924), and his description of their general characteristics may be summarized as follows: The building is usually quadrilateral in ground plan, and is provided with a single door and one small window. It is roofed with a vaulted dome. One or more niches in the wall, like elongated cupboards, provide places for lamps or bottles of oil. The floor is either left bare or covered with matting. The building usually has a crescent emblem on the roof. A *miḥrab* in the south wall marks the direction of Mecca.

According to Canaan, the preferred location for a *weli* is on high ground, dominating the landscape and visible from a distance. Hence, most *weli*s are found on tells or ancient sites. They are frequently situated in or near a cemetery, although it is not always clear which came first. Canaan indicates

that a cemetery either followed the building of the *weli* or greatly increased in size because of its presence. Burial near the tomb of a holy man offered the double benefit of greater blessing in the world to come and protection of the grave from desecration by enemies.

*Weli*s are frequently associated with a single large, green tree or with a small grove. Other features often found near a shrine are a spring, running water, a cistern, or a cave. The Wadi Hesi might qualify as a stream, and its bed contains springs, but no cave or cistern is associated with the *weli* at Hesi.

The shrine on the south ridge is clearly an example of the common form of Muslim holy place described by Canaan. On the basis of this description the reconstruction in Fig. 9 provides the building with a domed roof, surmounted by a crescent, and a barred window in the western wall. The walls have been represented as stonework, although the exterior of the building may have been plastered.

The *weli* is not mentioned by Bliss (1894) or by Petrie (1891) in their descriptions of the site, nor does it appear in the *Survey of Western Palestine* (Conder and Kitchener, 1883), in Robinson and Smith's *Biblical Researches in Palestine* (1856), or in Abel's *Géographie* (1933). However, two fragments of evidence may possibly relate to the shrine.

In an article entitled "Excavating from Its Picturesque Side," F. J. Bliss describes the nocturnal antics of Sheikh Salim, "a dear old gentleman, with a worn face, sweet and gentle":

As Sheikh Salim toiled in his deep trench who would recognize in this homely, quiet old man the wild figure seen at sunset dancing up to *the grave of a holy man near the camp*, shouting out guttural sentences, braying like a donkey, uttering the mingled roar and growl of an angry camel, then suddenly turning and darting off across country, to be brought back, swaying like a drunken man and almost as unconscious, by the young men who rushed after him? (Bliss, 1891b, 294; italics added.)

Bliss does not describe the shrine or locate it accurately. It could hardly have been at Tell Nagila, since it was within eyeshot of Bliss's camp. Bliss mentions no cemetery in connection with the shrine. Most likely the shrine was already in ruins in Bliss's time, although still capable by its antiquity and sanctity of inspiring religious fervor in an old man with a long memory for tradition.

The second possible reference to the *weli* is more pedestrian. The Survey of Palestine maps

(1945: 1:20,000 series, sheet 12-10 [Jamma]) indicate the location of the tamarisk, and to the west of it a place called *qabr el-'Ureibat*, "the grave of el-'Ureibat." The identity of this grave or tomb with the *weli* is left in doubt, since the *weli* lies actually to the east of the tree.

The discussion of the Field I cemetery showed that its graves reach their highest density in the southern part of the field. Initial probes in Fields V and VI suggested that graves occurred there at about the same frequency as in the southern part of Field I. The obvious explanation is that the favored burial places were on the high ground of the acropolis and the south ridge, nearest the tomb of the holy man.

Was the saint dead and buried before the Hesi cemetery came into existence, and was the cemetery established because of the shrine? Or had the cemetery been begun before the death of the holy man, so that he was buried near the graveyard of his people? The data available allow no firm answers to these questions. The Field I cemetery certainly covered the whole summit of the acropolis and probably originally had a symmetrical arrangement of its graves in rows. The regularity of the layout is broken everywhere by later burials, but the disturbance is greatest at the south of Field I. This may be taken as evidence that the crowding of the cemetery took place after it had been laid out and in use for some time. If this was the case, the burial of the holy man took place after the cemetery had been established and in use for a considerable period, and affected the frequency of the graves but not the general plan of the cemetery. On the other hand, the presence of clusters of the best-built graves, those with both stone cappers and liners, in the southern part of the cemetery (Fig. 5) may indicate that the wealthiest or most prestigious families claimed the most favored part of the cemetery. If this happened, the burial of the saint took place either before the establishment of the cemetery or early in its history. In either case the close relationship between the *weli* and the cemetery is evident.

CHAPTER 5

Grave Construction

Sections

The data presented in this chapter are best illustrated by the section drawings. Three sections have been selected for inclusion in this report. All three are north-south sections, running the full length of Field I. They are: the east-balk section of Areas 1-51 (Pocket Insert 2), the west-balk section of the same areas (Pocket Insert 3), and the west-balk section of Areas 2-32 (Pocket Insert 4). Because of the orientation of the graves, no east-west sections have been included. Since the axes of the burials were east-west, the north and south balks of the squares cut the graves lengthwise, and the burials appeared as elongated zones, merging with and intersecting one another. The east balk of Areas 2-32 has not been presented in section because it was only 1.00m removed from the west balk of Areas 1-51, and provided little additional information. The north-south balks of Areas 3-13 and of Area 4 were not included because the excavation of the cemetery was incomplete in those areas. The sections omitted from this report will be published in Bennett, forthcoming.

The legend provided with each section identifies and gives the phases of the layers through which the graves were cut; it should be read in conjunction with the stratigraphic chart (Table 1). However, this information is not greatly relevant to a study of the cemetery, since all graves were cut from above the latest period of settled occupation. For convenience of reference, the area and locus number of each grave is printed on the section, instead of the layer numbers used for the earlier occupational remains. The elevations printed at both ends of each section serve as a scale for the drawings.

Grave Shafts

During the 1970 season, when Stratum II graves began to appear in Field I, they were recognized only at the level of the skeleton or, in the case of stone-built cists, at the level of the covering stones. It was at first thought that the graves had been dug from the level of these stones, so that the capstones would have been exposed on the surface when the cemetery was in use, serving both as grave covers and grave markers. Evidence quickly accumulated to force a revision of this conclusion.

(1) Interments would have been in exceedingly shallow graves, the bodies being only 0.20-0.40m below the surface. The corpses, particularly those in simple earth graves, would have been easy victims of animal marauders.

(2) In several cases, burials were found directly above the covering stones of undisturbed graves. For this to have happened, the surface level of the cemetery would have had to build up 0.40-0.60m during the cemetery's period of use, an accumulation which seems improbably large (see p. 34).

(3) Observations recorded by the area supervisors showed that, in some cases at least, shafts were present above the cists in which the bodies rested. On the locus sheet of Burial I.2.013, for instance, the supervisor noted that 0.50m of loose soil covered the capstones of the burial. A similar observation was recorded for Burial I.2.018, where the depth of soft earth was given as 0.60m. These and corresponding field notes on other graves indicated that the burials had been at least half a meter below the surface at the time of inhumation.

(4) A study of the sections confirmed the acuteness of the supervisors' observations. The

shaft of grave after grave could be traced in section from the prepared cist in which the body lay to the disturbed surface soil, or even to the present surface of the mound. On the section shown in Pocket Insert 2, for example, the capped grave of an adult male (I.11.045) is seen at the base of a shaft that is inclined slightly to the north and filled with loose earth (Layer 13). In this soft soil the disturbed remains of two individuals (I.11.026A and B) were buried. Further south on the same section the shaft of the stone-built grave of a juvenile (I.21.063) rises vertically between that of Secondary Burial I.11.014 and that of a capped and lined adult burial (I.21.027). The section in Pocket Insert 3 shows the shaft of a child burial (I.11.058) just north of the shaft of an infant burial (I.12.127). Both graves were capped with flat stones. On the section shown in Pocket Insert 4 the vertical shaft of the simple earth grave of an adult female (I.12.021) has within it a capped grave empty of bones (I.12.006). The photograph in Pl. 17 shows the complexity which grave shafts assume when seen in section. The almost vertical shaft of I.41.217A and B has been disturbed and the capstones of the grave have been knocked askew by Burial I.41.211 directly above and by Burials I.41.076, .081, and .105 just to the south. Somewhere in the jumble are the shafts of I.41.052, .071, and .053 as well.

The failure to discern clear grave shafts for every burial was due in part to the nature of the soil in which the graves were dug and in part to the history of the cemetery itself. The Hellenistic Period (Stratum IV) is the last occupation of the site from which substantial structures survived. It is represented on the sections principally by a IVb stone wall (Pocket Insert 4, Layer 11). After this period the summit of the acropolis was under crops, and the accumulation of earth over Stratum IVb surfaces resulted from the deposition of loess soil. The slowness of this process is indicated by the fact that the top of the Hellenistic wall was barely below the present surface.

The fine yellowish-brown particles of loess are easily transported by the wind, and loess areas are thus exposed to two competing tendencies. The topsoil of the area may be carried away by the wind, or new soil may be deposited from the dust-filled air. Since Tell el-Hesi is on the northern edge of the loess zone, the net effect is a slow accumulation of soil. The process deposited approximately 0.60m of earth on the site between the Hellenistic occupation and the establishment of the cemetery. The result was not regular over the entire summit, however. The deposition of the particles by the wind had a leveling effect, leaving the tops of Hellenistic walls near the surface, while as much as 0.80m of earth accumulated in low places and depressions. The loess deposits appear as Layers 1 and 2 on the sections.

The grave shafts were dug through the loess layers until the more compact occupational debris was reached. In this firmer matrix the burial chambers were excavated. Grave I.11.058 (Pocket Insert 3) penetrated Loess Layers 1 and 68 and had its burial chamber in the highly compact surfaces of Stratum IV (Layers 70a, b, and d). Similarly, Burial I.41.134 (Pocket Insert 2) cut Loess Layer 1 and had its burial chamber against a Stratum VA wall (Layer 64). On the same section Burial I.11.045, after passing through the loess layer, encountered the soft soil in the top of a Stratum Va pit (Layer 14) and had to have its sides shored up with stones. The shafts of the graves were filled mainly with the fine-grained loess removed during their excavation, and so the outer edges of the shafts were difficult and sometimes impossible to discern. When new graves were added to the cemetery, their shafts frequently cut through earlier ones and confused the picture still further.

(5) The use of grave shafts was proven by graves such as I.22.090 (Pocket Insert 4). Its capstones were on a level with the base of the Hellenistic wall (Layer 11), and 0.60m of wall survived above them. The only explanation for the position of this grave is that it was at the bottom of a shaft cut from a much higher ground level. A similar argument applies to Burial I.41.217 (Pocket Insert 3), and Burials I.41.120 and .134 (Pocket Insert 2).

Burial Procedures

The method by which graves were constructed is reasonably clear, and a general description of the procedures employed may be useful before their details are considered.

The outline of the grave was laid out on the ground. Its axis ran either west-east or southwest-northeast, or somewhere between the two orientations. The grave took on roughly the size and shape of the deceased. Single graves appear on plan as long rectangles with rounded ends, occasionally with a slight constriction in the region of the waist.

When the grave outline was established, a shaft was dug in the shape of the grave to a depth of 0.50-1.20m. When the desired depth had been reached, the burial chamber was prepared. Five forms of cist were employed: simple earth burials in which the burial chamber was of bare earth, cists covered with flat stone slabs or field stones, cists both lined and covered with stone, cists lined with stones but without stone covering, and a single case in which the body was enclosed in a pottery jar.

Before the grave covering was applied, the body was laid on the earth floor of the burial chamber. No evidence of wood or nails was found in the graves. Hence, in all probability, no coffin was used, but the body was wrapped in a cloth shroud. The head of the deceased was almost invariably placed in the west end of the grave, often inclined on the right side. The face was turned to the south, so that the eyes looked toward Mecca. The covering of the cist, if any was used, was then put in place, and the shaft was filled with the earth that had been removed from it. A simple stone marker was probably placed at the head and foot of the grave (p. 26).

The details of skeletal position are treated in Chapters 8 and 9. The remainder of this chapter will be devoted to the particulars of grave construction and related questions.

Grave Orientation

"Orientation," as used here, refers to the direction of the long axis of the grave, read from the end in which the skull was found.

In the Stratum II cemetery, grave orientation, so defined, was remarkably consistent. Only 15 (5.1%) of the 296 typed burials had orientations outside of the 45° range from due west-east to southwest-northeast. The atypical burials were I.1.044 and .046; I.13.007; I.21.005A, B, and C, .017C; I.22.006, .008, .016, and .094; I.31.015; I.32.009; I.41.204; I.51.028; V.P-1a.006; V.P-1p.004. The percentage of real anomalies was even lower than 5.1%, however. Four of the graves listed (I.21.017C; I.22.008 and .016; I.32.009) were simple earth burials containing disarticulated bones which were obviously not in their original graves. Two others had their axes approximately 50° south of west (I.1.046; I.22.094), only 5° outside the 45° arc characteristic of the cemetery, and may be regarded as accidental variants.

Of the remaining nine graves with anomalous orientation, four (I.21.005A, B, and C; I.31.015; V.P-1a.006; V.P-1p.004) had their axes almost due north-south. All were burials of individuals less than eight years old. The two graves in Field V were simple earth burials. The grave in I.31 was capped and lined with stones, but the locus sheet notes that it was roughly constructed. Burial I.21.005A, B, and C was the multiple burial of three children. While the grave as a whole had a north-south axis, each of the skeletons within it lay on a west-east axis (see Pl. 8). The last five burials (I.1.044; I.13.007; I.22.006; I.41.204; I.51.028) were all interments of infants or children in simple earth graves.

Seven of the apparent anomalies (four secondary burials, two burials deviating only 5° from the normal range, and one multiple burial whose individual skeletons were oriented along the normal west-east axis) can be discounted. Since the remaining eight anomalies (2.7%) involved very young individuals and were, in all but one case, simple earth graves, it may be that burials of infants and children were not always made as carefully as those of adults. Therefore, a higher proportion of anomalies in all categories of burial data may be expected for burials of individuals under eight years.

Within the 45° angle between west-east and southwest-northeast the preferred orientation seems to have been south-southwest—north-northeast, but the practical difficulties involved in defining grave outlines exactly make this conclusion difficult to establish.

Theoretically at least, variations in grave orientation might have arisen from varying burial practices among different groups using the cemetery either simultaneously or at successive periods. In the first instance there might have been specific areas in the cemetery in which particular orientations predominated. In the second, older graves should have had consistently different orientations from more recent burials. Neither of these patterns can be established from the general plan of the Field I cemetery (Pocket Insert 1), and so the cemetery probably reflects only one practice of grave orientation from the beginning to the end of its history. The variations arose because the burials were not carried out with mathematical faithfulness to compass direction. The intention was evidently to place the body at right angles to a line running approximately south-southeast from Tell el-Hesi in the direction of Mecca. The purpose was carried out by rough visual estimate.

Many factors undoubtedly influenced the precision with which graves were oriented. If heavy stones were encountered by the diggers, they might skew the grave shaft to avoid the obstacle. Instructions from the family to avoid certain graves or, perhaps, to place the body "upon" a particular earlier burial (see p. 26) would influence the grave orientation within the limits allowed by tradition. The gravediggers would naturally take more care in the interment of a wealthy or respected adult than of a poor person or, as we have seen, of a child.

The grave orientation had a direct influence on one of the characteristics of skeletal position to be discussed later, namely, eye direction. After the body had been laid in the grave, the custom was to turn the face toward the south. The eyes, therefore, look along a line approximately at right angles to the axis of the grave; that is, they vary through a 45° angle from south to southeast (see pp. 66-68).

Grave Shapes

The general description "an elongated rectangle with rounded ends" adequately covers the shape of 94% of the graves in the cemetery. Variations resulted from accommodating grave shape to the size and shape of the body. The smaller the corpse the more ovoid the grave, until, in the case of a newborn or very young infant, it might be almost circular (I.51.038). The graves of bodies buried in a flexed position were usually wider at the foot to accommodate the bent knees. Those in an extended position were often wider at the head because of the breadth of shoulder. Some graves had a slight constriction near the center, where the waist of the corpse would have been.

The faithfulness of the grave shape to the outline of the human figure is positive evidence that the dead were buried in cloth shrouds, not in coffins. It supports the negative evidence of the absence of nails or wood remains from the graves.

Most of the peculiar shapes seen on the plan (Pocket Insert 1) are due to the reburial of disarticulated bones from earlier graves (I.22.107; I.31.021; I.32.040; I.41.045 and .077), where there was no motivation to follow the contours of the human form. Burial I.41.019, the cemetery's single surviving jar burial, had an almost circular cist. Multiple burials in the same grave or in intersecting graves (I.1.039; I.21.005A, B, and C;

I.32.024A and B) distorted the shape of the cist. I.51.028 is the careless and disoriented burial of an infant in a simple earth grave referred to on p. 35.

The plan (Pocket Insert 1) reflects also the difficulty of outlining the cists accurately during excavation. This explains the odd shape of Burials I.3.010; I.12.037; I.22.041; I.32.018. The wavy edge and rectangular shape of Burial I.22.015 is the result of drawing the cappers, rather than the outline of the cist, on the top plan.

Depth of Burials

The sections in Pocket Inserts 2, 3, and 4 show a wide variation in the depth to which graves were dug. Grave-depth cannot be measured precisely, because it is impossible to determine the actual surface from which the graves were dug. That surface has merged with the disturbed upper soil layer, and has become indistinguishable from the featureless loess.

A plot of the bottoms of the deepest graves follows closely the line of the present ground surface, rising where it rises and sinking where it slopes downward. The contours of the surface at the time the cemetery was in use, therefore, corresponded closely to those of the present ground level. Since the rate of accumulation of loess is slow on high ground, exposed to the full effect of the wind (see p. 34), not much soil would have been deposited on the acropolis after the cemetery was abandoned. A generous estimate would be 0.10m, so that a reasonably accurate calculation of grave depth can be made by taking the depth below present surface, less 0.10m.

Calculated in this way, the range of grave depths encountered in the cemetery was 0.40-1.40m. The majority of infant burials fell between 0.40m and 0.60m, those of juveniles and adults between 0.80m and 1.20m. Exceptional burials occurred in both categories. Deep infant and child burials were occasionally found, as well as shallow adult burials, and there were a few adult burials below the 1.20m limit. Burials with stone coverings were generally deep, falling in the lower parts of the ranges.

The discussion of grave clusters (pp. 22-23) indicated that the depth of a grave was a function of the age and, consequently, probably of the height of the deceased. The data on grave-depths generally reinforce this conclusion and make it more precise. Unfortunately, estimated heights of individuals based on the skeletal remains were not recorded on the locus sheets. One exception is the unusually large individual buried in Grave I.1.039, the simple earth grave of an adult male about 2.00m tall. This "Goliath," as the area supervisor named him, had the deepest grave in the cemetery, 1.40m, calculated as described above. In this case the ratio of grave-depth to body height would have been 7:10. At this ratio a grave 1.23m (four feet) deep would have been required for someone 1.75m (five feet nine inches) tall. That is, the combined cist and shaft would have reached chest height if the corpse had been placed upright in the grave.

Since the average grave depth for juveniles and adults is 1.00m, their average height would be 1.43m (about four feet eight inches), ranging from 1.14m (three feet nine inches) for a juvenile to 1.71m (five feet seven inches) for a tallish man. Immediately adjacent to "Goliath's" grave, and partly overlapping it, was the burial of an adult female in a stone-covered grave (I.1.066). The depth of this burial (0.90m) would have been suitable for someone 1.29m (four feet three inches) tall.

As so often in this report, the argument results in a strong case rather than in conclusive proof. The figures given are consistent with a burial practice which called for a grave proportionate in depth to the height of the dead person, at a ratio of about 7:10. The practical criterion would have been the length of the body from feet to chest, probably determined by an eye estimate rather than by actual measurement.

Position of Burial Chambers

In every case where the evidence was clear, the grave shafts were dug vertically and the burial chambers were prepared at their base immediately below the opening. Many examples appear on the sections (Pocket Inserts 2 and 3). Reading from left to right on each section, these graves are I.11.045; I.21.063 and .027; I.31.022, .029, and .053; I.41.223 and .134; I.51.065 (Pocket Insert 2); I.51.080, .125, and .057; I.41.114, .132, and .217; I.32.127 and .122; I.21.056 and .060; I.12.127; I.11.058 and .029 (Pocket Insert 3). Three graves seem to have had the burial chamber somewhat offset to one side of the shaft. I.41.081 (Pocket Insert 3), the interment of an adult male in a stone-covered cist, had the burial offset to the north and the capstones set at an angle. The exact delineation of the shaft of this grave was uncertain, however, since Burials I.41.045 and .211 were immediately adjacent to it, and I.41.081 itself disturbed two earlier burials (I.41.105 and .106; p. 25 and Pocket Insert 1 and Pl. 16). I.41.115, the stone-covered burial of an infant (Pocket Insert 2) had the chamber offset to the south and the cappers set at an angle across its mouth. Here again disturbances complicated the situation. The burial rested above and partially disrupted an earlier grave (I.41.120), and its shaft had another burial (I.41.106) in it and was consequently distorted and enlarged. Burial I.22.090, the capped grave of an infant, seemed to be a better example, but the burial chamber was only slightly offset in the shaft, perhaps because the gravediggers had made the shaft larger than necessary.

The most likely conclusion is that the burial practices of the users of the cemetery called for a vertical shaft with a prepared burial chamber below the opening, and that this practice was almost universally carried out.

Types of Burial Chambers

The form taken by the cist was obviously a matter of choice on the part of those responsible for the burial. Moreover, it is the grave characteristic most easily recognized during excavation. If a grave is identified at all, the form of its burial chamber is known, and so data on cist construction are available for every typed burial. For these reasons cist construction deserves to be the first element in the typological formula used to describe burials. Roman numerals are used to designate cist type.

Type I—Earth Burials (Pl. 5-A)

In these graves the burial chamber was prepared by the simple process of packing the bottom and lower sides of the shaft by pressure. The corpse was laid directly on the earth floor, and the shaft was then filled in. In a few graves the floor and lower walls of the shaft were consolidated with limestone chips, but this practice was not universally followed. The burial of an infant in this type of cist is shown in Pl. 18, and that of an adult male in Pl. 19.

Statistically the Type I grave is the cist form most frequently encountered in the cemetery. Of the 296 typed burials in all areas, 136, or 46%, belong to Type I (see Table 9).

Type II—Burials Capped but Not Lined
(Pl. 5-B)

Cists of this type had a rooflike covering of stone. The sides and bottom were bare earth, sometimes consolidated with limestone chips. Of the 296 typed burials, 108, or 36.5%, are classified as Type II (see Table 9).

In the construction of Type II cists the gravediggers constricted the shaft of the grave about 0.30-0.50m above the bottom, leaving a ledge of earth 0.05-0.10m wide along both sides but not at the ends of the grave (Pl. 17). After the body had been placed in the grave the covering stones were laid across the cist with their ends resting on the earth ridges.

The usual grave covering was slabs of flat stone, five generally sufficing to roof a grave. Limestone, sandstone, and conglomerate rock from the *wadi* were used. Occasionally, as in Burial I.22.066, a worked stone from an ancient building would be used. The gravediggers often robbed the cappers from earlier burials. I.1.066, I.2.021, I.12.054, and I.21.013 had only one surviving capstone, and I.41.134 had only half its cappers left (compare I.41.100, Pl. 21). The covering stones of I.32.018 and I.41.115 were disturbed and scattered from their original position. The locus sheets for Burials I.22.034 and I.41.114 note that these graves were probably once capped. The ledges for the support of the cappers were present, but no covering stones were found.

The best preserved of the Type II burials were I.2.020; I.3.043; I.4.007; I.21.012; I.32.027, .046, and .145; and I.41.090 (for descriptions see Appendix 2: Typological Catalogue). Pl. 15 shows Burial I.32.046 excavated to the level of the covering stones, five slabs and one field stone. Pl. 13 shows the skeleton after the cappers and grave fill had been removed. The meter stick rests on the ledge which supported the northern edges of the capstones. The flexed position of the skeleton explains why the grave widened at the foot.

Graves with well-laid covering stones were capable of protecting the body from the earth, but, with one exception, the burial chambers were full of earth when excavated. Burial VI.P-1a.005, whose cappers were tightly joined and had been undisturbed, was empty of earth (Pl. 20). The filling of the cists was probably due to the filtering of earth between the cappers over a long period of time. This would account for the observation, noted on many locus sheets, that the fill in the burial chambers was more finely sorted and less consolidated than the earth above the cappers. The assaults of animals and perhaps also of human vandals on graves exposed in section in the balks between seasons demonstrated the sturdiness of Type II (and Type III) grave construction. The culprits cleared the earth and skeletal remains completely from the graves, but the roofs remained standing under their heavy overburden. No instance of roof collapse was observed for a cist emptied in this way.

Instead of slabs, many Type II graves were covered with large, somewhat flat field stones, usually five or six in number. V.P-1b.006 had such a covering, composed of six stones, while I.4.020 was covered by four large stones and a re-used basalt grinder. I.41.096 was roofed with four field stones and a large slab. The field stones were wedged in place so that they would remain in position without support from beneath. They protected the body from earth almost as efficiently as a roof of stone slabs.

The poorest form of roofing is stones of large cobble size. Burials I.22.103 and .126, I.32.019A and B, and I.41.026, among others, were roofed in this way. The stones employed were unworked field stones or water-rounded *wadi* stones. The most elaborate example of this form of roofing was Burial I.22.065A and B. The covering consisted of two rows of stones, neatly parallel to one another. Unless small covering stones were laid with great care they would not likely remain in position without support. The body may have been covered with a thin layer of earth before the stones were put in place, although this would seem to defeat the obvious purpose of roofing the grave.

Type III—Capped and Lined Burials
(Pl. 5-C)

The construction of these stone-built "coffins" resembles that of Type II cists, except that the lower sides of the shaft were lined with stone slabs or flat field stones set on their narrow edges. The tops of the lining stones, like the earth ridge of the Type II burials, served to support the edges of the covering stones. The bottom of the grave was never stone-covered. Pl. 22 shows a Type III cist (I.32.048) with the capping stones removed and illustrates the main features of the lining.

The Type III cist was the most elaborate form of burial chamber found in the cemetery, and was usually constructed with care. Only one burial of this type was described on the locus sheets as "roughly" built (I.31.015). The roofing was always of good-quality slabs or field stone blocks. No cases of cobble-sized roofing stones were reported, and small stones were used only for the lining of a few chambers (e.g., I.41.070 and .100). The lining of I.41.100 (Pl. 21) illustrates the care taken in the construction of Type III burials. Although the lining was built of relatively small stones, they were precisely and securely placed in a double row around the burial. The liners thinned out almost to the vanishing point at the head and foot of the grave, where the cappers did not require support.

Pl. 23 shows the capstones of Grave I.12.017, with the edges of the lining stones visible on both sides. The stones overlapped in a corbel effect, and the interstices were carefully chinked with smaller stones. Such a grave cover would have been virtually earth-tight for a long time. Pl. 24 illustrates the same burial with the capstones removed and the skeleton in place. The liners surrounding the burial were large, flat, natural stones. No liners were present at the head or foot of the grave. The primary function of the stone lining was, therefore, to give firm support to the roof, rather than to protect the body from fall-in from the sides of the shaft.

Forty-three Type III burials occurred in the cemetery, accounting for 14.5% of the total (see Table 9).

Type IV—Burials Lined but Not Capped

The type presents no new construction features. A Type IV burial is, in fact, a Type III grave without the covering stones. This form of burial was infrequent in the cemetery, comprising only 2.7% of the typed burials, 8 out of 296 (see Table 9). The graves in question are I.12.019A; I.32.094; I.41.012, .013, .018, .057, .063, and .065.

Several lines of evidence converge to suggest that Type IV is not an independent cist type, that is, that the grave makers did not intend to produce a cist with a lining but no roof. The small number of graves in the type and the confused context in which they occurred raise the suspicion that the lack of capstones may have been the result of grave robbery to obtain stone for later burials. Six of the eight Type IV burials were found among the crowded graves of Field I, Area 41 (Pocket 1). The locus sheets note that three of these were cut into and the skeletal remains disturbed by later burials (I.41.012, .013, and .063). Two contiguous burials and the military

trenching intruded on I.12.019A. I.32.094 showed clear evidence of robbery (Pl. 25). The skull and pelvis of the skeleton were crushed. The liners were in place on the south side of the grave, but some of the northern liners were missing, although the indentations marking their original position were visible in the side of the grave. One of the type IV cists (I.41.057) had a capstone still in place.

In the study of Type III burials, it was established that the primary function of the liners was to support the roofing stones (p. 39). A grave with liners but no cappers is thus an inherent improbability. For purposes of analysis, therefore, Type IV burials will be combined with Type III.

Type V—Jar Burial

The cemetery contained only one example of the burial of an infant in a pottery jar (I.41.019). Pls. 26 and 27 show the details of the burial after the exposure of the jar. The outlines of the shaft or pit in which the jar was placed were not identified during excavation. From the descriptions on the locus sheet the jar probably lay at the bottom of a shaft about 0.40m deep. The shaft, filled with loose earth, was dug through a stony layer. Only two of the stones appear to have been associated with the burial, an upright slab near the bottom of the jar and a large field stone opposite its top. Since the upper part of the jar was only slightly below the present surface level (0.20-0.25m), the stone slab may have served as a grave marker (Pl. 26 and p. 26). The base of the shaft was consolidated by pressure.

The neck of the jar had been broken off in order to admit the body of an infant of six months or younger, possibly newborn. The remains were inserted into the jar head first and packed in place with loose earth. The jar was laid on its side in the bottom of the grave shaft with its base to the west. The body was thus in the position typical for the cemetery, head to the west.

F. J. Bliss mentioned jar burials in the upper levels of his excavations on the acropolis (Bliss, 1891a, 285-86). It is not clear from his description whether they were in the upper "rubbish" or in the debris of the latest city, which was founded at a depth of three and one-half feet (ca. 1.06m) at the north and six and one-half feet (ca. 1.98m) at the south of the excavation. The latter seems to be implied. The relevant parts of Bliss's account read as follows:

We found several jars, evidently buried with intention.... Near one of the ovens a jar, 24 inches in height, and 44 at its largest circumference, was found lying on its side. It seems to have been filled with fine earth after it had been put in position, as the earth seems to have been pressed down by hand, being lighter on top. It contained bones, a stone, a flint and a potsherd. Near it was a long cylindrical vessel with no handles. I do not feel sure of the purpose of these jar burials. (Bliss, 1891a, 285-86.)

Bliss's jar burials were at a lower level than I.41.019, but they were certainly at too high an elevation to be assigned to the Late Bronze Age, which is the archaeological context for other jar burials on the site. Although Bliss himself did not make the connection, they are almost certainly to be associated with his Arab cemetery.

The jar in which Burial I.41.019 was found is illustrated and discussed in Chapter 10, and its relationship to the closely parallel jar burials in the Muslim cemetery at Tel Mevorach (pp. 17-18) is considered there (p. 107).

burials of disarticulated or partly articulated bones, probably reburied from their original place of interment or disturbed by other graves or trenching. For purposes of this summary a more refined sample has been selected. It takes account only of articulated burials from the ten areas in Field I where excavation of the cemetery was complete. The reduced sample contains 203 burials. Types III and IV have been combined for the reasons given above.

It should be noted that robbery of stones from earlier graves renders even this sample misleading. Completely robbed Type II and Type III/IV cists would be recorded as Type I burials. The cemetery probably contained a higher percentage of stone-covered burials and stone-covered and stone-lined burials than the figures indicate.

Table 4 shows the distribution of the grave types by area, both in actual figures and in percentages of the total number of graves in each area.

Table 4.   Distribution of Cist Types by Area in Totals and Percentages

Area	Grave Type				Totals
	I	II	III/IV	V	
1	6 (46.2%)	6 (46.2%)	1 (7.7%)	0	13
2	3 (50.0%)	3 (50.0%)	0	0	6
11	5 (45.5%)	6 (54.5%)	0	0	11
12	11 (57.9%)	5 (26.3%)	3 (15.8%)	0	19
21	4 (30.8%)	4 (30.8%)	5 (38.5%)	0	13
22	11 (42.3%)	8 (30.8%)	7 (26.9%)	0	26
31	2 (28.6%)	3 (42.9%)	2 (28.6%)	0	7
32	5 (15.6%)	21 (65.6%)	6 (18.8%)	0	32
41	19 (37.3%)	12 (23.5%)	19 (37.3%)	1 (2.0%)	51
51	16 (64.0%)	7 (28.0%)	2 (8.0%)	0	25
Totals	82 (40.4%)	75 (36.9%)	45 (22.2%)	1 (0.5%)	203

Statistical Summary

The sample used in the study of cist types was the typed graves listed in Appendix 2: Typological Catalogue. This listing contains the data from Field I, Areas 3, 4, and 13, which were incompletely excavated, and from Fields V and VI, where the horizontal exposure was too limited to give meaningful results. The catalogue of typed burials includes all graves for which two or more elements in the four-part typological formula could be determined. Therefore, it lists numerous

The highest relative concentration of capped and lined graves (Type III/IV) was in Areas 21, 22, 31, and 41. The highest relative concentration of cists in whose construction stone was used (Types II and III/IV) was in Areas 21, 31, 32, and 41, with the maximum concentration in Area 32. These figures support the conclusion arrived at in the discussion of grave frequencies (pp. 21-22) that the most popular part of the cemetery was the southern portion of the acropolis, somewhat back from the *wadi* edges. Not only are the graves more frequent there, but the better-built graves are found in their highest concentration relative to other cist types. If the quality of the grave may be taken as an index of the social status of its occupant, Areas 21, 22, 31, 32, and 41 were slightly more favored as burial places by prominent citizens. This is probably because these areas are at the end of the acropolis nearest the *weli*. Taken as a whole, however, the cemetery shows a remarkably even distribution of cist forms.

Simple earth burials (Type I) are, as one would expect, relatively more frequent in Areas 1, 2, 11, and 12 than elsewhere in the cemetery. The unexpected statistic is the very high frequency of the poorest kind of burial in Area 51. This observation strengthens the tentative conclusion reached above (pp. 21-22) that Area 51 was an undesirable site for graves because of the proximity of the southern slope of the acropolis and the consequent danger of damage to the graves by erosion.

The correlation between grave structure and the other typological characteristics of the burials will be examined after the full typology of the burials has been developed (Chapter 8). However, since the likelihood that adults were buried in better-quality graves than infants or children has already been raised, a preliminary presentation of the relationship between age and grave form will be presented, using the same sample as was employed in the formulation of Table 4. This analysis is given in Table 5.

Table 5. The Distribution of Grave Types among the Various Age Groups

Age	Grave Type			
	I	II	III/IV	Totals
Infants	37 (50.0%)	20 (27.0%)	17 (23.0%)	74
Children	8 (34.8%)	8 (34.8%)	7 (30.4%)	23
Juveniles	1 (25.0%)	1 (25.0%)	2 (50.0%)	4
Adults	36 (35.6%)	46 (45.5%)	19 (18.8%)	101
Totals	82 (40.6%)	75 (37.1%)	45 (22.3%)	202

On the basis of Table 5, six conclusions are possible:

(1) The data available for juveniles are too small to be statistically meaningful.

(2) All grave types were used for individuals of all ages.

(3) Infants under the age of three years were more frequently buried in simple earth graves than any other age group, but the grave form for infants was probably dictated almost as much by economic and social factors as by age.

(4) The figures for infant burials are likely to be too low. A simple earth burial at a relatively shallow depth is more liable to disturbance than deeper, stone-constructed graves. An attempt to correct for this possibility is made in Chapter 8.

(5) For children older than three years, built cists were used for 65.2% of the burials. We may, perhaps, conclude from this that at the age of three or thereabouts a change in the child's status in the eyes of the family took place.

(6) A substantially higher percentage of children than of adults was buried in Type III/IV graves. The built grave of an adult was more likely to be stone-capped, but not stone-lined, perhaps because of the larger amount of stone required for an adult burial and the more frequent use of readily available small stones in the graves of children.

Inclusions

The graves generally contained nothing but the skeleton encased in earth. Seven types of inclusions were occasionally present, however: stone "pillows" under the skulls, jewelry and other articles of personal adornment, cloth fragments, pottery vessels, shells, flint and other stone objects, and miscellaneous, mainly unidentified, objects.

Stone Pillows

In seven burials the skull rested on a flat stone. The presence of these stones was clearly a deliberately planned feature of the burials and is, therefore, properly discussed in the present chapter. Three burials containing pillows were Type I infant graves (I.3.010; I.51.028 [Pl. 18]; V.P-1a.006 [Pl. 28]). Two were capped graves without stone lining (Type II), an adult male (I.51.067) and an adult female (I.22.207). The remaining two burials were Type IV (lined but not capped). The skeletons were those of an infant (I.41.012) and of a child (I.41.013).

Although the number of graves with stone pillows was small, the feature was found throughout the cemetery, from Area 3 in the north of Field I to Area 51 in the south, as well as in Field V. All cist types, except Type III, and all age ranges, except juveniles, could be associated with the pillows. The exceptions are probably accidental, due to the smallness of the sample.

These observations indicate that the placing of a stone pillow under the skull was not a mandatory part of the burial customs observed by the users of the cemetery, but an optional practice carried out in relatively few cases. The purpose of the pillow, if it were not simply a mark of affection, was to wedge the head in position, so that the eyes remained fixed in the direction of Mecca.

Artifacts

A full listing of the objects found with the burials is given in Appendix 3: Index of Artifacts. The objects are discussed and illustrated in Chapter 10. Only a preliminary statement of the distribution of artifacts is given here (Table 6), the purpose being to show the relationship, if any, to position in the cemetery and to grave construction.

indicate which grave types are most likely to contain artifacts. Of the graves containing artifacts 39.74% (31/78) belong to Type I as do also 40.6% (82/202) of the total graves. Forty-one percent (32/78) of the graves containing artifacts and 37.1% (75/202) of the total graves are Type II. Of the graves containing artifacts 19.23% (15/78) belong to Type III/IV as do 22.3% (45/202) of the total graves. The conclusion seems to be that all grave types are equally likely to contain artifacts. This conclusion is supported by a comparison of Columns 5 and 6 of Table 6. Except for Areas 1 and 32 the percentages of graves with artifacts and of total graves are virtually the same. Area 1 has too few graves to be a reliable sample. The Area 32 figures suggest that it was the richest part of the cemetery. The area is unusually high also in stone-built cists (Types II and III/IV).

A study of Table 6 leads to two significant conclusions:

Table 6. Data Comparing the Number of Graves Containing Artifacts with the Total Number of Graves and with the Cist Types Area by Area

| Area | Total Graves | Graves with Artifacts | | Number of Artifacts Per Grave Type | | | % of Total No. of Graves | % of Graves with Artifacts |
		No.	%	I	II	III/IV		
1	13	2	15.4	2	0	0	6.4	2.6
2	6	3	50.0	2	1	0	3.0	3.8
11	11	6	54.5	3	3	0	5.4	7.7
12	19	6	31.6	4	2	0	9.4	7.7
21	13	5	38.5	2	2	1	6.4	6.4
22	26	8	30.8	2	4	2	12.9	10.3
31	7	4	57.1	2	2	0	3.5	5.1
32	32	17	53.1	1	11	5	15.8	21.8
41	50	18	36.0	7	4	7	24.8	23.1
51	25	9	36.0	6	3	0	12.4	11.5
Totals	202	78	38.6	31	32	15	100.0	100.0

The totals in Column 3 of Table 6 show that approximately 40% of all articulated burials in the cemetery contained artifacts. Because of the accidents of preservation and the destruction wrought in the cemetery by the military trenching, the percentage figures for individual areas fluctuate widely. No consistent pattern of distribution by area can be discerned.

A comparison of the data given in Column 4 of Table 6 with the data provided by Table 4 should

(1) The deposition of jewelry or other articles of adornment in the grave seems to have been a matter of personal preference. The practice was not confined to or dominant in any particular part of the cemetery or any specific type of grave construction.

(2) The community which used the cemetery was "democratic" in its burial customs. No area reserved for the use of a wealthy or privileged class can be discerned from the data available.

Burials in the favored southern part of the cemetery may have been slightly richer in artifacts than those further to the north, but this conclusion is not beyond dispute. The evidence suggests a society without conspicuous social or economic stratification.

Comparative Data

The brief comparative sketch given below is far from complete, especially since it omits the important works of Lane (1860) on Egyptian practices and of Granqvist (1965) on Muslim burials in general. The authors cited here have been selected because their observations deal in some detail with the burial practices of nomads and semi-nomads, rather than city Arabs or Muslims in general.

H. P. R. Dickson (1951, 210-12), describing life among the Bedouin of Kuwait and Saudi Arabia, made some observations on burial customs. The grave was a trench not more than four feet deep. "A woman's grave must be deep enough to hide her breasts, if she were placed upright," a man's grave need only be up to his waist. The body was placed in a "nook . . . hollowed out in the side of the grave to take the body. . . ." The body was protected from the earth thrown into the shaft by a wall of brushwood. The depth of the grave accords well with the data presented on pp. 36-37, and the cist resembles that of Type I. The "nook" in the side of the grave was found in only a few of the Hesi burials (p. 37), however, and no traces of protective brushwood screens were found.

Anton Jaussen (1908, 95-105) gave an account of the grave construction employed by the semi-nomads of the Trans-Jordan region, near the northern end of the Dead Sea. The grave shaft was formed to the size and shape of the dead person and was of a depth equal to his or her height. The bottom was covered with stones, the sides were lined with stone, and a stone vault was built in the shaft over the burial chamber. After the grave was filled in, a stone marker was placed at the head and foot. These practices called for a grave deeper than those found at Hesi, and graves with stone bottoms were not represented in the Stratum II cemetery.

The semi-nomads of northern Palestine, according to T. Ashkenazi's account (1938, 110-13), wrapped the body in a shroud and placed it in a grave about as deep as the individual was tall. The corpse rested between two rows of stones, about 0.50m high, with its head on a stone. The burial chamber was covered with slabs, and the shaft was filled with earth. This is almost an exact description of a Type III burial from the Stratum II cemetery. The only discrepancy is the deeper grave shaft.

The nearest analogy to the Hesi graves is provided by the burials of the semi-nomads, rather than by those of Bedouin in the strict sense of the word. The chief occupation of the semi-nomads is herding, although they engage in sporadic agriculture. Their society shows little social or economic stratification, a feature which agrees with the conclusions arrived at from a study of the Hesi cemetery (pp. 42-43).

CHAPTER 6

Secondary Burials

Many of the graves in the Hesi cemetery cut into earlier burials, in some cases destroying the earlier interment completely, in others removing only a part of the skeleton. The locus sheets contain thirty-seven entries which specifically describe this phenomenon. Such expressions as "All but the skull cut off," "No pelvis or femur," "Skull and torso only," "Skull missing," etc. occur frequently. Thirty-seven is a minimum number and represents only the most clear-cut occurrences. Many more are listed in Appendix 2: Typological Catalogue under "Comments" and among the burials with insufficient data for classification. To attempt to describe every instance of intersecting burials would be unduly long and highly repetitious. Five of the best examples for which photographs are available will serve to illustrate the nature of the phenomenon:

(1) Pl. 29 shows the skeleton of an adult male, lying in a Type III (capped and lined) grave from which the covering stones have been removed (I.32.039). The skull and shoulder bones were missing, having been removed by the diggers of Grave I.32.037. The bones were clearly not crushed and destroyed *in situ*, but were deliberately taken away, since a pit of loose earth exists where the skull once rested.

(2) In Burial I.32.064 the opposite fate overtook the skeleton. Only its skull and a few bones of the upper torso survived (Pl. 30). In this case the robbery may have been done by the military trenching, not by another grave.

(3) Burial I.32.049, an adult female, has, like her male counterpart in I.32.039, lost her skull and upper torso, also to Grave I.32.037 (Pl. 31).

(4) The intersecting of the graves can, as the previous example shows, become complex and involved. Pl. 32 shows the burial of a child in a Type II grave (I.51.024). At the child's feet was all that remained of Burial I.51.039, a fragment of the pelvis and the lower limbs. But at an earlier stage I.51.039 had itself intruded on an infant burial (I.51.038) and removed part of the skeleton (Pl. 33).

(5) The most spectacular case of intersecting burials is shown in Pl. 34. The original interment was that of a young female in a Type III grave, carefully lined and capped (I.32.038). The later burial of an infant (I.32.040) intruded on this grave, breaking open the cist and removing the legs and parts of the pelvis. The stone liners and cappers of the first grave were rather carelessly rearranged to make a Type III grave for the infant, some of the original capping slabs being used as liners. The combined effect was the eerie juxtapositioning of the infant and the legless body of the adult in what appeared to be a common grave.

The removal of parts of skeletons from early graves raises the question, "How were such bones disposed of?" They do not seem to have been thrown over the *wadi* edge or otherwise disposed of with summary disrespect. Rather they were reburied with considerable care. This report refers to such reinterments as "secondary burials."

Incidence of Secondary Burials

In Appendix 2: Typological Catalogue, secondary burials form a major category (Section II), and the listing contains twenty-three entries. The actual number of secondary burials, however, greatly exceeds this modest figure. The discrepancy is due to the principles on which the catalogue was made up. If enough of the skeleton was preserved to allow two items of the four-part typological formula to be determined, the grave was entered as a typed burial. Seventy-seven of the typed burials contained disarticulated bones or bones on which the degree of articulation was not reported. While some of these burials were disturbed by the military trenching, a considerable number were secondary burials. A study of the locus sheets for these seventy-seven burials suggests that a minimum of twelve were secondary. Some of the burials with insufficient data (Appendix 2: Typological Catalogue, Section IV) were undoubtedly secondary as well. A conservative estimate of their number is nineteen. To these must be added the six burial pits (Appendix 2: Typological Catalogue, Section III), for a minimum total of fifty-nine secondary burials in the cemetery as a whole.

The distribution of the secondary burials follows closely the frequency pattern of the graves. No part of the cemetery is without secondary interments; they are sparsest in the least populous areas and thickest where the graves are most abundant. The practices of secondary burial thus represent the customs of the community as a whole, and not of any particular segment within it.

Types of Secondary Burials

Gravediggers who encountered the bones of previous burials dealt with them in one of three ways: (1) They sometimes reinterred the bones in the shaft of the new grave. (2) On other occasions they gathered the disinterred bones and buried them in a shallow grave near the new burial. (3) When many bones were encountered, a larger pit was dug to receive them.

Secondary Burials in Grave Shafts

The bones displaced by the new burial were set aside until the time came to fill in the shaft. A small amount of earth, usually only 0.05-0.10m, was thrown in above the body or the roof of the burial chamber. The bones were placed together, but in anatomical disarray, on this earth layer, and the filling of the shaft was completed. This type of secondary burial usually involved the skeleton or part of the skeleton of one individual, but occasionally parts of two skeletons were involved.

Ten examples of this type of secondary burial are listed in Appendix 2: Typological Catalogue (I.1.007; I.11.026B; I.12.005; I.31.016, .021;

I.41.071, .083, .092, .104, .108). To these may be added I.2.090; I.31.052; I.32.049; I.41.068, .081; I.51.013. In these cases there was an articulated primary burial, but disarticulated bones occurred either in the cist or in the shaft. The minimal total of secondary burials in grave shafts is thus sixteen. The area numbers of these graves show that secondary burials in the shafts of graves were not confined to, or typical of, any part of the cemetery.

In most cases the secondary burial consisted of disarticulated bones, too damaged to yield detailed information. From the few instances where age data could be obtained, it was clear that both adults and infants were reinterred in grave shafts. From this point of view, I.11.026B is of special interest. It contained the jumbled bones of an infant and an adult male. The long bones of the adult had been cut. The bones of the infant were jammed down on those of the adult, so that the pelvis of the former was crushed into the skull of the latter. Burial I.31.021, on the other hand, showed unusual care in the construction of the secondary cist. Located in the shaft of I.31.028, it contained disarticulated bones, but the secondary grave was crudely capped with stones. In I.2.090, the capped burial of an infant, the skeleton was intact and articulated, but the skull of a second individual was found *within* the cist. In this instance the secondary burial took place before the filling of the shaft began.

Secondary Burials in Separate Graves

Rather than dispose of disinterred bones in the shaft of the new grave, the gravediggers frequently placed them in a shallow, irregularly shaped pit nearby. Thirteen cases are listed under secondary burials in Appendix 2: Typological Catalogue, Section III (I.1.029; I.2.011, .066; I.11.014, .023, .027A and B, .028; I.21.009, .017B and C; I.22.024; I.32.067). To these may be added I.11.029 from among the typed burials, and other examples are probably to be found in the graves with insufficient data.

Secondary burials of this type generally contained the remains, usually incomplete and always disarticulated, of a single individual. Burial I.21.009 held the skeleton of a juvenile male. The skull was missing, the legs pointed in opposite directions, and the vertebrae were in the pelvis. I.21.017B and C were secondary burials of adults in two adjacent pits, one disarticulated skeleton to a pit. Burial I.32.067 consisted of the feet only of an adult, thrust into a cranny of the Hellenistic wall. The area supervisor suggested that the bones were the feet of I.32.038, removed by I.32.040 (Pl. 34).

Other secondary burials in separate graves included the fragmentary remains of more than one individual. Burial I.11.023, for example, contained the partial and disarticulated skeletons of two infants and an adult, and Burial I.11.028 was a round pit containing parts of a young male and an infant. The sides of the pit were consolidated with stones.

A small group of secondary graves contained animal bones. Two held the remains of animals only. In I.1.029 the type of animal was not identified. In I.22.024 the bones were mostly sheep/goat. In Burials I.2.066 and I.11.014 a mixture of human and animal bones was found. Those in I.2.066 were numerous and included sheep/goat, gazelle, horse, and deer. The human bones derived from several individuals, both infants and adults.

The secondary burial of animal bones was almost certainly not intentional. The gravediggers lacked the ability or the inclination to separate the animal from the human remains which they encountered when excavating a grave. They disposed of all bones with equal respect, without investigating their nature too closely.

Burial Pits

The cemetery contained six burial pits (see Appendix 2: Typological Catalogue, Section III). These did not differ in kind, but only in size, from secondary burials in separate graves. Two of these pits (I.31.036, .051/53) have already been discussed (p. 21). Pit I.41.077 was quite shallow and contained a jumble of bones. Among them were the bones of humans of all age groups as well as animal bones. Like Pit I.31.051/53, Pit I.41.077 was stone-lined. Pit I.51.015 was small and might have been classified among the secondary burials in separate graves. It held the partial and fragmented skeletons of two infants, together with some bones of adults. The only secondary burial in Fields V and VI was V.P-1c.008. It consisted of a deep pit dug through the brickwork of an Early Bronze Age wall and covered by a large slab of white chalk. The bones within it were too badly damaged to allow identification, except that they derived from both animal and human skeletons.

Empty Graves

Eight pits in the Field I cemetery were at first identified as graves, but, upon excavation, were found to contain no bones. Five empty cistlike pits (I.1.045; I.2.014, .015; I.32.023; I.51.018) may have been graves that had been robbed of their contents by later burials or by the military trenching, but more probably they were grave shafts misidentified as cists during excavation. Two partially capped graves (I.12.006; I.32.022) had no burials beneath the covering stones. One capped and lined grave (I.12.014) was also found empty. Graves found empty of bones may have been prepared for burials which never took place, or they may have been robbed of their skeletons by later gravediggers. In the latter event it is difficult to see why the diggers would have removed the skeleton without at the same time claiming the valuable stones for reuse. With Burials I.32.022 and I.12.014 it would have been difficult, if not impossible, to remove the skeleton, since the capstones were found in place. One hopes that these graves represent fortunate recoveries from the point of death.

Interpretation

An observation of Ashkenazi's (1938, 112) provides a starting point for the interpretation of the secondary burials of Stratum II, "De nombreuses fractions de tribus suivent l'usage d'enterrer leurs morts dans le même tombeau familial. A chaque mort, le tombeau est découvert et le corps du mort est recouvert par les ossements de ceux qui l'on précédé dans la tombe." In the light of this comment, the secondary burials in the shafts of graves may have been made when a relationship was recognized between the corpse to be buried and the bones dug up from the earlier grave. The practice would then have been an understandable reversal of placing the body of the dead "upon" that of a chosen relative (p. 26). The distribution of secondary burials in grave shafts followed the same pattern as the distribution of the graves themselves, and they had the same characteristics throughout the cemetery. They thus bore a close relationship to the primary burials. These features are in accord with the hypothesis that the individuals in the primary burials were related by blood ties to those whose remains were found in the shafts.

The theory may be pushed a step further, and the secondary burials in separate graves may be regarded as conscious attempts *not* to put the exhumed bones "upon" the new burial. This would imply that no family relationship was recognized between the dead person and the body disturbed in the burial. The exhumed bones were those of "strangers," to be treated with respect, but not to be associated in the grave with the newly dead. The Hesi cemetery had a long history, and burial plots, particularly in the more popular southern part of the cemetery, must sometimes have passed from the hands of one family into those of another.

Support for the second step of the hypothesis is slight. The sole evidence is the distribution of the secondary graves and burial pits. Secondary burials in separate graves began in Area 1, but extended no further south than Areas 31/32. By con-

trast, burial pits were not found north of Areas 31/32 but did occur in Areas 31, 41, and 51, as well as in Field V, i.e., in the most heavily used portion of the cemetery. Thus, secondary graves containing the remains of one to three skeletons occurred where the graves were less crowded and where, consequently, fewer burials would be encountered in digging a new grave. The burial pits were merely secondary graves adapted to receive the larger quantity of bones inevitably disturbed in gravedigging in the southern part of the cemetery. Burial pits and secondary graves were both simply devices for the disposal of unwanted bones, but secondary burials in grave shafts resulted from a relationship, probably familial, between the individuals involved in the primary and secondary burials.

CHAPTER 7

Field Recording and Computer Coding

An account of the techniques adopted for the field recording of the Stratum II cemetery and the computer code which resulted from them should, perhaps, have come at the beginning of this report. However, some understanding of the cemetery's structure, of the volume of data which had to be dealt with, and of the special problems encountered in the excavation of the graves was necessary before the factors which led to the development of these techniques could be appreciated. Moreover, the recording system leads directly to the burial typology which will be presented in the succeeding chapters and provides an appropriate introduction to that typology.

In 1970, when the excavation of the cemetery began, the expedition was faced with a major decision. Should the graves, appearing in profusion in every square, be treated in individual detail, or should a small representative sample be excavated carefully, and the rest disposed of without full analysis? It was decided to treat each grave as a discrete locus and to excavate it with the same thoroughness shown on a surface or a wall. This decision raised a series of thorny problems.

The expedition was not set up to handle burial data in the large volume in which they began to appear. It was an obvious physical impossibility for the osteologist to give his personal attention to the excavation and reporting of every grave and, at the same time, to deal with the skeletal remains in the field laboratory. The area supervisors, though experienced field personnel, were not trained in the excavation of skeletal material or in the full range of observation and recording necessary for its subsequent study. The locus sheets with which they were provided were designed for reporting on soil layers or architectural features, but not on burials. In order to record the essential characteristics of the graves and the skeletal remains, the supervisor was required to write a long prose paragraph under the heading "General Description." The inevitable result, under the pressure of field conditions, was that the descriptions were not consistent in items recorded, uniform in terminology, or complete in the data reported. It was difficult in later examination of the locus sheets to determine whether two supervisors meant the same thing by the same wording, or whether omissions resulted from the absence of remains or from failure to record what was there.

By the end of the 1970 season it was clear that the supervisors needed a recording device which would indicate what observations ought to be made on each burial and enable them to record these observations rapidly, accurately, and completely. In addition, in order to relieve the osteologist of the impossible burden of personally excavating every burial, teams had to be trained in the special techniques used to expose and remove skeletal remains.

The Development of the Burial Code

During the interval between the 1970 and 1971 seasons the author and Patricia Koeber, a graduate student in archaeology at Wilfrid Laurier University, made a preliminary study of the field recording of burials.

The first step was to develop a checklist of observations necessary for the full recording of a burial and to group the items under two major categories: grave data and skeletal data. The required observations on the graves were organized under ten headings: (1) field identification,

(2) number of burials in a grave, (3) vertical relationship to other graves, (4) shape of cist, (5) length of cist, (6) width of cist, (7) depth of cist, (8) type of covering, (9) type of lining, (10) excavatability. The skeletal data were similarly grouped in ten categories: (1) field identification, (2) type of remains, including the individual's sex, (3) age, (4) degree of articulation, (5) position of arms, (6) position of legs, (7) direction of eyes, (8) position of body, (9) location in area, (10) orientation of skeleton.

It was evident that the recording demanded would become an intolerable burden on the already overworked area supervisors if they were asked to write prose descriptions incorporating all the required observations, and so a simplified recording form was worked out. The form provided a box for each category of data, and each entry was made in the form of a one-digit or two-digit number. The area supervisors needed only to make the observations called for and enter the corresponding numbers in the appropriate boxes. The data would be treated thoroughly, uniformly, accurately, and with a minimum loss of time in note-taking. Only anomalous items or data not suited to the prepared forms had to be entered on the locus sheet.

When this stage had been reached, what had started as a labor-saving device began to look very much like a computer code. It preserved the burial data in a mathematical language which could be transferred directly to a computer, but a further revision of the recording system would be needed before analytical programs could be efficiently applied to the material.

When the recording system had been developed in a preliminary form, an extended conference was held with the expedition's osteologist, Dr. Jeffrey Schwartz. The suggested procedures were reviewed point by point, and the categories were examined and rearranged. At his suggestion the range of data to be reported was enlarged to include items not provided for in the original projection, particularly in relation to the position of the body, of the arms, and of the legs; and such entries as age were brought into conformity with the limits and possibilities of field determination. The code as used in the field is dependent in large measure on Schwartz's skill and good counsel.

The Code as Used in the Field

The report form, illustrated in Fig. 10, provided fourteen boxes for recording skeletal data and twelve for grave data. Each area supervisor was provided with a supply of these forms which, when filled in, were stapled to the locus sheets on which the more generalized data of the burial as well as its associated pottery and material culture items were recorded. This system of reporting was used in the 1971 and, with minor modifications, subsequent seasons.

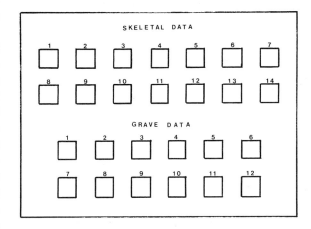

Fig. 10. Field form used for reporting skeletal and grave data from a single burial. This form was used in the 1971 and subsequent seasons. Designed by L. E. Toombs.

The numerical code used for the completion of this form, a copy of which was in the hands of every area supervisor, is as shown in Table 7.

Notes on Skeletal Data

Boxes 1-3

The field data entries are required in case the burial sheet becomes separated from its locus sheet. Boxes 1-3 allow a stray sheet to be associated with its proper locus sheet, photographs, top plans, and material culture and object registries.

Box 2

The three-digit number applied easily to Field I, but the system of plot designation adopted for Fields V and VI in 1975 needed modification for expression as a three-digit number. Since only one plot was excavated in each field, and its 1m × 1m squares were given letter designations, the numeral "1" was omitted and the letter was translated into its numerical equivalent. Thus, V.1-d was recorded as 504, and V.1-p as 516. For all subsequent seasons, a numbering system similar to that of Field I has been adopted for Fields V and VI.

Table 7. Burial Code as Used in the Field

Skeletal Data

Box 1	Year	Given by a two-digit number (e.g., 70, 71, 73, 75).	Box 11	Direction of eyes	−1. no record 01. face up 02. face down 03. facing north 04. facing south 05. facing east 06. facing west 07. decapitated 08. facing north-northeast 09. facing east-northeast 10. facing east-southeast 11. facing south-southeast 12. facing south-southwest 13. facing west-southwest 14. facing west-northwest 15. facing north-northwest 16. facing northeast 17. facing southeast 18. facing southwest 19. facing northwest	
Box 2	Field and area	Given by a three-digit number (e.g., 112 = Field I, Area 12).				
Box 3	Locus number	Given by a three-digit number (e.g., 026 = Locus 26).				
Box 4	Type of skeletal material	1. animal 2. human—sex not distinguishable 3. human—male 4. human—female				
Box 5	Age	−1. no record 01. 0-6 mos. 02. 6-18 mos. 03. 18 mos.-3 yrs. 04. 3-4 yrs. 05. 4-6 yrs. 06. 6-8 yrs. 07. 8-10 yrs. 08. 10-12 yrs. 09. 12-17 yrs. 10. 17-24 yrs. 11. over 24 yrs.				
			Box 12	Body position	−1. no record 1. extended on front 2. extended on back 3. extended on left side 4. extended on right side 5. flexed on front (kneeling) 6. flexed on back 7. flexed on right side 8. flexed on left side	
Box 6	Articulation	−1. no record 1. articulated 2. disarticulated 3. disemboweled				
Box 7	Right arm	−1. no record 01. pronation 02. supination 03. wrist flexed medially 04. wrist flexed laterally 05. flexed elbow 06. arm across chest 07. arm across abdomen 08. arm across pelvis 09. hand on pelvis 10. hand in pelvis 11. hand on femur 12. arm extended	Box 13	Position by quadrant	−1. no record 1. northeast 2. southeast 3. southwest 4. northwest	
			Box 14	Orientation (based on head direction)	−1. no record 01. north 02. north-northeast 03. northeast 04. east-northeast 05. east 06. east-southeast 07. southeast 08. south-southeast 09. south 10. south-southwest 11. southwest 12. west-southwest 13. west 14. west-northwest 15. northwest 16. north-northwest	
Box 8	Left arm	Same entries as for right arm				
Box 9	Right leg	−1. no record 1. abducted 2. adducted 3. flexed 4. medial rotation 5. lateral rotation 6. extended 7. ankle crossed over left 8. leg crossed over left				
Box 10	Left leg	−1. no record 1. abducted 2. adducted 3. flexed 4. medial rotation 5. lateral rotation 6. extended 7. ankle crossed over right 8. leg crossed over right				

Table 7—Continued

		Grave Data				
Box 1	Year	Given by a two-digit number (e.g., 70, 71, 73, 75)	Box 7	Shape of cist	−1. no record 1. rectangular 2. kidney-shaped 3. pear-shaped 4. oblong 5. circular
Box 2	Field and area	Given by a three-digit number (e.g., 112 = Field I, Area 12)			
Box 3	Locus number	Given by a three-digit number (e.g., 026 = Locus 26)	Box 8	Length of cist	Three digits; measurement in centimeters
Box 4	Excavatability	−1. no record 1. totally in square 2. partially in balk—distinguishable 3. partially in balk—not distinguishable 4. totally in balk	Box 9	Width of cist	Three digits; measurement in centimeters
			Box 10	Depth of cist	Three digits; measurement in centimeters
			Box 11	Covering	−1. no record 1. small field stones 2. large stones 3. stone slabs 4. capstones 5. fill 6. mud 7. brick
Box 5	Number of skeletons	−1. no record 1. single 2. multiple (2) 3. multiple (3) 4. multiple (4)			
Box 6	Vertical relationship to other burials	−1. no record 1. single 2. upper of 2 3. lower of 2 4. upper of 3 5. middle of 3 6. lower of 3	Box 12	Lining	−1. no record 1. field stones 2. stone slabs 3. fill 4. mud 5. brick

Box 3

The three-digit number is used in all cases (001 for Locus 1, 010 for Locus 10, 100 for Locus 100).

Box 4

The entries distinguish grossly between human and animal remains. When the remains are human, the sex data may be included without confusion and without overburdening the entries. For identification of the animal(s) represented in animal remains, the locus sheet must be consulted. If mixtures of animal and human remains need to be recorded, further entries may be created.

Box 5

The age divisions were developed by the osteologist so as to reflect the changes which occur with the development of the skeletal structure. With advancing age these changes take place less rapidly and are less pronounced. Consequently the age span involved in each entry progressively increases, and only in rare cases can the age of an adult over twenty-four years of age be determined with greater precision. In these cases the more precise data are entered on the locus sheet.

Box 6

Articulation is reported only in the positive or negative sense. This information is the minimum needed to allow a distinction to be made between disturbed and undisturbed, or between primary and secondary burials. However, the form of the code used in the field does not report on partial skeletons, nor does it tell whether such incompletely excavated or preserved remains are articulated or not. This has to be inferred by comparing Box 6 under skeletal data with Box 4 under grave data. The latter indicates cases where only part of the skeleton could be excavated.

Boxes 7 and 8

The entries include a miscellany of information: the position of the hand, the flexation of the wrist and elbow, the position of the arm in relation to the body. A full set of entries provides a fairly complete picture of the positions of both arms. However, double or triple entries in the same box are usually required.

Boxes 9 and 10

The entries descriptive of the legs are similarly comprehensive, but also require multiple entries in the same box.

Box 11

The strange order of the entries reflects the growth of the reporting system. In its 1971 form the entries gave only the cardinal points of the compass. In 1973 four more directions were added, and in 1975 the boxing of the compass was completed. In each season the additional directions were added to the end of the list so that no conflict would develop with the sheets filled out in previous years. Ideally, observation of eye direction should be made with the use of a compass, but this was not always done.

Box 12

Not all theoretically possible body positions are covered by the entries, but the list does include all the cases actually encountered in the cemetery. In fact, no skeletons flexed on the front (Entry 5) were found. The main omission from the category is any device for expressing the degree of flexation. Observations on degree of flexation were entered directly on the locus sheets.

Box 13

Information on the general location of the burial in the square is of great assistance in relating the code sheet to the appropriate top plans, photographs, and section drawings, and this is the chief reason for its presence in the code.

Box 14

The orientation of the skeleton is the direction of the axis of the body, read from the head to the feet. Since the body may be assumed to have been placed in the grave with the spine relatively straight, the orientation can be adequately indicated by specifying the direction of the head in relation to the rest of the skeleton. The entries, therefore, consist merely of the points of the compass, read clockwise from north. Badly twisted

skeletons, if any were encountered, would require a separate entry on the locus sheet.

Notes on Grave Data

Boxes 1-3

See "Notes on Skeletal Data" (pp. 49, 51).

Box 4

The awkward word "excavatability" indicates the purpose of the category—to show to what degree the burial was accessible to the excavators. If it was partially in the balk, Entries 2 and 3 tell whether or not its main features could be distinguished with sufficient accuracy to be reported. Box 4 thus serves to explain the absence of data in other categories.

Box 5

These entries deal with multiple burials by giving the number of skeletons found in a common grave. Four is sufficient to deal with any case actually found, but the numerical sequence could be extended indefinitely without altering the form of the code. In cases of multiple burial, each skeleton must be given a sub-locus number and reported on a separate form for skeletal data.

Box 6

The vertical relationship of a grave to other burials appears primarily on the top plans, from which it is transferred to the general plan of the cemetery. It is also seen in the section drawings, if the grave intersects a balk. Box 6 gives an additional check on these recording devices by alerting the student of the burial sheets to the fact that a case of superimposed graves is being dealt with. The form of the code used in the field provides for only three superimposed burials. The experience of the 1975 season demonstrated that this should be extended to four.

Box 7

Cist shapes are given in somewhat subjective terms, but the uniformity of the cemetery and the small number of grave shapes actually found make the general and rather vague descriptions adequate.

Boxes 8-10

The measurements, given in centimeters, never require more than three digits. The depth of the cist is the measurement from the top of the covering stones to the bottom of the cist. For uncapped graves the upper measurement is taken from the point at which the existence of the cist was recognized. Length and width measurements are maximum readings. All measurements should be examined in conjunction with those shown on the top plans, for which they serve as a valuable check. The absolute levels of the top and floor of the grave at several points appear on the locus sheets and top plans.

Boxes 11 and 12

The entries in these categories were developed on the basis of the types of covering and lining material found in 1970. There is no reason for the lists to differ in numbering and content of entries. The fact that they do so is a source of unnecessary confusion, introduced by inadvertence and perpetuated from a desire to keep the forms consistent from season to season.

Revision of the Code

The foregoing comments on the form of the code used in the field are both explanatory and critical. They point to a number of changes desirable in order to increase the efficiency of the reporting system. During the winter of 1974-75, two graduate students in archaeology at Wilfrid Laurier University, Sandra Woolfrey and Prince Chitwood, worked under the author's direction to revise the code in the directions which field experience had shown to be advisable, especially with a view to effective computer analysis.

Revised Structure

The data to be recorded have been broken down under four headings instead of the original three: field data, grave data, skeletal data, and artifactual data. The grave data are put first, because the excavation of the grave precedes that of the skeleton. The artifactual data come last, because they are not recorded in the field but in the field laboratory. The filling out of this part of the form is time-consuming, but it does not intrude on the area supervisor's other duties, since it is not done during excavation.

A new form for recording the data was drawn up (Fig. 11). It lays out the entries in a way closely corresponding to the columns which they would occupy on an IBM computer card. The single-sheet format is also convenient for field use. Since the system requires 104 columns, two computer cards must be used for each burial.

New Categories

"Artifactual data" is a new general heading, involving three new categories: the functional classification of associated artifacts, the materials composing those artifacts, and the types of animal bones found in the grave.

The first category's entries include all the functional types found thus far in the cemetery; further alternatives can be added as needed. Up to ten different types can be recorded on the form (Fig. 11). If further space is needed, a second form can be used to continue the record.

The second new category identifies the material of which each object is composed. In order to report this category a two-digit number is placed on the form (Fig. 11) directly below the number classifying a given artifact. Forty-seven possibilities are suggested, based on the finds made to date in the cemetery, and other alternatives can be added as needed. Entry 2, "composite," is provided in order to deal with objects composed of several materials. A string of beads, for example, may contain beads made of different materials. Rather than listing each bead separately, the code alerts its user to the composite character of the necklace, and leaves him or her to study the details from the necklace itself or from the object registry.

The third new category describes the types of animal bones associated with the burial. The category contains twenty-one entries and provides for as many as five animal types in connection with each burial (see Fig. 11).

Reorganization of Categories

In order to obtain a more logical and useful arrangement of categories, the grave data have been placed before the skeletal data, and categories which apply to both grave and skeleton have been brought to the head of the listing. Thus, "position by quadrants" has been transferred from skeletal to grave data and given the first position. The arrangement of categories under skeletal data has been adjusted so that the reporting moves from more general to more specific observations and

FIELD DATA

1   2   3   4   5

□ □□ □□ □□□ □□□

GRAVE DATA

6 7 8 9 10 11 12 13 14 15

□ □ □ □□ □ □□□ □□□ □□□ □ □

SKELETAL DATA

16   17   18   19   20   21

□ □□ □ □□ □□ □□

22   23   24   25

□□□□ □□□□ □□□□ □□□□

ARTIFACTUAL DATA

26 26 26 26 26 26 26 26 26 26

□□ : □□ : □□ : □□ : □□ : □□ : □□ : □□ : □□ : □□

27 27 27 27 27 27 27 27 27 27

□□ : □□ : □□ : □□ : □□ : □□ : □□ : □□ : □□ : □□

28 28 28 28 28

□□ : □□ : □□ : □□ : □□

LEGEND

1. Site
2. Year
3. Field
4. Area
5. Locus

6. Position in quadrants
7. Excavatability
8. Number of skeletons
9. Vertical relationships
10. Shape of cist
11. Length of cist
12. Width of cist
13. Depth of cist
14. Covering
15. Lining

16. Type of skeletal material
17. Orientation
18. Articulation
19. Age
20. Body position
21. Eye direction
22. Right arm
23. Left arm
24. Right leg
25. Left leg

26. Artifact type
27. Artifact material
28. Associated animal bone

Fig. 11. Suggested field form for reporting field, grave, skeletal, and artifactual data for a single burial in cemeteries similar to that of Tell el-Hesi, Stratum II. Designed by S. Woolfrey.

attempts to follow the natural order in which the observations would be taken in the field. The new order of categories is: type of skeletal material, orientation of skeleton, articulation, age, body position, direction of eyes, position of right arm, left arm, right leg, and left leg.

The general heading for field data now begins with a new category to identify the particular site.

This will allow burial data from other cemeteries comparable to the one at Tell el-Hesi to be computerized under the same system, so that comparative studies may be made more easily. Each site will receive its own identification number. Hesi has been arbitrarily identified as Site 8, the numerical equivalent of its initial letter.

Table 8. Burial Code, Revised Form

Field Data

1. Site (one column)	For Hesi always 8
2. Year (two columns)	Two-digit number (e.g., 70, 71, 73, 75)
3. Field (two columns)	Two-digit number (e.g., 01)
4. Area (three columns)	Three-digit number (e.g., 021)
5. Locus (three columns)	Three-digit number (e.g., 046)

Grave Data

6. Position in quadrants (one column)	1. no record 2. northeast 3. southeast 4. southwest 5. northwest	10. Shape of cist (one column)	1. no record 2. rectangular 3. kidney-shaped 4. pear-shaped 5. oblong 6. circular
7. Excavatability (one column)	1. no record 2. totally in square 3. partially in balk—distinguishable 4. partially in balk—not distinguishable 5. totally in balk	11. Length of cist (three columns)	Measurement in centimeters
		12. Width of cist (three columns)	Measurement in centimeters
		13. Depth of cist (three columns)	Measurement in centimeters
8. Number of skeletons (one column)	1. no record 2. single 3. multiple (2) 4. multiple (3) 5. multiple (4)	14. Covering (one column)	1. no record 2. small field stones 3. large field stones 4. stone slabs 5. natural earth or fill 6. mud 7. brick
9. Vertical relationship to other burials (two columns)	01. no record 02. single 03. upper of 2 04. lower of 2 05. upper of 3 06. middle of 3 07. lower of 3 08. upper of 4 09. second of 4 10. third of 4 11. lower of 4 12. side by side	15. Lining (one column)	1. no record 2. small field stones 3. large field stones 4. stone slabs 5. natural earth or fill 6. mud 7. brick 8. unlined

Skeletal Data

16. Type of skeletal material (one column)	1. no record 2. animal 3. human (male) 4. human (female) 5. human (sex not distinguished)	6. animal + human (male) 7. animal + human (female) 8. animal + human (sex not distinguished)

Skeletal Data—Continued

17. Orientation (two columns)
01. no record
02. north
03. north-northeast
04. northeast
05. east-northeast
06. east
07. east-southeast
08. southeast
09. south-southeast
10. south
11. south-southwest
12. southwest
13. west-southwest
14. west
15. west-northwest
16. northwest
17. north-northwest

05. facing north-northeast
06. facing northeast
07. facing east-northeast
08. facing east
09. facing east-southeast
10. facing southeast
11. facing south-southeast
12. facing south
13. facing south-southwest
14. facing southwest
15. facing west-southwest
16. facing west
17. facing west-northwest
18. facing northwest
19. facing west-northwest

18. Articulation (one column)
1. no record
2. articulated
3. disarticulated
4. partial skeleton—articulated
5. partial skeleton—disarticulated

19. Age (two columns)
01. no record
02. 0-6 mos.
03. 6-18 mos.
04. 18 mos.-3 yrs.
05. 3-4 yrs.
06. 4-6 yrs.
07. 6-8 yrs.
08. 8-10 yrs.
09. 10-12 yrs.
10. 12-17 yrs.
11. 17-24 yrs.
12. over 24 yrs.

20. Body position (two columns)
01. no record
02. extended on front
03. extended on back
04. extended on right side
05. extended on left side
06. loosely flexed on front
07. loosely flexed on back
08. loosely flexed on right side
09. loosely flexed on left side
10. moderately flexed on front
11. moderately flexed on back
12. moderately flexed on right side
13. moderately flexed on left side
14. tightly flexed on front
15. tightly flexed on back
16. tightly flexed on right side
17. tightly flexed on left side

21. Eye direction (two columns)
01. no record
02. face up
03. face down
04. facing north

22. Right Arm:
Group A (one column)
1. no record
2. pronation
3. supination
4. wrist flexed medially
5. wrist flexed laterally
Group B (one column)
1. no record
2. arm extended
3. arm across chest
4. arm across abdomen
5. arm across pelvis
Group C (one column)
1. no record
2. hand on pelvis
3. hand in pelvis
4. hand on femur
Group D (one column)
1. no record
2. wrist crossed over left
3. arm crossed over left

23. Left Arm:
Same groupings and entries as for right arm. Modify Group D, entries 2 and 3, appropriately. Four columns in all.

24. Right Leg:
Group A (one column)
1. no record
2. abducted
3. adducted
Group B (one column)
1. no record
2. extended
3. loosely flexed
4. moderately flexed
5. tightly flexed
Group C (one column)
1. no record
2. medial rotation
3. lateral rotation
Group D (one column)
1. no record
2. ankle crossed over left
3. leg crossed over left

25. Left Leg:
Same groupings and entries as for right leg. Modify Group D, entries 2 and 3, appropriately. Four columns in all.

Artifactual Data

26. Functional classification (20 columns are provided for the entry of 10 artifacts)	01. no record 02. anklet 03. beads 04. bell 05. blade 06. buckle 07. button 08. chain 09. coin 10. coin, punctured 11. comb 12. cosmetic implement 13. disk 14. earring 15. gem 16. mirror 17. perfume juglet or bottle 18. ring 19. pin 20. pottery 21. scraper 22. pipe (smoking) 23. toe ring 24. wristlet	24. silver 25. tin *Fiber* 26. basket 27. net 28. rope 29. textile *Bone* 30. burned 31. cut 32. gnawed 33. worked *Other* 34. antler 35. ash 36. charcoal 37. faience 38. frit 39. glass 40. ivory 41. leather 42. plaster 43. plastic 44. pollen 45. pottery clay 46. shell 47. wood
27. Material of artifact (10 artifacts, 20 columns)	01. no record 02. composite *Stone* 03. agate 04. alabaster 05. amber 06. basalt 07. carnelian 08. chert 09. coral 10. jade 11. limestone 12. marble 13. obsidian 14. porphyry 15. sandstone 16. travertine 17. tuffa 18. turquoise *Metal* 19. bronze 20. copper 21. gold 22. iron 23. lead	
28. Associated animal bone (5 possibilities, 10 columns)		01. no record 02. aves (bird) 03. bos (cow) 04. camelus (camel) 05. canus (dog) 06. capra (goat) 07. capreolus (roebuck) 08. carnivore (small) 09. cervus (red deer) 10. crustacea 11. equus (horse) 12. felix (cat) 13. gazella 14. hrax (conie) 15. lupus (wolf) 16. ovis (sheep) 17. ovis/capra (sheep/goat) 18. pisces (fish) 19. rodentia (rodent) 20. sus (pig) 21. ursus (bear)

Revision of Entries

(1) To simplify the recording of the field data the field and area entries have been separated, and three boxes (or IBM columns) are assigned to "area" in order to provide for area numbers of three digits.

(2) The entry −1 has been eliminated, and 1 is uniformly used to signify "no record." The negative number causes no problem in field recording, but is awkward in a computer-oriented code. "No record" is used when *for any reason* the data required for the entry are unavailable.

(3) "Vertical relationships to other burials" has been expanded to include six new entries that enable the category to deal with four superimposed burials and with burials side by side.

(4) The entries under "covering" and "lining" of cists have been made consistent with each other, except that a new entry ("unlined") has been introduced under "lining" for graves where, in the excavator's judgment, no attempt was made by the gravediggers to alter the earth into which the cist was dug.

(5) To make provision for graves which contain both animal and human bones, three entries have been added to "type of skeletal material."

(6) Two additional entries have been provided under "articulation" to cover the occurrence of partial skeletons. The entry "disemboweled" has been removed from the category. It was inspired by one dramatic occurrence. Since the phenomenon did not recur, and since, in any case, it is more properly confined to a special note on the locus sheet, the entry was judged superfluous.

(7) "Body position" has been enlarged by nine new entries which spell out the degree of flexation more precisely.

(8) The only change in the category "eye direction" is the regularizing of the compass directions so that they read clockwise from north.

(9) The principal problem in describing arm and leg positions with the older form of the code was that multiple entries had to be made in the same box. This has been corrected by subdividing the category and assigning a separate box to each of the sub-categories. The leg descriptions yielded four sub-categories: foot position, leg position, rotation of limb, and relative position of legs. The arm descriptions yielded only three sub-categories: position of wrist, arm, and hand. A fourth sub-category was added to indicate the relative position of the arms as well. Both arm and leg descriptions thus require four boxes (or columns) for each limb.

General Observations

The code presented here is not, and was not intended to be, an instrument for the recording of any and all burials. It was designed for the specific purpose of dealing with the type of burial found in the Stratum II cemetery at Tell el-Hesi and is, therefore, a one-site, or even a one-stratum, instrument. Its specificity resides mainly in the categories listed under grave data. In the sections dealing with skeletal remains and artifacts it is more widely useful, since skeletal remains and artifacts have much the same characteristics in any type of grave. Burials in caves or in built

sepulchres would require that new categories be developed, and even earth burials in coffins would necessitate modifications of the system, but these alterations and additions could be made readily in ways which would be compatible with the structure of the code. The author hopes that other researchers who intend to computerize burial data may find this code a useful starting point. If computerized burial data are kept in compatible form, a common pool of information directly accessible to all interested scholars may be built up.

The data obtained from the code as used in the field are now being transferred to the revised form. When this work is complete, the data will be analyzed for significant clusters of attributes in a more comprehensive way than has been possible up to this stage.

Training of Excavation Teams

The large number of graves that had to be dealt with simultaneously required the training of a special team composed of excavators who could expose and remove the skeletal remains rapidly and with a minimum loss of data. Ten volunteers, one for each of the areas in which graves would be found, were selected on the basis of their background and interest in anthropology. They were taken off their regular field assignments and given a week of intensive instruction in the excavation of burials. The program, which was initiated and directed by Schwartz, included a brief refresher in physical anthropology, with special reference to the type of material found in the Stratum II cemetery. This was followed by field practice in the recognition of burials, the excavation of skeletons, the crucial observations to be made, the most expeditious method of making these observations, and the techniques of removing a skeleton from the earth in such a way as to preserve the material for later laboratory study. In the field program the volunteers worked under the direct supervision of Schwartz.

At the end of the week the trainees were reassigned to their areas, and a second group of volunteers entered the program. At the end of two weeks each area had two persons trained to deal with burials, and the excavation of the graves became their principal responsibility. This system was begun in 1971. Its successful operation contributed greatly to the speed and thoroughness with which the cemetery was cleared.

Photography

Ideally, every grave should have been photographed for the permanent record. The insistent pressures of many other tasks on the photographer's time, however, made this counsel of perfection a physical impossibility and forced a compromise solution to the problem. Graves in which the remains were well preserved were selected for photography. The basic principle of selection was that the full range of typical and recurring phenomena should be covered by the photographic record. In practice the varieties of cist structure and of body position carried the greatest weight in determining the choice. In addition, all graves which showed marked deviations from the normal patterns of burial practices were regularly photographed.

The photographic record is naturally weakest for the 1970 season. That year was largely experimental, and the characteristics of the graves were being learned by the excavators. It improved in 1971, although in that year it was limited by the sheer number of graves encountered. The photographic record of the burials in 1973 and 1975 is much more complete, since the number of graves had drastically diminished, and the excavators knew in advance what features to look for.

These remarks should not be taken as apology for the photographic recording of the burials. The record is much more comprehensive than is normally the case for a Muslim cemetery, and the possibility of making this report owes much to the photographers who worked on the expedition's staff, Theodore Rosen (1970 and 1971), William Nassau (1973), Eugenia Nitowski (1975), and James Whitred (1975).

CHAPTER 8

Typology of Burials

Excluding field data, the coded burial sheets (described in Chapter 7) provide for twenty pieces of information relating to each burial for which all observations could be made. In addition, the locus sheets and daily top plans give the bottom level of each burial, and often contain valuable notes on grave construction and on the relationship of graves to one another. Thus, for a fully reported burial upwards of twenty-five pieces of information may be available.

These field observations are those which experience and common sense indicated ought to be made. Clearly, not all are of equal significance in determining the burial customs of the community which used the Hesi cemetery. The purpose of this chapter is to derive from the raw data gathered in the field the practices which gave the cemetery its observed form. The first stage in this process is to isolate what may be called the "primary characteristics" of the burials, that is, those which are not derivative from other characteristics and which were observed frequently enough to provide a statistically useful sample.

Preliminary Examination of the Data

Invariable Characteristics of the Burials

Certain features of the burials are to all intents and purposes universal in the cemetery. Burials are invariably at the bottoms of shafts. The grave is almost always oblong, tending somewhat to the rectangular. The graves are oriented with the long axis between northwest-southeast and southwest-northeast. The body was placed in the grave with the head in its western end. Almost all undisturbed graves contain the body of a single individual. These categories represent invariable elements in the burial customs. The same practice was carried out whatever the age, sex, or social status of the individual.

Variable Characteristics Regarded as Primary

The only observed variable features of the burials which were beyond the direct control of the burial parties were the sex of the deceased and his or her age at time of death. Other factors of this kind, such as wealth, social position, and religious convictions, were undoubtedly present, but were not directly observable. Age and sex are both among the primary characteristics of the burials; it will be important for the cemetery analysis to determine their relationship to humanly controlled burial features. In the coded sheets sex data were combined with type of remains, that is, whether the bones were animal or human. Since only human bones are considered in this report, the sex data may conveniently be detached from the type of remains and combined with the age data by means of such entries as "child, male," or "adult, female."

Three humanly controlled characteristics of the burials may also be regarded as primary. These are: the structure of the grave, the position of the body in the cist, and the direction of the eyes. All three are independent of other variables in the burial practices, and all were observed with sufficient frequency to provide a large statistical sample. To be sure, the position of the body puts a general limitation on the direction of the eyes, but in the Hesi cemetery the natural position of the head was often altered to make the eyes look in the desired direction.

In order to condense the data on grave structure the coded entries for grave covering and grave

60

lining have been combined into a single entry, such as "capped and lined" or "capped but not lined."

The other characteristics have been classified as "secondary" for a variety of reasons.

Variable Characteristics Regarded as Secondary

Observations Implied in Other Data

The size of the grave and the depth to which it was dug are functions of the size of the dead person, which in turn is closely related to his or her age at time of death. Thus, in a general way at least, the age data imply the grave size and depth, and so the physical dimensions of the grave may be omitted from the primary characteristics of the burials.

Observations Unduly Affected by Chance

Except for secondary burials, a skeleton's degree of articulation did not result from any burial custom, but from the accidents of preservation. Since secondary burial was adequately discussed in Chapter 6, it need not reappear in the present chapter.

The relationship of a grave to other burials may either result from deliberate design or be caused by the accidental juxtaposition of later and earlier burials. Since excavation does not discriminate in this matter between accident and design, the vertical relationship of burials must for the present purpose be regarded as the result of chance.

The bottom levels of graves are of dubious significance. As has been shown (pp. 36-37), the depth of the grave is a function of the height of the deceased. It has no stratigraphic significance unless the level from which the grave was dug is known. Since this level was never directly observed, the bottom level of the cist has no independent importance.

The number and nature of artifacts associated with the graves constitute a problem. Objects not originally associated with a burial may be introduced into a grave during the process of filling the shaft. The intersection of graves with one another creates an ambiguity as to which burial is the source of a particular artifact. Moreover, the presence or absence of artifacts may not be as significant as the type of artifact found. On the whole, the artifactual data contain too many uncertainties to be included among the primary characteristics of the burials. A comprehensive discussion of the artifacts is given in Chapter 10.

Observations Too Infrequently Made

The positions of the arms and hands and of the legs and feet are, for a variety of reasons, noted only infrequently on the data sheets. To include these among the primary characteristics would mean reducing the number of burials in the statistical sample to a very small percentage of the total number of graves in the cemetery.

The Typological Formula

The foregoing analysis has isolated four primary characteristics of the Hesi burials: (1) the type of covering and/or lining of the cist (i.e., "grave structure"), (2) the age and sex of the individual, (3) the position of the body in the grave, and (4) the direction of the eyes. The order in which the categories are listed is a logical one. The first is the only category which applies to the grave itself. The second is a category determined by nature and not by design. The third and fourth include data produced by the burial customs of the community. The listing is also in order of decreasing frequency of observation.

The designations used for the categories of information are: Roman numerals for grave structure, block capitals for age and sex, Arabic numbers for body position, and lower case letters for eye direction.

The following paragraphs give the nature and scope of the entries in each category.

Grave Structure

This category includes five possibilities:

    I. Graves which are neither capped nor lined with stones;

    II. Graves which are capped but not lined;

    III. Graves which are both capped and lined;

    IV. Graves which are lined but not capped;

    V. Jar burials (one occurrence only).

The detailed description of the phenomena associated with grave construction has been given in Chapter 5 (pp. 33-41). In the pages which follow, grave structure will be studied in relation to the other categories of information provided by the primary characteristics of the burials.

Age and Sex

The combined age and sex data are presented by dividing the life span into four age brackets: infant, child, juvenile, and adult. These divisions were suggested by the expedition's anthropologist, Jeffrey Schwartz. They correspond to the most readily observable changes in the skeletal structure with age. Each bracket is repeated three times, once for the skeletons of males and once for those of females. The third repetition covers the many cases in which the sex of the deceased could not be determined. This division of the data produces twelve possibilities:

A. Infant (0-3 yrs.), male;
B. Infant (0-3 yrs.), female;
C. Infant (0-3 yrs.), sex undetermined;
D. Child (3-10 yrs.), male;
E. Child (3-10 yrs.), female;
F. Child (3-10 yrs.), sex undetermined;
G. Juvenile (10-17 yrs.), male;
H. Juvenile (10-17 yrs.), female;
J. Juvenile (10-17 yrs.), sex undetermined;
K. Adult (over 17 yrs.), male;
L. Adult (over 17 yrs.), female;
M. Adult (over 17 yrs.), sex undetermined.

The letter I is omitted to avoid confusion with Type I of grave structure.

Body Position

This category combines flexation of the skeleton and the manner in which the body was laid in the grave. Flexation is described under two possibilities only: "extended" and "flexed." To have refined the degree of flexation further, using such entries as "lightly flexed," "moderately flexed," and "tightly flexed," would have complicated and extended the category. The degree of flexation will be discussed below under "Secondary Characteristics" in Chapter 9.

The position in which the body rested was reduced to four possibilities: on the front, on the back, on the left side, and on the right side. These decisions created eight possibilities for body position:

1. Extended on the front;
2. Extended on the back;
3. Extended on the left side;
4. Extended on the right side;
5. Flexed on the front;
6. Flexed on the back;
7. Flexed on the left side;
8. Flexed on the right side.

Eye Direction

The problem in this category, as in that of body position, was: "How complex should the entries be permitted to become?" To box the compass

would have given thirty-four possibilities. This exactitude exceeds the limits of accuracy of the measurement and is too precise to allow for slight shifts of the body in the earth. Accordingly, only the eight principal points of the compass and the designations "looking up" and "looking down" were used, for a total of ten possibilities:

a. Looking up;
b. Looking down;
c. Looking north;
d. Looking northeast;
e. Looking east;
f. Looking southeast;
g. Looking south;
h. Looking southwest;
i. Looking west;
j. Looking northwest.

The primary characteristics of any grave may now be summarized in a four-part formula. For example, III.K.2.f signifies a burial which was both capped and lined with stones, and which contained the body of an adult male, extended on the back with the eyes directed to the southeast. I.C.4.g refers to a grave without stone capping or lining in which the body of an infant of undetermined sex lay extended on the right side with the eyes looking to the south.

In many cases information regarding one or more of the categories in the formula is missing altogether. The presence of "0" in any position in the formula indicates that information is lacking. For example, I.L.8.0 represents a grave without capstones or liners, containing the skeleton of an adult female, flexed on her right side, the direction of the eyes being unknown.

The four-part formula is referred to in the pages which follow as a "typological formula." The author does not wish to enter into the debate concerning the archaeological meaning of the word "type." The term is used because it has general currency in Palestinian archaeology, particularly in ceramic studies, in the sense in which it is employed here. Still less does the author wish to imply that each grave type represents a different form of interment known to, and consciously practiced by, the community which used the cemetery. The formula allows for 4,800 types of burial. It is patently absurd to think of the burial parties holding 4,800 models in mind and deliberately selecting one of them. The types are theoretical possibilities created, not by the ancient community, but by the manner in which the observed data are organized. The task of analysis from this point on is to determine which of these theoretical possibilities were, in fact, options permissible within the burial customs of the community.

In Appendix 2: Typological Catalogue, Section I (typed graves), the typological formula constitutes the first column. The items excluded from the typological formula, for the reasons given above (pp. 60-61), follow in the other columns of the catalogue. The one exception is the position of the legs and feet. This element was omitted from the catalogue because the relevant data are only infrequently reported. Secondary burials (Section II of the catalogue) cannot be expressed in the typological formula, but the remainder of the data is given in tabular form. Prose descriptions are used for burial pits and burials with insufficient data (Sections III and IV of the catalogue), since the observations were too fragmentary to permit tabulation.

Statistical Samples

The separate burial types contain too few examples to be used directly for purposes of analysis, since many types are represented by a single example. Statistical study must involve cross-comparisons of the four categories of information expressed in the typological formula for a selected sample larger than the individual types. For this purpose the only valid sample is the burials for which all four elements of the typological formula are known (i.e., the fully typed burials). To use all typed burials (Section I of the catalogue) would be to include many graves for which one or more of the categories are missing. If, for example, eye direction were being compared with body position across the typed graves as a whole, the individual members of the eye-direction sample would be different from those of the body-position sample, and the comparison would be between two substantially different groups of burials. The total graves in the cemetery (all catalogue entries) would obviously be an even more unreliable sample for statistical purposes.

Selection of the fully typed burials as the sample to be used sharply decreases the number of individuals involved. The total catalogue contains 410 entries. Of these, 296 are typed burials and only 141 are fully typed burials. Does the reduction in sample size mean that the fully typed burials are not representative of the cemetery as a whole? To answer this question, goodness-of-fit tests were run between the fully typed and the

typed burials (Snedecor and Cochran, 1967, 228-31). The results of these tests are summarized in Tables 9-14 and Figs. 12-16.

The author's thanks are due to Dr. Rick Elliott of the Mathematics Department of Wilfrid Laurier University and to his student assistant, Paula Burden, who conducted the mathematical tests reported in this chapter, and whose advice on statistical matters was of the greatest assistance in its preparation.

Comparison of Typed and Fully Typed Burials

Grave Structure

Table 9 summarizes the data on grave structure. If the single example of a jar burial (Type V) is omitted from the goodness-of-fit test, a chi-square value of 0.61 with three degrees of freedom is obtained, indicating a close fit between the two samples. This correspondence is illustrated graphically in Fig. 12.

Table 9. Comparison of the Occurrence of Cist Types between Typed Burials and those Having Full Typological Data (Totals and Percentages)

Grave Structure	Typed Burials	Full Typology
I. neither capped nor lined	136/46.0%	62/44.0%
II. capped, not lined	108/36.5%	52/36.9%
III. capped and lined	43/14.5%	22/15.6%
IV. lined, not capped	8/2.7%	5/3.5%
V. jar burials	1/0.3%	0/0.0%
Totals	296/100%	141/100%

Omitting V, chi-square value 0.61 with 3 D.F.; $p \approx 0.90$

These results indicate that three types of grave structure (Types I, II, and III) were employed in the cemetery and that, the more complicated the grave structure, the less frequent is its occurrence. The Type IV graves may not represent the intention of the users of the cemetery. They are most likely graves, originally capped and lined (Type III), which have lost their cappers to later burials. Some Type I burials may have originally been capped (Type II), and the cappers removed by later gravediggers. Since there is no empirical way of checking this possibility, however, it has been left out of account in the calculations.

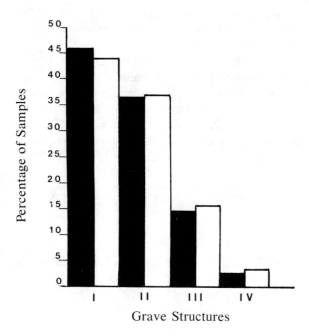

Fig. 12. Histogram illustrating the percentage of each cist type among the typed burials (black bars) in comparison with the percentage among the burials with full typological data (white bars). Drawn by L. E. Toombs.

Age and Sex

Table 10 shows that the sex data are statistically unreliable. Sex differentiation in the skeletal structure is not clearly developed until the age of about ten years. All the infants and 95% of the children are, therefore, reported as "sex undetermined." Among the adults the sex of 11.3% of the individuals could not be determined. A goodness-of-fit test on the total data of Table 10 gives a chi-square value of 12.13 with eight degrees of freedom, a large value, but nevertheless consistent with agreement between the samples. However, since chi-square may be unreliable if there are fewer than five specimens in the category, the sex data and the age category "juvenile" ought to be omitted, and only the age groupings infants (A-C), children (D-F), and adults (K-M) used. This simplification results in Table 11 and Fig. 13. The chi-square value, indicating excellent agreement, is now 0.77 with two degrees of freedom.

Table 11.   Comparison of the Occurrence of Age Groupings between Typed Burials and those Having Full Typological Data (Totals and Percentages)

Age Brackets		Typed Burials	Full Typology
A-C	infants	119/41.3%	60/42.9%
D-F	children	40/13.9%	22/15.7%
K-M	adults	129/44.8%	58/41.4%
	Totals	288/100%	140/100%

Chi-square value 0.77 with 2 D.F.; 0.75 > p > 0.50

The figures presented in Table 11 and their graphic counterpart at the left of Fig. 13 present an almost terrifying picture of the high death rate among infants and children. Of the population 42.6% died before reaching three years of age, and 52.8% before their eleventh birthday. Column 8 of Appendix 2: Typological Catalogue indicates that the highest mortality rate occurred between 0 and 6 months and that many infants died at or near the time of birth. The death rate remained high during the first three years and continued at a high level into early childhood, dropping off dramatically in late childhood and in the juvenile years. These observations agree with the probability of a high mortality rate among mothers during child-

Table 10.   Comparison of the Occurrence of Age and Sex Groupings between Typed Burials and those Having Full Typological Data (Totals and Percentages)*

Age and Sex	Typed Burials	Full Typology
A. infant, male	0/0.0%	0/0.0%
B. infant, female	0/0.0%	0/0.0%
C. infant, sex undetermined	119/40.8%	60/42.6%
D. child, male	0/0.0%	0/0.0%
E. child, female	2/0.7%	1/0.7%
F. child, sex undetermined	38/13.0%	21/14.9%
G. juvenile, male	1/0.3%	0/0.0%
H. juvenile, female	1/0.3%	0/0.0%
J. juvenile, sex undetermined	2/0.7%	1/0.7%
K. adult, male	45/15.4%	23/16.3%
L. adult, female	51/17.5%	31/22.0%
M. adult, sex undetermined	33/11.3%	4/2.8%
Totals	292/100%	141/100%

Chi-square value 12.13 with 8 D.F.; 0.25 > p > 0.10

*Categories A, B, and D were not considered in calculating chi-square.

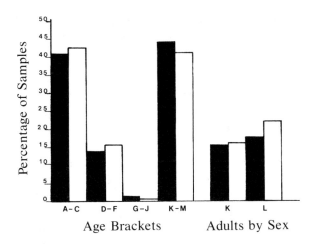

Age Brackets   Adults by Sex

Fig. 13. Histogram illustrating the percentage of each age bracket among the typed burials (black bars) in comparison with the percentage among the burials with full typological data (white bars). The last four columns show the percentages of adult males and adult females in the two samples. Drawn by L. E. Toombs.

birth, indicated by the preponderance of adult females over adult males in the cemetery.

It follows from the above discussion that the only valid comparison in the matter of sex is between adult males and adult females. These age/sex groups are compared in Table 12 and on the right of Fig. 13. The relative number of individuals for which the sex was determined is higher in the fully typed than in the typed burials. This is because the skeletons in the fully typed burials are in a better state of preservation than in the typed graves, and the sex of the deceased can be determined more frequently. As a result, the burials with full typology probably represent the proportion of adult males to adult females more accurately than the typed burials.

Table 12.   Comparison of Adult Male and Adult Female Burials between Typed Burials and those Having Full Typological Data (Totals and Percentages)

Adults by Sex	Typed Burials	Full Typology
K. adult, male	45/46.9%	23/42.6%
L. adult, female	51/53.1%	31/57.4%
Totals	96/100%	54/100%

Chi-square value 0.40 with 1 D.F.; p ≈ 0.50

Of the adults in fully typed burials, 57.4% were female. More girls are born than boys, but the divergence usually does not reach the proportions witnessed in the cemetery. For example, figures provided by the Bureau of Census of the United States for 1969 show that the general population consisted of 51.9% females and 48.1% males (Delury, 1973, 140). Comparable figures for Canada (1971) indicate a slight preponderance of males over females, but the Canadian figures are influenced by large-scale immigration in recent decades (Information Canada, 1975, 145). The American figures are less likely to have been skewed by immigration, since the number of immigrants was relatively small and was received into a very large population pool. The preponderance of females over males in the adult population of the cemetery is thus approximately 6.7% greater than the expected ratio at birth.

A number of factors could explain this situation. If the number of males who died in infancy substantially exceeded the number of females, more females than males would reach adulthood. If a considerable number of adult males died and were buried away from the community, perhaps as a result of military campaigns, the proportion of adult male interments in the cemetery would be reduced. A third potential reason for the preponderance of women over men in the cemetery is the Muslim practice of polygamous marriage. Extensive practice of polygamy would probably have resulted in a percentage of adult females higher than the observed 57.4%, however. Although polygamy is socially and religiously acceptable to a Bedouin or fellahin community, the brute facts of economics keep its incidence low. Finally, the death of a mother in childbirth, particularly at the birth of her first child, would frequently lead the husband to take a second wife. If a considerable number of mothers died at childbirth, this could have been a further reason for the preponderance of adult females in the Hesi cemetery.

Column 8 of Appendix 2: Typological Catalogue gives the age at time of death for some of the adults buried in the cemetery. Unfortunately, many entries necessarily give the age in such vague terms as "over 24 years." These entries cannot contribute to a study of age at time of death. Taking only cases where age is specified within a five-year range, and using the highest figure given, the average age at time of death for adult males is 35.3 years and for adult females 27.9 years. In cultures with advanced medical knowledge women tend to outlive men. If the figures given for the cemetery can be taken as approximately accurate, the opposite was true at Hesi. The most probable explanation is that death at childbirth was a common phenomenon. This conclusion is strengthened by the substantial number of newborn infants buried in the cemetery. However, since so many age entries in the catalogue were not specific enough to be used, the conclusion cannot be regarded as proved.

The age and sex data from the Hesi cemetery are consistent with a community in which the standards of sanitation and medical care were low, in which the deaths of mothers and infants at childbirth were frequent, and in which the death rate among infants and young children was high. They may also point to a limited practice of polygamous marriage within the community.

Body Positions

The histogram for body positions (Fig. 14, cf. Table 13) shows peak occurrences in positions 2, 4, and 8. The remaining five possibilities are represented by only a few examples. A goodness-of-fit test on the body-position table as a whole gives a chi-square value of 1.69 with six degrees of freedom. The highest percentages of the chi-square value are contributed by variations in the rare positions 1, 3, 6, and 7. When these are lumped together as "other," the chi-square value drops to 0.78 with three degrees of freedom. This reorganization of the data brings the samples into good agreement with one another.

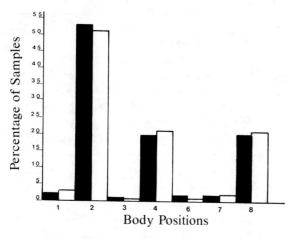

Fig. 14.   Histogram illustrating the percentage of each body position among the typed burials (black bars) in comparison with the percentage among the burials with full typological data (white bars). Position 5 is not represented in either sample. Drawn by L. E. Toombs.

Table 13.   Comparison of Body Positions between Typed Burials and those Having Full Typological Data (Totals and Percentages)*

Body Positions	Typed Burials	Full Typology
1. extended on front	4/2.2%	4/2.8%
2. extended on back	96/53.0%	72/51.1%
3. extended on left side	2/1.1%	1/0.7%
4. extended on right side	36/19.9%	30/21.3%
5. flexed on front	0/0.0%	0/0.0%
6. flexed on back	3/1.7%	1/0.7%
7. flexed on left side	3/1.7%	3/2.1%
8. flexed on right side	37/20.4%	30/21.3%
Totals	181/100%	141/100%

Chi-square value 1.69 with 6 D.F.; $p \approx 0.95$

Body Positions	Typed Burials	Full Typology
2. extended on back	96/53.0%	72/51.1%
4. extended on right side	36/19.9%	30/21.3%
8. flexed on right side	37/20.4%	30/21.3%
Other	12/6.7%	9/6.3%
Totals	181/100%	141/100%

Chi-square value 0.78 with 3 D.F.; $p \approx 0.95$

*The data for all positions are given separately in the upper part of the table. The data with the infrequent positions combined are given in the lower part of the table.

It is reasonable to conclude that any of the three major positions (2—extended on the back, 4—extended on the right side, or 8—flexed on the right side) was acceptable within the burial customs of the community. The body was placed on the back or on the right side with about equal frequency. When the position on the right side was chosen, it was a matter of indifference whether the body was flexed or extended. The two variations of the position occur almost equally. The other four body positions must be regarded as in some sense anomalous.

Eye Directions

Eye directions fall into a distinctive and informative pattern. As Fig. 15 and Table 14 show, 91% of the observed eye directions are between east (e) and southwest (h), with 80% of the skeletons looking either southeast (f) or south (g). If all the eye directions represented in the cemetery are considered separately, the samples are in agreement (chi-square 4.63 with eight degrees of freedom), but categories a, b, c, d, i, and j each contain a small number of individuals and hence may render the chi-square unreliable. If directions e-h are combined and the remaining orientations grouped together as "other," the samples fit almost perfectly (chi-square 0.06 with one degree of freedom). Eye direction e-h may therefore be regarded as the only one permitted by the burial customs, and the other eye directions may be considered as rarely occurring anomalies.

Mecca. As has been pointed out (pp. 35-36), the graves were not laid out to a precise compass direction, and several factors influenced the grave orientation and eye direction. Within these limits, however, the direction of the eyes is consistent and indicates an intent to orient the body and particularly the eyes in the direction of Mecca.

The position of the head in the western end of the grave and the direction of the eyes toward Mecca had a determinative effect on other characteristics of the burials, particularly the orientation of the grave and the position of the body. To

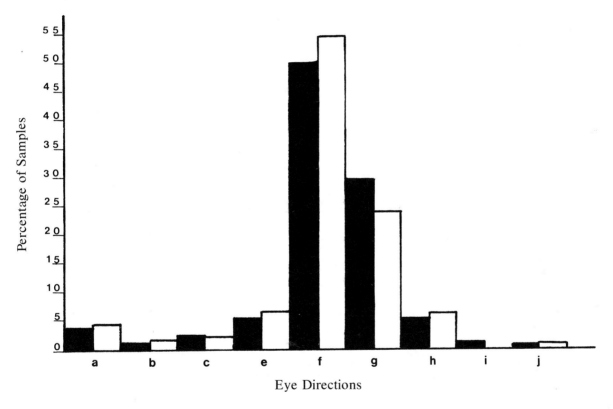

Fig. 15. Histogram illustrating the percentage of each eye direction among the typed burials (black bars) in comparison with the percentage among the burials with full typological data (white bars). Eye direction d is not represented in either sample. Drawn by L. E. Toombs.

The distribution of eye directions provides the surest evidence that the Hesi cemetery was used by a Muslim community. Mecca lies to the south-southeast of Hesi. The eye directions cluster thickest around this orientation, and taper off as one moves away from it (Fig. 16). Other features of the burials, such as grave structure and body position, may vary, but one procedure was virtually always carried out in a burial. The head was placed in the western end of a grave oriented east-west, and the eyes were directed toward

achieve the right eye direction with the head in the western end of the grave, the grave would have to be dug roughly at right angles to the direction of Mecca. The body could then be placed on the back or front and the face turned toward the south-southeast, although positioning the body on the front would make this more awkward. The body could also rest on the right side, but placing it on the left side would be ruled out. The statistics summarized in Tables 9-14 support these conclusions. Of the burials 51.8% are on the back, and

42.6% are on the right side. Half of the remainder are on the front (2.8%). All other positions account for only 2.8% of the total.

Table 14. Comparison of Eye Directions between Typed Burials and those Having Full Typological Data (Totals and Percentages)*

Eye Direction	Typed Burials	Full Typology
a. looking up	6/3.6%	6/4.3%
b. looking down	2/1.2%	2/1.4%
c. looking north	4/2.4%	3/2.1%
d. looking northeast	0/0.0%	0/0.0%
e. looking east	9/5.4%	9/6.4%
f. looking southeast	84/50.3%	77/54.6%
g. looking south	50/29.9%	34/24.1%
h. looking southwest	9/5.4%	9/6.4%
i. looking west	2/1.2%	0/0.0%
j. looking northwest	1/0.6%	1/0.7%
Totals	167/100%	141/100%

Chi-square value 4.63 with 8 D.F.; 0.90 > p > 0.75

e, f, g. h	152/91.0%	129/91.5%
Other	15/9.0%	12/8.5%
Totals	167/100%	141/100%

Chi-square value 0.06 with 1 D.F.; 0.90 > p > 0.75

*The data for all positions are given separately in the upper part of the table. The lower part of the table shows the data with the directions toward Mecca combined, and the rest clustered as "other."

Conclusions

(1) If the various categories of data are reorganized as suggested in the foregoing analysis, the burials with full typology are representative of the cemetery as a whole. This sample may therefore be used with a high degree of confidence in making cross-comparisons of the various categories of data.

(2) The analysis permits a precise definition of the types of burials permitted within the framework of the burial customs. A "typical" burial might be in any one of the grave structures, but reasons have been given why Types III and IV should be combined. Type V, with only one occurrence, is too small a sample to be statistically valid. The sex groupings, except for adults, have

been shown to provide insufficient data for comparative purposes, and the number of individuals in the juvenile grouping is too small to be reliable. Body positions 2, 4, and 8 and eye directions e-h are within the normal burial customs of the cemetery. The characteristics of a typical burial may be summarized in the following formula:

I, II, III/IV. A-C, D-F, (G-J), K-M. 2, 4, 8. e-h.

Any burial not included in the formula constitutes an anomaly. Within the terms of the formula a burial can be anomalous only in respect to body position and/or eye direction.

The remainder of this chapter will present: (1) a cross-comparison of the categories of data included in the typological formula, (2) illustrations and descriptions of typical burials, and (3) a discussion of anomalous burials.

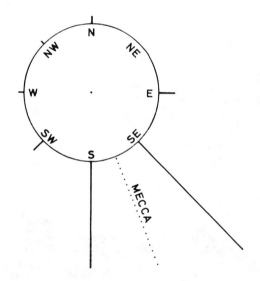

EYE DIRECTION

(1mm = 2 individuals)

Fig. 16. The compass rose illustrates the distribution of eye directions among the typed burials in relation to the direction from the site to the city of Mecca. Drawn by B. Zoughbi from an original by L. E. Toombs.

Cross-comparison of Categories

The relevant data for burials with full typology are presented in Table 15. The columns show grave structure in combination with age and sex. The rows give the combined data for body position and eye direction. The totals for any one of these categories may easily be derived from the table.

Table 15. Analysis of the Graves Having Full Typological Data in Terms of the Elements in the Typological Formula

	I C	II C	III C	IV C	II E	I F	II F	III F	IV F	I J	I K	II K	III K	I L	II L	III L	IV L	I M	II M	
1b																		1		1
1f														1						1
1g													1							1
1h													1							1
2a	1	2	2															1		6
2c													1							1
2e	3	1	1			1		1												7
2f	8	2	3	1		5	4	3			1	1		2	5	1	2	1		39
2g	1	1						1		1	1	3	1	2	3	1			1	16
2h				1	1											1				3
3j		1																		1
4f	3	5				3					3	2		1						17
4g	2	2				1					2	1		1	1					10
4h															2	1				3
6f													1							1
7c	1													1						2
7g															1					1
8b	1																			1
8e	1		1																	2
8f	7	4	1	1								2		1		3				19
8g	2		1									1	1	1						6
8h	1												1							2
	31	18	9	2	1	10	6	4	1	1	9	11	3	8	15	6	2	3	1	141

Each of the four elements in the typological formula was compared with every other element by means of "tests for independence of rows and columns in row and column contingency tables" made up from Table 15 (Snedecor and Cochran, 1967, 250-53). In every case the results showed a high degree of independence. Practically speaking, this means that within the general framework of the burial customs the burial parties exercised a large measure of freedom of choice in selecting the grave structure and body position to be used in the interment of individuals of any age or of either sex. That is, in any specific grave any combination of the elements defined in the typological formula may be found.

Two questions of considerable importance are not answered by the foregoing statement. Did the two characteristics of a burial over which the community had no control, viz., the age and sex of the deceased, have any influence on the way in which the burial customs were applied? Do the Hesi burials give any evidence of social stratification in the community which used the cemetery?

Influence of Age and Sex

In order to answer the first question, a series of histograms was prepared comparing the observed and expected occurrences of the three age brackets (infants, children, and adults) in the various grave structures (Fig. 17), body positions (Fig. 18), and eye directions (Fig. 19). The expected values are those arrived at by assuming independence of the two factors involved (Snedecor and Cochran, 1967, 1950-53). Both the observed and expected values are plotted as percentages of the burials with full typology. The single juvenile in the sample is omitted from the histograms, and in Fig. 17 the Type IV cists are also omitted (see p. 63). The percentage differences between the observed and expected values are in every case small, but the following tendencies may be noted.

Infants are buried more frequently than expected in simple earth graves (Type I), and less frequently than expected in capped graves (Type II). Their occurrence in capped and lined graves (Type III) is almost precisely as expected (Fig. 17). The preferred body position for infants is flexed on the right side (8). In all other positions the occurrence is less than expected (Fig. 18). The eyes of infants are directed towards Mecca slightly less frequently than in the other age groups, and proportionately more anomalies occur (Fig. 19).

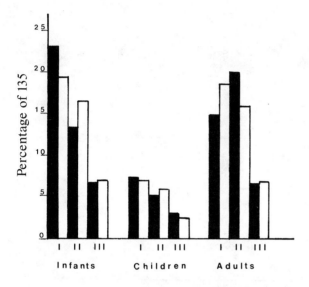

Fig. 17. Histogram comparing the occurrence of the various age brackets in the three principal grave structures. Black bars show observed frequencies, white bars expected values, assuming independence of age and grave structure. The juveniles and the Type IV cists have been omitted from the histogram. Drawn by L. E. Toombs.

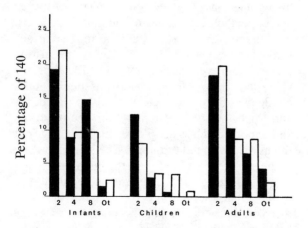

Fig. 18. Histogram comparing the occurrence of the various age brackets in the three principal body positions. All remaining body positions are lumped together as "other" (Ot). Black bars show observed frequencies, white bars expected values, assuming independence of age and body position. Juveniles have been omitted. Drawn by L. E. Toombs.

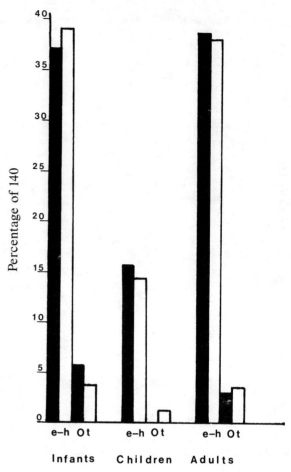

Fig. 19. Histogram comparing the occurrence of the various age brackets in respect to the eye direction towards Mecca (e-h) and other eye directions (Ot). Black bars show observed frequencies, white bars expected values, assuming independence of age and eye direction. Juveniles have been omitted. Drawn by L. E. Toombs.

Child burials are distributed among grave structures in almost precisely the expected ratios (Fig. 17). The extended position on the back (2) is preferred for children. Extension on the right side (4) is about as expected, but the flexed position on the right side (8) occurs less frequently than expected (Fig. 18). The standard eye direction is found more often than expected and no anomalies occur.

Adults were buried more frequently than expected in capped graves (Type II), less frequently than expected in simple earth graves (Type I), and about as expected in capped and lined graves (Type III/IV; see Fig. 17). The body positions are close to the expected values, but when the body rests on the right side it is more likely to be in the extended (4) than in the flexed position (8). There is an unexpectedly high incidence of anomalous body positions among adults (Fig. 18). This phenomenon probably has a simple explanation. The body of an adult, because of its bulk, is harder to handle in the narrow confines of the cist and, consequently, occasionally defied the efforts of the burial party to get it into the desired position. The eye directions of the adults are about as expected (Fig. 19).

Adult interments may be broken down into adult males and adult females. The histogram shown in Fig. 20 compares the percentages of adult males (black bars) and adult females (hatched bars) in respect to grave structure and body position. Eye direction is omitted from the histogram since only one individual of each sex looks in an anomalous direction.

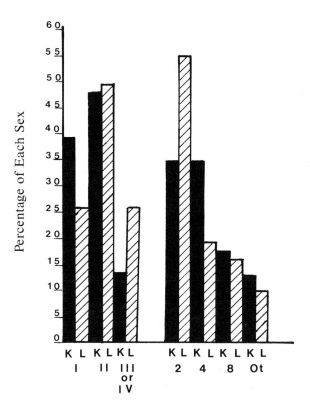

Fig. 20. Histogram comparing the distribution of adult males and adult females in each grave structure and in each body position. Black bars indicate adult males, hatched bars adult females. Drawn by L. E. Toombs.

Adult males are buried in simple earth graves (Type I) more frequently and in capped and lined graves (Type III/IV) less frequently than are women. Women are buried in the extended position on the back (2) more frequently than men. The tendency to bury women in the supine position may be accounted for by the custom of folding the hands of a woman over the region of the genital organs (see pp. 84-85). This is much more easily done if the body lies on the back. When the burial of a man is on the right side (4, 8), the extended position (4) is preferred to the flexed (8). More anomalous body positions occur in the burials of men than of women. The standard eye direction is almost uniformly achieved.

Judged on the basis of cist construction and anomalies in eye direction, the care taken in interment increases in the following order: infants, children, adult males, adult females.

On page 41 it was suggested that a change in the child's status in the eyes of the family took place at about the age of three. The data summarized in the histograms support this conclusion. Infants are buried in the simplest type of grave with a degree of frequency higher than expected (Fig. 17). The preference for the flexed position in the burial of infants (Fig. 18) may result, not from design, but from the practice of placing the small body in the grave without carefully composing the limbs (see p. 85). Since eye direction was a basic element in the burial customs, the relatively high incidence of anomalous eye directions in infant burials (Fig. 19) is additional evidence of slipshod interment.

The unexpected feature of the sequence is that women are buried more frequently than men in the most elaborate grave structures. No certain reason can be given for this phenomenon, although several possibilities suggest themselves. The extra care in the burial of women could be due to respect for their role as mothers. It could also reflect the earlier age at time of death of women in the community. The husband would frequently outlive the wife and be present at the time of her death to look after the funeral arrangements. A widow might not be in a position to do the same for her husband, and surviving sons might not display the same concern for the burial of a father as a husband might for his wife. However, there is an alternate and perhaps more likely explanation for the preponderance of women in the Type III/IV graves. Since stone had to be brought to the site for the construction of this type of grave in greater quantity than for capped graves (Type II), the Type IV graves would have been expensive to build and were probably used by a prestigious and economically advantaged group. Polygamy, permitted by Muslim law, would probably be more frequent among the wealthy and influential segment of society, and the higher incidence of adult females in this type of grave would be expected.

Muslim and, particularly, Bedouin society with its veiling of women and their careful seclusion in the tent or home has become for the Western world the prime example of a society in which the position of women is denigrated. The burials in the Hesi cemetery urge caution in drawing the conclusion that in such societies women are poorly valued or little esteemed, although the cynical mind might attribute the care taken in the burial of women to the husband's desire to look good in the eyes of the community.

Social Stratification

The possibility that the Type III graves were used by an "upper class" within the community suggests a closer study of the relationships between grave structure and the other elements in the typological formula. These relationships are shown in Figs. 21-23. The histograms compare the observed with the expected values as determined in the tests for independence.

Theoretically, the three types of grave structure could represent three strata of society, distinguished from one another on the basis of wealth or prestige. If this were the case, the observed and accepted values for the various age brackets should coincide for each grave structure. This happens only in the case of capped and lined graves (Type III; see Fig. 21). Apparently, then, the well-to-do of the community (about 20% of the population; see Table 9) buried all members of the family, including infants, in lined or capped and lined graves. Of course, the choice of the stone-built cist may not have been entirely due to superior economic resources. This group may have included the social pace-setters or political leaders of the community who would have used the better-built graves as a visible sign of family prestige. The group may also have been more tradition-minded or religiously oriented than the rest of the community and therefore more willing to invest a considerable portion of their resources in meticulously proper burials. Indeed, all of these factors may have been operative.

The Type II (capped) graves have fewer infants and more adults than expected (Fig. 21). The group which used these graves probably formed a kind of "middle class" in wealth or status. They buried their adults and children, and some of their infants, in the capped graves, but interred a portion of the infants in simple earth graves (Type I). This practice makes it difficult to calculate the size of the group. On the basis of Table 9 it was probably about 35% of the population.

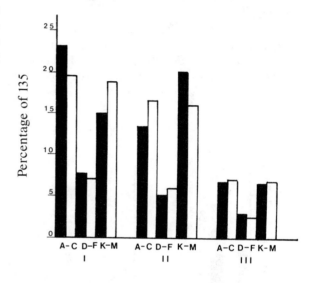

Fig. 21. Histogram comparing the distribution of the various age brackets among the types of grave structure. Black bars show observed frequencies, white bars expected values, assuming independence of age and grave structure. The juveniles and the Type IV cists have been omitted from the histogram. Drawn by L. E. Toombs.

A large number of infants and children were buried in simple earth graves (Type I; see Fig. 21). This practice is probably to be associated with the least advantaged and least influential part of the community (approximately 45% of the population). This group used the simple earth grave for the burial of all members of the family.

The upper stratum of society only rarely used the flexed position on the right side (4; see Fig. 22). The apparent preference for the extended position on the back (2; Fig. 22) is due to the preponderance of adult females in this group, possibly because of a larger number of polygamous marriages in this segment of society (see pp. 71-72). The "middle class," roughly represented by the Type II graves, seems to have used the extended position on the right side (4) more often and the flexed position on the right side (8) less often than expected (Fig. 22). In this respect, however, the histogram is misleading. Many infants in this group were buried in Type I graves, and flexation is a characteristic of infant burials (pp. 69-70). Therefore, the practice of burying infants in simple earth graves reduced the occurrence of the flexed position in the capped graves. If allowance is made for the burial of "middle-class" infants in simple earth graves, the "lower class" used all three of the acceptable body positions about as expected.

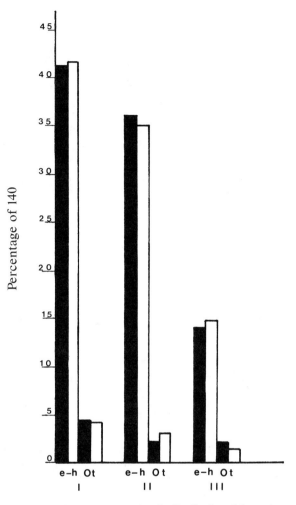

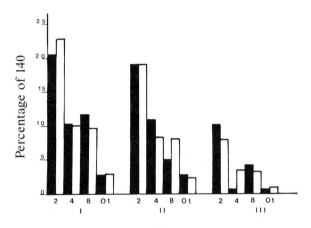

Fig. 22. Histogram comparing the distribution of the various body positions among the types of grave structure. Black bars show observed frequencies, white bars expected values, assuming independence of body position and grave structure. The juveniles have been omitted from the histogram. Drawn by L. E. Toombs.

Fig. 23. Histogram comparing the distribution of the various eye directions among the types of grave structure. Black bars show observed frequencies, white bars expected values, assuming independence of eye direction and grave structure. The juveniles have been omitted from the histogram. Drawn by L. E. Toombs.

The eye directions of all three groups closely approximate expected values (Fig. 23) and indicate that the desire to have the dead look toward Mecca was common to all levels of the community.

The possibility of dividing the community which used the Hesi cemetery into groups based on grave structure does not demonstrate, or even indicate, the existence of a highly stratified, class-conscious society. The eye directions confirm that the community was Muslim, and the simplicity of the burials suggests that it was a Bedouin or peasant farming culture. Societies of this type show little social or economic stratification, and the layout of the cemetery testifies to a remarkable democracy in death (pp. 42-43).

Typical Burials

A typical burial is one which falls within the range of the typological formula given on page 68. Table 16 shows this formula and tabulates the possibilities involved under each of its four categories. Table 17 summarizes the typical burials for which full typological data are available. There are 124 such burials, constituting 87.9% of the 141 burials for which the full typological data are known. These have been analyzed statistically in the previous sections of this chapter. This section will present the available photographs of typical burials, and discuss them in terms of the visual evidence. The order of presentation will be by age groups.

Table 16. Typological Formula*

Grave Structure I, II, III/IV	Age and Sex Groups A-C, D-F, (G-J), K-M	Body Position 2, 4, 8	Eye Direction e-h

Grave Structure—This category includes five possibilities:
   I. Graves which are neither capped nor lined with stones
  II. Graves which are capped but not lined
 III. Graves which are both capped and lined
  IV. Graves which are lined but not capped
((V. Jar burials))

Age and Sex Groups—This category includes twelve possibilities. G-J occur only rarely:

A. Infant (0-3 yrs.), male
B. Infant (0-3 yrs.), female
C. Infant (0-3 yrs.), sex undetermined
D. Child (3-10 yrs.), male
E. Child (3-10 yrs.), female
F. Child (3-10 yrs.), sex undetermined

G. Juvenile (10-17 yrs.), male
H. Juvenile (10-17 yrs.), female
J. Juvenile (10-17 yrs.), sex undetermined
K. Adult (over 17 yrs.), male
L. Adult (over 17 yrs.), female
M. Adult (over 17 yrs.), sex undetermined

Body Position—This category includes eight possibilities, three of which are typical:

((1. Extended on the front))
 2. Extended on the back
((3. Extended on the left side))
 4. Extended on the right side

((5. Flexed on the front))
((6. Flexed on the back))
((7. Flexed on the left side))
 8. Flexed on the right side

Eye Direction—This category includes ten possibilities, four of which are typical:

((a. Looking up))
((b. Looking down))
((c. Looking north))
((d. Looking northeast))
 e. Looking east

 f. Looking southeast
 g. Looking south
 h. Looking southwest
((i. Looking west))
((j. Looking northwest))

*The typological formula is given at the top of the table. Below are tabulated the possibilities under each of the four categories. Double parentheses indicate the possibilities which are regarded as anomalous and are therefore not included in the typological formula. The presence of a "0" in any position in the formula indicates that information for that category is lacking.

Typical Burials of Infants

Pls. 28 and 33 (Type I cists), Pl. 10 (Type II cist), and Pl. 35 (Type III cist) illustrate the burials of infants in the extended position on the back (2), a position less frequent among infants than burial on the right side (Fig. 18 and pp. 69-70). All the examples shown in the photographs display considerable deterioration of, and damage to, the bones. Moreover, Pl. 10 is complicated by the presence of a newborn child on the chest and abdomen of the older infant. Three of the photographs (Pls. 10, 33, and 35) show deliberate turning of the head so that the eyes look to the southeast. The eye direction of the infant shown in Pl. 28 is east, probably because the skull has slipped downward on the stone pillow. The infants illustrated in Pls. 28 and 35 are inclined slightly to the right side. The arm positions vary widely.

Typical infant burials in the extended position on the right side (4) are shown in Pl. 36 (Type I cist) and in Pls. 9 and 37 (Type II cists). The position does not occur in burials of infants in Type III/IV cists. Pl. 9 shows two infants in the same grave (see p. 24). Both are extended on the right side, but the legs of both appear to be slightly flexed. The same characteristic is evident in Pls. 36 and 37. This observation supports the conclusion, advanced on page 70, that, when an infant was buried on the right side, the legs were normally flexed, although in some cases the degree of flexation was slight. This feature of infant burials contrasts with adult interments, where the fully extended position on the right side (4) was more common. The arm positions are again varied.

Typical infant burials in the flexed position on the right side (8), the most common body position among infant burials, are illustrated in Pls. 18 and 38 (Type I cists), Pl. 39 (Type II cist), and Pl. 8C (Type III cist). Pl. 18 is the most informative of these photographs. The skeleton is well preserved. The head rests on a stone pillow. The flexation of the legs is pronounced. Marked flexation occurs also in Pl. 39, but its presence or absence is not clear in Pls. 8 and 38.

There are no photographs illustrative of child burials in the flexed position on the right side, which is relatively rare among children.

Table 17. The Typical Graves among the Burials with Full Typological Data*

Typological Classification	Number of Individuals	Plate Numbers	Typological Classification	Number of Individuals	Plate Numbers	Typological Classification	Number of Individuals	Plate Numbers
I.C.2.e-h	12	28, 33	II.C.2.e-g	4	10	III/IV.C.2.e-f	5	35
I.C.4.f-g	5	36	II.C.4.f-g	7	9, 37			
I.C.8.e-h	11	18, 38	II.C.8.f	4	39	III/IV.C.8.e-g	4	8
			II.E.2.h	1	none			
I.F.2.e-f	6	7, 40	II.F.2.f, h	5	30, 32, 41	III/IV.F.2.e-g	5	none
I.F.4.f	3	none	II.F.4.g	1	42			
I.F.8.g	1	none						
I.J.2.g	1	43						
I.K.2.f-g	2	none	II.K.2.f-g	4	44	III/IV.K.2.g	1	none
I.K.4.f-g	5	19	II.K.4.f-g	3	45			
I.K.8.f	2	none	II.K.8.g-h	2	12			
I.L.2.f-g	4	6	II.L.2.f-h	9	12, 14, 16	III/IV.L.2.f-g	4	11, 21, 25
I.L.4.g	1	none	II.L.4.f-h	4	31, 46	III/IV.L.4.h	1	34
I.L.8.f	1	47	II.L.8.g	1	48	III/IV.L.8.f	3	24, 49, 50
I.M.2.f	1	none	II.M.2.g	1	none			

*Only the number of individuals in each category is given. The reader may identify the locus numbers of the individual graves by consulting Appendix 2: Typological Catalogue.

Typical Burials of Children

Pl. 40 (Type I cist) and Pls. 32 and 41 (Type II cists) represent typical child burials in the extended position on the back. Pl. 40, the burial of a child of three to four years, shows the same inclination toward the right side and the same slight flexation of the legs as is common in infant burials. The burial of a child of four to six years, illustrated in Pl. 41, shows a fully extended position of the arms and legs, except that the right leg is slightly flexed. Pl. 32, the burial of a child of four to six years, has the body placed directly on the back with the legs fully extended. Both features are characteristic of adult burials on the back, especially those of women (p. 71).

Only one photograph of a typical child burial in the extended position on the right side is available (Pl. 42, Type II cist). The individual is only three to four years old, but the adult characteristic of full extension of the legs is present.

Typical Burial of a Juvenile

There is only one juvenile among the burials with full typological data (see Table 15). The individual, eleven to fifteen years of age, is of unknown sex. The body (Pl. 43) is reported as resting in the extended position on the back in a simple earth grave (Type I). The lower part of the body was, however, cut away by the military trenching, and the position of the lower limbs is uncertain.

Typical Burials of Adult Males

The typical burial of an adult male in the extended position on the back is illustrated in Pl. 44 (Type II cist). The body was placed flat on the back in the grave, and the head was turned so that the eyes looked to the southeast. Both arms were laid on the body, so that the hands rested in the pelvic area. This position is more characteristic of women than of men. The legs were fully extended with the toes pointing upward. The position is in all respects a natural one for a person lying on the back.

Pl. 19 (Type I cist) and Pl. 45 (Type II cist) illustrate typical burials of adult males in the extended position on the right side. In both cases the legs are fully extended, and the body rests squarely on the right shoulder. In this position the eye direction to the south or southeast is the natural one, requiring no adjustment of the head. The arm positions are virtually the same in both photographs, except that in Pl. 19 the left hand is on the pelvis, whereas in Pl. 45 the left arm is across the lower abdomen.

There is only one illustration of an adult male in the flexed position on the right side (Pl. 12B, Type II cist). The body lies in a natural position of sleep with the legs slightly flexed and the left arm resting easily across the chest. The position on the right side guarantees that the eyes will be directed to the south or southeast.

Typical Burials of Adult Females

Eight photographs show typical burials of adult females in the extended position on the back (Pl. 6A, Type I cist; Pls. 12A, 14, and 16, Type II cists; Pls. 21 and 22, Type III cists; Pls. 11 and 25, Type IV cists). In all cases the body is flat on the back, except that the skeleton in Pl. 11 inclines slightly to the right side. The deliberate turning of the head over the right shoulder is clear in all the photographs. Except for the burial shown in Pl. 12A, where both arms are extended, all the individuals have at least one hand in the pelvic region.

Typical burials of adult females in the extended position on the right side are illustrated in Pls. 31 and 46 (Type II cists) and in Pl. 34 (Type III cist). Pl. 46 is the best representative of the type. The legs of the skeleton are fully extended. The lower limbs of the skeleton depicted in Pl. 34 were cut off by a later infant burial (I.32.040), but enough of the long bones remained to suggest that this skeleton also was fully extended. The legs of the skeleton illustrated in Pl. 31 were so slightly flexed that the burial was reported on the code forms as being in the extended position. In all three cases one or both of the hands rested in the pelvic area.

Typical burials of females in the flexed position on the right side are illustrated in Pl. 47 (Type I cist), Pl. 48 (Type II cist), and Pls. 24, 49, and 50 (Type III cists). The photographs show that the manner and degree of flexation of the legs varies.

The skeletons pictured in Pls. 24 and 50 have both legs slightly flexed. That shown in Pl. 48 has the right leg slightly flexed, but the left leg almost straight. In Pl. 49 there is only a suggestion of flexation. In all four burials the left elbow is flexed, so that the forearm lies across the abdominal region. The position on the right side virtually ensures the direction of the eyes to the south or southeast.

Although the burial shown in Pl. 47 (Type I cist) is a "typical" adult female burial in terms of the typological formula, it has several unusual characteristics which arise from attributes not included in the formula. The cist is a simple earth grave without capstones or liners, and it is too small to contain the body in an extended or slightly flexed position. To accommodate the body to the grave, the legs were pushed upward until the knees were just below the chin. The hands do not lie in a natural position across the abdomen or in the pelvis. Instead, the elbows are tightly flexed, bringing the hands close to the chin, and the wrists are bent, so that the hands lie palm downward with the fingers pointing toward the neck. There is no certain explanation for this unusual treatment of the body. The fact that the burial is in a simple earth grave indicates that the woman belonged to the less advantaged class of society. She was a woman over twenty-four years of age. Possibly this was merely a hasty and careless burial of a woman who had no immediate family to provide a proper interment.

Conclusions

The norms of the burial customs and procedures appear most clearly in the adult burials. The positioning of the head in the western end of the grave and the orientation of the eyes to the south or southeast appear to have been mandatory. The burial party had a choice of three body positions. Having selected one of these, they adjusted the head, if necessary, and composed the limbs in a natural position resembling that of sleep. When the body lay on the back, the legs were fully extended, and the arms were usually extended at the sides. However, the right arm was often flexed, so as to bring the right hand over the pelvis in a kind of final gesture of modesty. Sometimes both arms were treated in this way. When burial was on the side, the legs were either extended or slightly flexed. The right arm was usually extended just in front of the body, and the left bent.

so that the arm lay across the chest or abdomen. Frequently an attempt was made to cover the genital region with the left hand.

The burials of infants were not made with the same care as those of adults, and, consequently, numerous variations from adult norms occur. However, for children over the age of four or five years, more care seems to have been taken to give the burial an adult form. One fairly consistent tendency in infant burials is a preference for interment on the right side with the legs flexed.

The conclusions regarding arm and leg positions given above are based on the photographed burials. This is a small and, in some respects, random sample. In Chapter 9 these conclusions will be re-examined in the light of the full range of available data.

Atypical Burials

In terms of the typological formula (p. 68), a burial may be atypical in body position, in eye direction, or in both. The atypical burials among the interments with full typological data are listed in the upper part of Table 18, the nature of the anomaly is stated, and the figure number, if any, is given. The lower part of Table 18 supplements this list by tabulating the anomalous burials among the typed graves.

Burials Anomalous in Body Position Only

Five interments among the burials with full typological data are anomalies in body position only. The anomalies are: extended on the front (position 1, Burials I.1.111, I.32.080, I.51.133), flexed on the back (position 6, Burial I.32.037), and flexed on the left side (position 7, Burial I.32.046). All the burials extended on the front involve adults: a woman of seventeen to twenty-four years (I.1.111) in a simple earth grave (Type I) and two mature males (I.32.080 and I.51.133) in capped but unlined cists (Type II). Although the bodies lie on the front, they do not face down. The heads have been turned so that the eyes look in a generally southerly direction. The legs are fully extended. The female (I.1.111) has both arms extended at the sides. The arm position of one of the males (I.51.133) could not be determined. The burial of the other male (I.32.080) is illustrated in Pl. 51. The turning of the head and the extension of the legs are clear in the photograph, but the position of the hands and arms cannot be distin-

guished. The osteologist reported that the left arm was extended and the right arm bent under the body so that the hand covered the genital region. Neither age, sex, nor cist type seems to account for burial on the front. Most probably this position was not considered to be a serious departure from the normal burial customs. It was, nevertheless, a rare and unpopular position.

Table 18. Anomalous Burials among the Graves with Full Typological Data and among the Typed Graves*

Typological Classification	Grave Number	Plate Number	Nature of Anomaly
Burials with Full Typology			
I.C.2.a	I.32.011	none	Eye direction only
I.C.7.c	I.22.006	none	Body position and eye direction
I.C.8.b	I.22.036	none	Eye direction only
I.L.1.f	I.1.111	none	Body position only
I.L.7.c	I.11.211	55	Body position and eye direction
I.M.1.b	I.51.134	none	Body position and eye direction
I.M.2.a	I.31.175	none	Eye direction only
II.C.2.a	I.12.015	53	Eye direction only
	I.12.127	none	Eye direction only
II.C.3.j	I.32.032A	none	Body position and eye direction
II.K.1.g	I.51.133	none	Body position only
II.K.1.h	I.32.080	51	Body position only
II.L.7.g	I.32.046	13	Body position only
III.C.2.a	I.32.040	34	Eye direction only
	I.41.051	none	Eye direction only
III.K.2.c	I.22.102	54	Eye direction only
III.K.6.f	I.32.037	52	Body position only
Typed Burials			
I.C.3.0	I.22.150	none	Body position only
I.C.6.0	I.41.212	none	Body position only
I.F.0.i	I.21.017A	none	Eye direction only
I.K.0.c	I.1.024	none	Eye direction only
III.F.0.i	I.31.015	none	Eye direction only
III.K.6.0	I.32.039	29	Body position only

*The upper part of the table shows the atypical burials with full typological data. The lower part shows additional anomalies among the typed graves (see Appendix 2: Typological Catalogue).

When burial was on the back, the legs were almost invariably fully extended. The single exception among the burials with full typological data is I.32.037 (Pl. 52). The legs are flexed and twisted to the right in a manner reminiscent of an infant burial. The skeleton is that of a mature male buried in a capped and lined cist (Type III). Both hands rest in the pelvic region. Two other examples of flexation on the back occur among the typed burials. I.41.212 is the burial of an infant in a simple earth grave (Type I), and I.32.039 (Pl. 29) is that of a mature male in a capped and lined cist (Type III). Unfortunately, in both cases the eye direction could not be determined. The variant represented by flexed burial on the back (6) may not be deliberate. It may result from a failure on the part of the burial party to compose and adjust the legs when the body was placed in the grave.

Flexation on the left side (7), unlike burial on the front and flexed burial on the back, is a radical departure from the norms of the cemetery. If the head were placed as usual in the west end of the grave, such a position would cause the eyes to look northward, as is the case with Burials I.11.211 and I.22.006, discussed below. Burial I.32.046 (Pl. 13) is a peculiar case. Although the body was flexed on the left side, the normal eye direction was achieved by placing the head in the *east* end of the grave. The interment is that of a female, aged seventeen to twenty-four years, buried in a capped but unlined grave (Type II). Her left arm is extended, but her right is strongly flexed at the elbow, bringing the hand just below the chin. There is no ready explanation for this end-to-end reversal of the body in the grave. It seems to be deliberate, since only an incredibly careless burial party would make an error of such magnitude.

Burials Anomalous in Eye Direction Only

Anomalies in eye direction only, occurring among burials with full typological data, are: direction a, looking up (six examples); direction b, looking down (one example); direction c, looking north (one example).

All the skeletons whose eyes look upward are extended on the back (2). Five are infant burials. Of these one (I.32.011) is in a simple earth grave (Type I), two (I.12.015 and I.12.127) are in capped but unlined graves (Type II), and two (I.32.040 and I.41.051) are in capped and lined graves (Type III). The remaining example (I.31.175) is the burial of an adult of unknown sex in a simple earth grave (Type I). Two of these burials may be illustrated by photographs. Pl. 53 shows the burial of an

infant (I.12.015) in a capped but unlined grave (Type II). The eyes look up. The arms are extended at the sides, and the right leg is slightly flexed to the south. Pl. 34 illustrates the burial of an infant (I.32.040) in a capped and lined grave (Type III). The eyes are directed upward. The arms are slightly flexed. The right hand rests on the pelvis, but the left hand is missing. The left leg bends slightly to the north. The obvious explanation of this anomaly is that those in charge of the burial failed to turn the head when the body was placed in the grave, leaving it in the position natural to a body lying on the back. The error occurred most frequently in the burial of infants, where meticulous attention was not always paid to the burial procedures. The single instance of an adult burial showing this anomaly (I.31.175) is in the poorest class of grave.

The only example of a burial with the eyes directed downward (b) is the interment of an infant (I.22.036) in a simple earth grave (Type I). The body is flexed on the right side (8) with the right arm extended and the left across the chest. This anomaly is the result of failure to adjust the head properly when the body was placed in the cist.

The same explanation probably applies to the single instance (I.22.102) among the burials with full typological data of an interment in which the only anomaly is that the eyes are directed to the north (c). The skeleton (Pl. 54) is that of an adult male buried in a capped and lined grave (Type III). It lies supine on the back, legs fully extended, right arm at the side, left arm bent so that the hand rests on the pelvis. The head, however, lolls over the left shoulder, directing the eyes to the north. The other two examples of bodies looking north (I.22.006 and I.11.211) occur along with flexation on the *left* side. Burial I.1.024 may be left out of account, since the body position could not be observed, and consequently it was impossible to tell whether it was extended on the back or placed on the left side.

When not combined with anomalous body positions, all irregularities in eye direction may be explained as failures on the part of those conducting the interment to turn the face toward Mecca after the body was placed in the grave. This oversight could easily occur in a few cases if the bodies were wrapped in shrouds before burial.

Examples of anomalous eye direction i (looking west) occur only among the typed burials. In both instances (I.21.017A and I.31.015) the body position is not known, and consequently the nature of the anomaly cannot be determined. Both are, perhaps by coincidence, child burials.

Burials Anomalous in Both Body Position and Eye Direction

The anomalies in this category are: 1b, on the front, looking down (one example); 3j, extended on the left side, looking northwest (one example, and another whose eye direction can only be inferred); 7c, flexed on the left side, looking north (two examples).

The single case of burial face down on the front (1b, I.51.134) is the interment of an adult of unknown sex in a simple earth grave (Type I). The legs and right arm are extended. The position of the left arm is unknown. Since the face-downward position is natural when the body is extended on the front, the anomaly is not a serious one and may be attributed to carelessness in the disposition of the body in the grave.

The remaining four cases are at once more interesting and more difficult to interpret. All involve burial on the left side with the head in the west end of the grave, a position which forces the eyes to look to the north or northwest. These four burials, then, appear to be deliberate reversals of the customary burial practices.

The first of these burials (I.32.032A) is the interment of an infant in a Type II cist (capped but not lined). The skeleton is extended on the left side (3), with the right arm straight and the left forearm across the lower chest. The eyes look to the northwest. Another example (I.22.150) of burial in the extended position on the left side occurs among the typed burials. Unfortunately, in this case the infant's eye direction is unknown. The third reversed burial (I.22.006) is an infant in a simple earth grave (Type I). The body is in a flexed position on its left side and the eyes look directly to the north. Both arms are bent at the elbow, so that the forearms lie across the chest. The last of these reversed burials is that of an adult female (I.11.211) in a simple earth grave (Type I). The skeleton, shown in Pl. 55, lies on the left side, looking north. The legs are somewhat more strongly flexed than is customary. The left arm is extended and the right elbow is bent, bringing the forearm across the chest.

From the description of these interments it is clear that they resemble typical burials in several ways. The graves are oriented from west to east. The head is in the western end of the grave. The arrangement of the limbs follows standard patterns. The crucial variant from the norm is the direction of the eyes to the north or northwest. To achieve this direction required placing the body on the left side.

The explanation of this peculiar phenomenon is not obvious. Numerous suggestions of varying seriousness have been offered. One hypothesis is that the individuals buried in these graves were members of families out of favor with the community. The reversed burials would then be a mark of hostility or contempt. Others have suggested that heretical or religiously indifferent individuals might be buried in this way, in order to signify their exclusion from true Islam. The presence of children in these anomalous burials makes either supposition hard doctrine indeed.

The direction of the eyes may be the clue to the significance of these reversed burials. Jerusalem, lying to the north-northeast of Hesi, is sacred to Muslims as well as to Jews and Christians. It is unlikely that even a small Jewish or Christian element existed in the Hesi community. Even if such a group did exist, it is improbable that its dead would be buried in the community cemetery. We are left with the hypothesis that a small minority of families preferred, for religious or other reasons, to be buried facing the Holy City of Jerusalem.

CHAPTER 9

Secondary Characteristics

The primary characteristics of the burials in the Hesi cemetery have been discussed in Chapters 5 and 8. The present chapter deals with those characteristics which were not included in the typological formula and which may, for the reasons stated on pages 60-61, be regarded as secondary. Two of these, grave orientation and grave shape, are features of cist construction that were discussed on pages 35-36. The remaining secondary characteristics are: (1) the orientation of the skeleton in the grave, discussed in a preliminary way on pages 35 and 60, (2) the position of the arms, (3) unusual positions of the legs, especially extreme flexation, which the typological formula does not distinguish from slight or medium flexation, (4) skull shape and coloration of the bones, characteristics which seem to be related to one another, (5) unusual positions of the skull, and (6) diseases and trauma.

Orientation of the Skeleton in the Grave

The normal orientation of the skeletons in the Hesi cemetery is along an axis lying between west-east and southwest-northeast with the head usually in the western end of the grave (see pp. 35-36). In the development of the typological formula this orientation was regarded as "invariable" (p. 60) and was therefore left out of account. Actually there are eighteen cases of anomalous skeletal orientation among the typed burials, ten of them burials with full typological data. They can be grouped into four classes:

   (1) *Head to the northwest*: I.3.051 (I.K.0.0), I.13.007 (I.F.8.g), I.32.009 (I.C.2.g), I.32.010 (I.C.0.0), I.41.016 (III.F.2.g), I.41.204 (I.C.0.f), I.51.028 (I.C.8.h);

   (2) *Head to the south*: I.3.097 (I.C.2.0), I.31.015 (III.F.0.i), V.P-1a.006 (I.C.2.e), V.P-1p.004 (I.F.2.f);

   (3) *Head to the southeast*: I.22.016 (I.C.2.0);

   (4) *Head to the east*: I.22.036 (I.C.8.b), I.22.107 (I.F.4.f), I.22.150 (I.C.3.0), I.32.046 (II.L.7.g), I.41.057 (IV.C.4.0), I.41.068 (III.L.2.f).

Of the burials with the head to the northwest, two (I.3.051 and I.32.010) were badly disturbed graves in which the bones were disarticulated, and the position of the skull in the grave is likely to have been accidental. Four of the remaining burials (I.13.007, I.32.009, I.41.024, and I.51.028) owe the abnormal orientation of the skeleton to the fact that the cist was dug on a northwest-southeast axis. The skeleton took on the normal orientation of the grave. The only case of a skeleton with the head to the northwest in a normally oriented grave is Burial I.41.016. This capped and lined grave contained the skeleton of a child of three to four years of age. The body was extended on the back with the right hand in the pelvis and the left arm extended, and the eyes looked to the south. Other than the relatively rare arm position, the only anomaly in the burial was the orientation of the skeleton. It may safely be concluded that the young child was merely buried somewhat askew in a normally oriented grave.

One of the burials with the head to the south (I.3.097) was disarticulated. The other three were in cists oriented almost due north-south. In each case the body has taken on the orientation of the cist. Eye directions were normal in V.P-1a.006 and V.P-1p.004, but the eyes of the skeleton in Burial I.31.015 looked to the west, at a right angle to the axis of the cist.

The single burial with the head to the southeast (I.22.016) contained a disarticulated skeleton.

Thus, in the first three classes of anomalous skeletal orientation, only one articulated burial occurred in a normally oriented grave (I.41.016).

One of the burials with the head to the east (I.22.150) contained a disarticulated skeleton. The remaining five, all articulated burials, constitute a curious sub-group representing an apparently deliberate reversal of the normal orientation. All three of the principal body positions are included. In Burial I.41.068 an adult female lay in a capped and lined grave, prostrate on the back with the right arm extended and the left hand in the pelvis. With the head in the east end of the grave the normal eye direction was achieved by turning the head so that the eyes looked over the *left* shoulder. The burial is typical in every respect except the orientation of the body.

Two of the burials with the skull to the east had ambiguous eye directions. Burial I.22.036, an infant in a simple earth grave, was flexed on the right side, but the head had been turned so that the face was down. The right arm was extended and the left was across the chest. Burial I.41.057 was the interment of an infant in a Type IV grave (lined but not capped). The body was extended on the right side, but the position of the arms and the direction of the eyes could not be determined. With the skull in the east end of the grave the eyes should have been looking north.

Unlike the other burials with the head to the east, I.32.046 had an anomalous body position. The body was flexed on the *left* side, so that, in spite of the fact that the skull was in the wrong end of the grave, the eyes looked toward Mecca. This burial is illustrated in Pl. 13 and discussed on page 78.

Burial I.22.107, a child in a simple earth grave, was described on the report sheets as resting in an impossible position. The body was extended on the right side with the eyes directed to the southeast. With the head at the eastern end of the grave this eye direction could only be obtained by turning the head through 180°, so that the eyes looked directly to the rear. In this case, the orientation of the skeleton was probably incorrectly reported, but unfortunately no photograph is available as a check.

The placing of the head in the wrong end of the grave is a mistake not easily made by a burial party. The practice does not seem to indicate that those buried with this orientation were outcasts from the community or heretics from Islam, since in the burials where eye direction could be determined the eyes looked toward Mecca. The burials contained the remains of two adult females and two infants. Three of the four burials were in stone-built cists. In the light of these facts it is likely that a small minority of the families using the cemetery adhered, for whatever reason, to the deviant tradition of burial with the head to the east.

Arm Positions

The discussion of typical and atypical burials on pages 73-79 included some treatment of arm position and arrived at preliminary conclusions. Since the discussion was limited to burials for which photographs were available, it was based on the small sample of graves with adequate skeletal preservation. The sample used in the following studies is the burials with full typological data. Of course, not all 141 individuals figure in the treatment, since in 37 cases the position of the arms was not reported.

The data for arm position are less frequent and less reliable than for body position. The decay of the flesh may have caused the arms to shift further from their original position than the rest of the skeleton. The arms and hands have often suffered damage because of the shifting of the body in the earth, the collapse of capstones on the skeleton, the action of rodents, or the process of excavation itself. Consequently, the field observations may not have been able to recover and accurately reflect the position in which the arms were placed at the time of interment. Moreover, if the position of the arms was not as closely prescribed by the burial customs as that of the body or eyes, wider variations in the observed positions would be expected.

These factors are reflected in the diversity of arm positions reported in Appendix 2: Typological Catalogue. In order that the arm positions may be tabulated, the varied terminology of the catalogue must be simplified.

Analysis of the Terminology

An initial step toward the simplification of the terminology is the assumption that entries reading "arm across chest" and "arm across abdomen" represent variations on the same position. A natural arm position for a person lying on the back or side is with one or both of the elbows flexed. The degree of flexation determines whether the hand lies in the region of the lower abdomen or high up under the chin. If the intention of the burial party was simply to place the body in a position of repose, then no particular degree of flexation would have been required or preferred. This assumption allows "arm across chest" and "arm across abdomen" to be combined under the general category "arm across chest or abdomen."

A second assumption, warranted by the nature of the field observations, is that an entry reading simply "flexed at elbow" means that the elbow was bent so as to bring the arm across the chest or abdomen. On this assumption, entries reading "flexed at elbow" may be combined with those reading "arm across chest or abdomen." This conflation may eliminate some cases where the hand originally rested on the pelvis, but the number will not be great, since the location of the hand on the pelvis was usually diligently reported by the area supervisors.

A third assumption is that such entries as "arm across pelvis," "hand in pelvis," and "hand on pelvis" all indicate attempts at the time of the burial to cover the genitals with the hand and may therefore be combined in a single entry, "hand in pelvis." This simplification may lose a few cases where the intention was to place the arm in an extended position or to flex it low across the abdomen.

A fourth assumption is that the presence of the hand on the femur is an insignificant variant of the fully extended position. Instead of allowing the arm to lie at the side with the hand on the ground, the burial party placed the hand on the upper thigh. On the basis of this assumption, entries reading "hand on femur" may be combined with those reading "arm extended." The combination may absorb some cases where the original intention was to place the hand in the pelvis, but where the decay of the flesh caused the hand to slip onto the thigh.

Each of these assumptions introduces possible sources of error into an already small sample. The cumulative effect of these errors is to reduce the proportion of burials with the hand in the pelvis and to increase that of burials in an extended position. The most serious criticism that can be raised against the simplification is that it builds an important conclusion into the assumptions, namely, that the burial rites aimed at placing the body in a position of repose. The photographs presented in the preceding chapter support the assumption, however, as do the impressions gained by viewing in the ground the many burials not included in the photographs.

On the whole, the errors introduced by the simplification of the categories of arm position should not seriously distort the figures given in Tables 19, 20, and 21.

Varieties of Arm Position

If the combinations indicated in the foregoing paragraphs are made, three basic arm positions may be distinguished: (1) "arm extended" (including "hand on femur"), (2) "arm across chest or abdomen" (including "arm flexed at elbow"), (3) "hand in pelvis" (including "hand on pelvis" and "arm across pelvis").

Bringing together the positions of both arms produces nine possibilities:
1. Both arms extended;
2. Both hands in pelvis;
3. Both arms across chest or abdomen;
4. Right arm extended, left hand in pelvis;
5. Right arm extended, left arm across chest or abdomen;
6. Right hand in pelvis, left arm extended;
7. Right hand in pelvis, left arm across chest or abdomen;
8. Right arm across chest or abdomen, left arm extended;
9. Right arm across chest or abdomen, left hand in pelvis.

This classification will be used to analyze the varieties of arm position in relation to (a) body position (which includes the position of the legs), (b) age and sex, and (c) grave structure. The eye direction is so uniform that a study of its relationship yields no useful results. Only the arm positions in burials with anomalous eye directions will be examined. It should be noted that arm position 9 does not occur in the sample.

Arm Position in Relation to Body Position
(Table 19)

Table 19 shows that of the nine possible arm positions three are preferred in the sample as a whole. Both arms extended (arm position 1), right arm extended, left hand in pelvis (arm position 4), and right arm extended, left across chest or abdomen (arm position 5) taken together account for 78.8% of the burials. The remaining six arm positions contribute only 21.2% of the total, and none has a greater incidence than 6.7%.

Table 19. Frequency of Occurrence of the Various Arm Positions among the Eight Body Positions

Body Positions	Arm Positions*								Totals
	1 Both arms extended	2 Both hands in pelvis	3 Both arms across chest or abdomen	4 Right arm extended, left hand in pelvis	5 Right arm extended, left across chest or abdomen	6 Right hand in pelvis, left arm extended	7 Right hand in pelvis, left arm across chest or abdomen	8 Right arm across chest or abdomen, left arm extended	
1 Extended on front	1 50.0%	0 0.0%	0 0.0%	0 0.0%	0 0.0%	1 50.0%	0 0.0%	0 0.0%	2 100%
2 Extended on back	24 46.2%	3 5.8%	1 1.9%	14 26.9%	5 9.6%	0 0.0%	4 7.7%	1 1.9%	52 100%
3 Extended on left side	0 0.0%	0 0.0%	0 0.0%	0 0.0%	1 100%	0 0.0%	0 0.0%	0 0.0%	1 100%
4 Extended on right side	3 14.3%	0 0.0%	0 0.0%	11 52.4%	5 23.8%	0 0.0%	0 0.0%	2 9.5%	21 100%
6 Flexed on back	0 0.0%	1 100%	0 0.0%	0 0.0%	0 0.0%	0 0.0%	0 0.0%	0 0.0%	1 100%
7 Flexed on left side	0 0.0%	0 0.0%	1 33.3%	0 0.0%	0 0.0%	0 0.0%	0 0.0%	2 66.7%	3 100%
8 Flexed on right side	3 12.5%	0 0.0%	5 20.8%	5 20.8%	10 41.7%	0 0.0%	0 0.0%	1 4.2%	24 100%
Totals	31 29.8%	4 3.8%	7 6.7%	30 28.8%	21 20.2%	1 1.0%	4 3.9%	6 5.8%	104 100%

*Arm position 9 (right arm across chest, left hand in pelvis) and body position 5 (flexed on front) do not occur in the sample.

The three preferred arm positions all have the right arm extended. In burial on the right side the right arm is below the body, and the left arm above. The common practice in burial on the right side (body positions 4 and 8) was to extend the right or lower arm fully and to flex the left or upper arm. The flexation of the left arm could vary from virtually fully extended to extremely flexed at the elbow, so that the arm lay high across the chest.

The figures given in Table 19 show that body position was the principal factor determining the arm position chosen for a burial. Although burials in each of the body positions displayed a variety of arm positions, each of the most common body positions (2, 4, and 8) preferred, more or less strongly, a specific arm position.

Burials extended on the back (body position 2) favored the extension of both arms along the sides (arm position 1). This combination of arm and body positions is illustrated in Pls. 12A, 25, 41, and 53. The most frequent variant from the preferred position was to extend the right arm and to place the left hand over the genital region (arm position 4), illustrated in Pls. 21, 32, 33, 44, and 54. A minor variant was to extend the right arm and to place the left arm across the chest or abdomen (arm position 5, see Pl. 28). In a relatively rare variant, the right hand was used to cover the genitals, and the left arm was allowed to lie across the chest or abdomen (arm position 7, see Pl. 34B). By pure chance, all three individuals with both hands in the pelvis region (arm position 2) are shown in the photographs (Pls. 10B, 11, and 14). Only one instance each of arm positions 3 and 8 occurred among burials in the extended position on the back.

Burials extended on the right side (body position 4) tended to have the right arm extended and the left hand in the pelvis (arm position 4). Burials with this combination of arm and body positions are illustrated in Pls. 34A, 36, 37, 42, 45, and 46. The two most common variants are with the right arm extended and the left across the chest or abdomen (arm position 5, see Pl. 19) or with both arms extended along the sides (arm position 1). There are two instances in which the left arm was extended at the side, and the right elbow bent, so as to bring the arm under the chest or abdomen (arm position 8).

Bodies flexed on the right side (body position 8) might reasonably be expected to have the arms disposed in the same way as bodies extended on the right side (body position 4), but this was not the case. The flexed burials showed less concern for covering the pelvic region. The preferred position was with the right arm extended and the left across the chest or abdomen, well away from the pelvic region (arm position 5, see Pls. 12B, 24, 38, 49, and 50). The two most common variants were with the right arm extended and the left hand covering the pelvis (arm position 4) or with both arms across chest or abdomen (arm position 3). The latter combination (illustrated in Pl. 18) is surprisingly frequent in view of the fact that the arm position occurred only twice more, once among bodies extended on the back (body position 2) and once among bodies flexed on the left side (body position 7). It did not occur at all among bodies extended on the right side (body position 4). The other variants in arm position for individuals flexed on the right side are three instances of arm position 1 (both extended) and one instance of arm position 8 (right arm across chest or abdomen, left arm extended).

Atypical body positions were not consistently accompanied by rare or atypical arm positions. Of

the two bodies buried in the extended position on the front (body position 1), one individual had both arms extended at the sides (arm position 1), a very common arm position. The other burial on the front is the only instance of arm position 6 (right hand in the pelvis, left arm extended, see Pl. 51). The one example of a body flexed on the back (body position 6) had both hands in the pelvis (arm position 2, see Pl. 52), a rare arm position, but not unnatural for a body lying on the back. Another flexed burial on the back (Pl. 29) had both arms extended (arm position 1). It does not appear in Table 19, since its eye direction is unknown. Burials on the left side show the same mixture of common and unusual arm positions. One burial was extended on the left side (body position 3). It had the right arm extended and the left across the chest (arm position 5), one of the three preferred positions. Of the three skeletons flexed on the left side (body position 7) one had both arms across the chest (arm position 3), an arm position most commonly associated with flexed burials on the *right* side. This burial (I.22.006) has been discussed on page 79. The remaining examples of flexation on the left side had the arms in the rare position 8 (right arm across chest, left extended; see Pls. 13 and 55). In these two cases the anomaly of the arm position is more apparent than real, since the position preserves the practice of extending fully the arm which is under the body and treating the upper arm as mobile.

An overview of the data just presented confirms the assumption that the main concern of the burial parties in arranging the arms was to give the impression of repose. Almost without exception the arm positions adopted are the natural ones for each body position.

One conspicuous feature, apparent in Table 19, is the covering of the pelvis with one or both hands. Four of the arm positions (2, 4, 6, and 7) involve this practice. The covering of the pelvis was by no means a universal custom, since it appears in only 39 of the 104 burials, but it occurs often enough to warrant a brief discussion.

The Muslim, and particularly the Bedouin, has a strong aversion to exposing the body to public view, and this feeling applies especially to the genital organs. The practice of covering the pelvic area with one or both hands at the time of burial may be a reflection of this aversion.

The left hand alone is used to cover the genital region in thirty of the thirty-nine burials in which the practice is found. The right hand alone is used in only five cases, and both hands are used in four cases.

Among the Bedouin, as in many other cultures, the left hand is regarded as the inferior member and is used for base or menial tasks. For example, the cleansing of the body after defecation is done with the left hand. Consequently, gestures made with the left hand are hostile or derogatory, and the left hand is the natural choice for covering the genitals at the time of burial. Moreover, in burial on the right side the left arm is the upper or mobile limb and is more readily available for the purpose.

probably due to lack of care in composing the arms, which were simply allowed to fall naturally into an extended position. In the case of child burials the extended position on the back occurs more frequently than expected (Fig. 18). In this body position extension of both arms predominates (Table 19).

In the burial of adults the preference was for the extension of the right arm and the placing of the left arm across the pelvis, chest, or abdomen (arm positions 4 and 5), probably because more care was taken with the arrangement of hands and arms in adult burials.

Table 20. Frequency of Occurrence of the Various Arm Positions among the Age/Sex Groups

Age Groups	Arm Positions*								Totals
	1 Both arms extended	2 Both hands in pelvis	3 Both arms across chest or abdomen	4 Right arm extended, left hand in pelvis	5 Right arm extended, left across chest or abdomen	6 Right hand in pelvis, left arm extended	7 Right hand in pelvis, left arm across chest or abdomen	8 Right arm across chest or abdomen, left arm extended	
A-C Infants	15 35.7%	1 2.4%	4 9.5%	10 23.8%	8 19.1%	0 0.0%	1 2.4%	3 7.1%	42 100%
D-F Children	6 42.9%	1 7.1%	2 14.3%	4 28.6%	0 0.0%	0 0.0%	1 7.1%	0 0.0%	14 100%
K Adult Males	4 20.0%	1 5.0%	1 5.0%	6 30.0%	6 30.0%	1 5.0%	0 0.0%	1 5.0%	20 100%
L Adult Females	5 18.5%	1 3.7%	0 0.0%	10 37.1%	7 25.9%	0 0.0%	2 7.4%	2 7.4%	27 100%
M Adult Sex UD	1 100%	0 0.0%	0 0.0%	0 0.0%	0 0.0%	0 0.0%	0 0.0%	0 0.0%	1 100%
Totals	31 29.8%	4 3.8%	7 6.7%	30 28.8%	21 20.2%	1 1.0%	4 3.9%	6 5.8%	104 100%

*Arm position 9 (right arm across chest, left hand in pelvis) and age group G-J (juveniles) do not occur in the sample.

Arm Position in Relation to Age and Sex

The data summarized in Table 20 show that extension of both arms (arm position 1) was preferred for the burial of infants and children. The preference for this position in the case of infants was

The covering of the pelvic region (arm positions 2, 4, 6, and 7) was most common in the burial of adult females (48.2%, see Table 20). Child burials are a close second (42.8%). The occurrence drops only slightly among the adult males (40.0%) but is strikingly less among the infant burials

(28.6%). The somewhat higher incidence of the practice among adult females than among adult males was probably the result of the almost universal belief that modesty in relation to the genital organs is more rigorously demanded of the female than of the male. The frequency of the covering of the pelvis in child burials is more difficult to explain. Since the total number of such burials in the sample is small, the sample may not be representative of the child burials in the cemetery as a whole. It was previously suggested that soon after the age of three the child passed into a new status in the eyes of its family and thus that more care would have been taken in the burial of children than of infants (pp. 41, 71). Parents might therefore have found it more appropriate to apply the final gesture of modesty in the burial of a child than in that of an infant. The low frequency of the practice of covering the pelvic region in the burial of infants is of a piece with the general lack of concern for niceties of the burial customs in the interment of infants (pp. 68-73).

Arm Position in Relation to Grave Structure

As Table 21 indicates, the three principal arm positions (1, 4, and 5) occur with virtually equal frequency in all types of cists. The same also appears to be true of the less frequent arm positions, but there the numbers are too small to permit general conclusions.

The Preferred Body-Arm Combinations

The isolation of three preferred combinations of body and arm positions (pp. 83-84) raises the question of whether these combinations reflect divergent burial customs used by sub-groups within the community. Such groupings could be based on age or sex, on economic or social status, or on tribal or clan affiliations.

The presence of such sub-groups may be tested by tabulating the three most frequent body-arm combinations (namely, 2-1, prostrate on the back with both arms extended; 4-4, extended on the right side with the right arm extended and the left hand in the pelvis; and 8-5, flexed on the right side with the right arm extended and the left across the chest or abdomen) against age and sex groups, cist types, and position in the cemetery.

The better-built cists could give an index of economic status, and a position in the southern end of the cemetery in closer proximity to the tomb of the holy man might indicate the burials of

Table 21.   Frequency of Occurrence of the Various Arm Positions among the Types of Grave Structure

Grave Structure	Arm Positions*								Totals
	1 Both arms extended	2 Both hands in pelvis	3 Both arms across chest or abdomen	4 Right arm extended, left hand in pelvis	5 Right arm extended, left across chest or abdomen	6 Right hand in pelvis, left arm extended	7 Right hand in pelvis, left arm across chest or abdomen	8 Right arm across chest or abdomen, left arm extended	
I	13 29.5%	0 0.0%	5 11.4%	12 27.3%	10 22.7%	0 0.0%	1 2.3%	3 6.8%	44 100%
II	12 30.7%	3 7.7%	1 2.6%	12 30.8%	7 17.9%	1 2.6%	0 0.0%	3 7.7%	39 100%
III/IV	6 28.6%	1 4.8%	1 4.8%	6 28.6%	4 18.9%	0 0.0%	3 14.3%	0 0.0%	21 100%
Totals	31 29.8%	4 3.8%	7 6.7%	30 28.9%	21 20.2%	1 1.0%	4 3.8%	6 5.8%	104 100%

*Arm position 9 (right arm across chest, left hand in pelvis) does not occur in the sample.

individuals more prestigious for either economic or social reasons.

The relevant figures are given in Tables 22, 23, and 24. The true totals in Table 24 (ignoring the doubling of the figures for Areas 41 and 51) are smaller than those in the other two tables because Field I, Areas 3, 4, and 13, and Fields V and VI have been omitted in order to involve only the fully excavated eastern lines of squares in the tabulation. The relatively small number of individuals included in these tables makes them unreliable for many of the categories tabulated, and only major percentage differences can be regarded as significant.

Table 22. Frequency of Occurrence of the Three Commonest Body-Arm Combinations among the Various Age Groups

| Age Groups | Body-Arm Combinations | | | |
	2-1 Extended on back; both arms extended	4-4 Extended on right side; right arm extended, left hand in pelvis	8-5 Flexed on right side; right arm extended, left across chest or abdomen	Totals
A-C Infants	11 52.4%	5 23.8%	5 23.8%	21 100%
D-F Children	5 83.3%	1 16.7%	0 0.0%	6 100%
K Adult Males	4 44.5%	3 33.3%	2 22.2%	9 100%
L Adult Females	4 44.5%	2 22.2%	3 33.3%	9 100%
Totals	24 53.3%	11 24.5%	10 22.2%	45 100%
K+L Adults	8 44.4%	5 27.8%	5 27.8%	18 100%

Table 22, which gives the occurrences of the commonest body-arm combinations among the various age groups, shows that within the limits of accuracy all combinations occur with about the same frequency in all age groups. The one exception is the preference in child burials for combination 2-1 (extended on the back with both arms

extended). The prevalence of this position in the burial of children merely reflects the fact that burial on the back occurs more frequently than expected among children (Fig. 18). Apart from this, no age group favors a particular body-arm combination.

The figures showing the frequency of the most popular body-arm combinations in the three types of cist (Table 23) indicate a close correspondence between Type I (simple earth graves) and Type II (graves capped but not lined) with some divergence in the Type III/IV (capped and lined) cists. The low incidence in Type III/IV cists of body-arm combination 4-4 (extended on the right side with the right arm extended and the left hand in the pelvis) is due to the relatively infrequent presence of body position 4 in conjunction with Type III/IV cists (Fig. 22).

Table 23. Frequency of Occurrence of the Three Commonest Body-Arm Combinations among the Various Types of Grave Structure

| Grave Structure | Body-Arm Combinations | | | |
	2-1 Extended on back; both arms extended	4-4 Extended on right side; right arm extended, left hand in pelvis	8-5 Flexed on right side; right arm extended, left across chest or abdomen	Totals
I	9 56.3%	4 25.0%	3 18.7%	16 100%
II	9 47.4%	6 31.6%	4 21.0%	19 100%
III/IV	6 60.0%	1 10.0%	3 30.0%	10 100%
Totals	24 53.3%	11 24.5%	10 22.2%	45 100%

If grave structure is taken as an index of economic or social status, the wealthier or more prestigious members of the community seem to have preferred to bury their children and some adults in the extended position on the back with both arms extended (2-1) and to employ flexation on the right side with its attendant arm positions (8-3, 8-4, 8-5) for most of the remaining adults. They tended to avoid the extended position on the right side with its associated arm positions.

The tabulation of the most popular body-arm combinations against position in the cemetery (Table 24) yields inconclusive results. There are too few well-preserved burials in the northern areas to permit valid comparison with the southern part of the cemetery, and the figures for the southern part are distorted because Areas 42 and 52 were not excavated. No firm conclusions can be drawn from these data.

Table 24.   The Concentration of the Three Commonest Body-Arm Combinations in the Field I Cemetery by Areas

Position in the Cemetery by Areas*	2-1 Extended on back; both arms extended	4-4 Extended on right side; right arm extended, left hand in pelvis	8-5 Flexed on right side; right arm extended, left across chest or abdomen	Totals
1-2	1 100%	0 0.0%	0 0.0%	1 100%
11-12	4 57.1%	1 14.3%	2 28.6%	7 100%
21-22	2 25.0%	4 50.0%	2 25.0%	8 100%
31-32	5 62.5%	1 12.5%	2 25.0%	8 100%
41×2	16 72.7%	4 18.2%	2 9.1%	22 100%
51×2	6 50.0%	0 0.0%	6 50.0%	12 100%
Totals	34 58.6%	10 17.2%	14 24.2%	58 100%

*Areas 41 and 51 show doubled figures in order to make their totals compatible with the pairs of areas excavated to the north.

The overall impression left by the data just reviewed is that of a homogeneous society with a strong tendency toward democracy in its burial practices.

Arm Positions in Burials with Anomalous Eye Directions

Arm positions are reported for nine burials where the eye directions were atypical.

Four of the nine, all infant burials (I.12.015, I.12.127, I.32.040, I.41.051), were extended on the back (body position 2) looking up (eye direction a). In Burials I.12.015 and I.41.051 the arms were in the extended position normal for burials on the back. The other two had less frequent arm positions. In Burial I.12.127 the right arm was extended, and the left was across the chest or abdomen (arm position 5). This position is not common in burials on the back (Table 19). In Burial I.32.040 the right hand was in the pelvis and the left arm across the chest or abdomen (arm position 7), again a rare arm position for burials on the back (Table 19).

An adult male (I.22.102) buried in the extended position on the back (body position 2) and looking north (eye direction c) had the right arm extended and the left hand in the pelvis (arm position 4), the second most favored arm position for burials on the back (Table 19).

An infant (I.22.036) flexed on the right side (body position 8) had the eyes directed downward (eye direction b). The right arm was extended and the left was across the chest or abdomen (arm position 5), the commonest arm position for flexed burials on the right side.

In the cases just discussed the arm positions followed normal patterns. Indeed, the anomalous eye directions probably resulted from carelessness during the burial, from the shifting of earth in the grave, or from the action of rodents, and do not represent the intention of the burial practices.

The three truly anomalous cases are those in which burial was on the left side (I.11.211, I.22.006, and I.32.032A). These burials reversed both the normal body position and the normal eye direction. They have been discussed above on pages 78-79. One of these burials (I.32.032A) was extended on the left side (body position 3), looking northwest (eye direction j). The right arm was extended, and the left was across the chest (arm position 5), the second most common position for bodies extended on the *right* side. The other two burials were flexed on the left side (body position 7) looking north (eye direction c). I.22.006 had both arms across the chest (arm position 3), a rare arm position but one easy to achieve in any body position. I.11.211 had the right arm across the chest and the left arm extended (arm position 8). This reverses the normal position for a body flexed on the right side, but is the natural one for a body flexed on the left side.

These data support the conclusion, arrived at

on page 79, that the determining factor in these burials was the intention to direct the eyes to the north. Both body and arm positions were adapted to this intention.

Unusual Leg Positions

For the purposes of this discussion, a skeleton is slightly flexed if the angle formed by the upper and lower legs is clearly obtuse, moderately flexed if the angle approximates 90°, and extremely flexed if the angle is sharply acute. In the overwhelming majority of cases where flexation occurred, the degree of flexation was slight.

Among bodies in the prone position either on the back (body position 2) or on the front (body position 1), flexation of any kind was rare. The legs were usually extended side by side with both feet resting on the ground (Pls. 11, 14, 16, 25, and 44). The skeleton pictured in Pl. 53 had slight flexation of the right leg only (for a similar leg position see Pl. 48). Pl. 52 illustrates a case of moderate flexation of both legs from the prone position. The legs were flexed to the right, and the left foot overlapped the right. The skeleton illustrated in Pl. 29 was classified as flexed on the back (body position 8), but the apparent flexation was caused by the crossing of the left leg over the right at the knee. A similar leg position, this time in a burial extended on the front (body position 1), is shown in Pl. 51.

Bodies in an extended position on the right side (body position 4) had both legs straight. The feet sometimes lay side by side (Pl. 42), but more commonly the left foot overlapped the right (Pls. 19, 45, and 46).

Among bodies flexed on the right side (body position 8), slight flexation with the left foot overlapping the right was the general rule (Pls. 12B, 49, and 50). In Pl. 48 only the right leg was flexed, and the left foot rested on the right. The skeleton in Pl. 24 had moderate flexation of both legs, but the left leg was twisted so that the left foot was *under* the right leg just above the ankle. Pl. 18 shows a case of moderate flexation in an infant burial. Pl. 47 is the highly unusual case of extreme flexation discussed above on page 76. A second case of extreme flexation was reported (I.32.018-II.M.8.0), but no photograph is available, and no further details are given on the locus sheets.

Two skeletons were flexed on the left side. They belong to the very small group of burials which have been a mystery in the study of each of

the typological categories, since they persistently constitute exceptions to the norms of the cemetery (see pp. 77-79, 81, 88). The principal anomaly in the burial shown in Pl. 13 was the placing of the body on its left side with the skull in the eastern end of the grave. The *left* arm was extended, and the *right* was flexed high across the chest. The legs were moderately flexed, and the right foot overlapped the left. Arm and leg positions were thus the opposite of those customary in bodies buried in the flexed position on the right side, but may be regarded as adaptations to the rare body position and orientation chosen for the interment. The burial illustrated in Pl. 55 had the head in the west end of the grave and the skeleton flexed on the left side, with the result that the eyes looked to the north. Like the skeleton shown in Pl. 13, the arm position has been accommodated to burial on the left side, the left arm being extended and the right flexed across the chest. The flexation of the legs was greater than usual, and the body appeared to be in a crouching or kneeling position.

Aside from a few minor variants, leg positions, like arm positions, are generally natural to a body in repose and probably imitate sleep. The major exceptions cluster in those burials with anomalies of eye direction or body orientation and point once again to a small group of cemetery users whose burial customs deviated from the norm.

Conversations with Bedouin and fellahin indicate that in these communities, where trained doctors are scarce or unavailable, persons are frequently pronounced dead prematurely. Many harrowing tales are told of bodies on their way to the cemetery displaying unexpected and terrifying signs of life. One persistent story, told in a variety of forms, describes the revival of a presumed corpse on the top of a crowded bus, to the consternation of its passengers.

From this point of view one burial deserves special mention. Grave I.41.058 (Pl. 56) contained the body of a male juvenile in a capped and lined grave. The legs were flung out in a striding position, the hands seemed to be clutching at the stone lining of the cist, and the torso was twisted to the right. The unique position of the skeleton was suggestive of action, in contrast to the impression of repose given by the other burials in the cemetery. It is possible that the teenager interred in this grave was buried alive, and that his struggles in the earth account for the unusual position of the body.

Skull Shape and Coloration of Bones

Four of the skeletons found in the cemetery (I.22.079, I.22.084, I.32.060, I.32.064) had relatively longer skulls than those of the other burials. These longer-headed individuals were found in two closely contiguous pairs in Areas 22 and 32, near the center of the excavated part of the cemetery and removed from the portion nearest the *weli*. The proximity of Burials I.32.060 and I.32.064 is striking. In Pl. 48, Burial I.32.060, an adult female, has been completely excavated. Burial I.32.064, a child of undetermined sex, has just begun to appear about a meter to the south and directly in line with Burial I.32.060. The arrangement, age, and sex suggest that the two individuals may have been members of the same family.

Three of the four burials in question were adult females. Two (I.22.079, Pl. 50, and I.32.060, Pl. 48) were flexed on the right side with normal eye directions and arm and leg positions. The body position of the third (I.22.084) is unknown, but the eye direction and arm and leg positions were normal. All three cist types are represented. Thus, the burials of all the longer-headed individuals conform closely to the standards of the cemetery.

The bones of two of the adult females of this group (I.22.079 and I.22.084) were stained red, probably with ochre which was on the skin at the time of burial and was transferred to the bones at the decay of the flesh. One other burial (I.41.072), consisting of disarticulated remains, showed the same red coloration of the bones.

The number of individuals in the long-headed group was small, and any conclusion must be merely in the nature of a suggestion. The fact that all the adults were female raises the possibility that a few women from a different tribal group,

characterized by longer crania, entered the community which used the cemetery by marriage, and that these women adorned their skin with ochre in a manner not practiced by the other women of the community.

Unusual Positions of the Skull

Three burials in the cemetery showed displacement of the skull from its normal position. Twice this apparently resulted from accidental disturbance of the skeleton. In Burial I.41.035 an infant was interred in a flexed position on the right side, but the skull rested on its base. The peculiar stance of the skull resulted from the settling of the skeleton's shoulders into a depression in the uneven floor of the grave. Burial I.1.046 contained the disturbed skeleton of a young woman in a capped and lined grave under two layers of capstones. Only the hands and feet were articulated, and the skull rested on the vault. The source of the disturbance within this sealed cist is unknown.

The most peculiar case of skull displacement was found in Burial I.1.031. The skull of the young woman buried in this grave had been deliberately severed from the spinal column and placed, vault up, on the abdomen. Execution by decapitation was, according to local report, a common punishment for adultery among the Bedouin of the region.

Diseases and Trauma

A full report on the evidence for disease and trauma obtained from the skeletal remains will be given in a subsequent volume of this series. The locus sheets mention only one instance of disease. The adult female buried in Grave I.3.043 had curvature of the spine.

CHAPTER 10

Artifacts

Ninety-four of the burials listed in the Typological Catalogue (Appendix 2) contain artifacts other than stone pillows. Of these burials eighty-six are typed graves, two are secondary burials, one is a burial pit, and five have insufficient data for classification. The graves containing artifacts are listed and the artifacts briefly described in Appendix 3: Index of Artifacts. The stone pillows are described on pages 41-42 as features of grave construction.

General Description

This chapter should not be construed as a final report on the artifacts recovered from the Field I cemetery. It lacks both laboratory analysis and comparative studies of the objects. The glass and faience artifacts have not been subjected to microscopic or spectroscopic analysis. The artifacts in metal have been stabilized, but have not been cleaned and examined by specialists. Objects in other materials, such as bone and shell, have received only examination in the field, and have not been studied under laboratory conditions. Rather than wait for the completion of these studies, which will appear in a later volume of the Hesi series, it seemed desirable to present a preliminary overview of the artifactual contents of the cemetery, illustrated by representative examples of each type of artifact. It is hoped that the presentation given here is in sufficient detail to provide the reader with a working knowledge of the types of artifacts associated with the burials and of their distribution in the cemetery.

Jewelry and articles of personal adornment constitute the most common class of artifact. These include beads in a variety of materials,

sizes, shapes, and colors; pendants, probably used as centerpieces in necklaces; bell-shaped bronze objects; coins, often bored for stringing in a necklace or headband; finger, toe, and ear rings, usually in bronze or iron; bracelets in bronze, iron, or glass; and anklets in bronze or iron. A mother-of-pearl band, possibly used as a hair fastener, and a leather strap, probably part of an arm band, may also belong to the category of personal adornments. The few needles and/or pins recovered were probably fastenings for garments or shrouds.

The ceramic vessels found in three of the graves constitute a particularly interesting type of artifact. In one case (I.41.019) the pottery vessel was used as the coffin for an infant. Chert blades and loom weights, occasionally encountered in the grave fills, are probably accidental inclusions. The function of several objects, particularly of bone, could not be determined. Glass fragments may indicate that occasionally glass vessels were included among the grave furnishings, but no intact examples have been recovered. Remnants of cloth, usually found adhering to copper/bronze jewelry, undoubtedly came from the garments or shrouds which covered the bodies.

Pl. 58 shows a typical collection of jewelry from a single grave (I.22.207). It is not the largest or most complete grouping found in the cemetery, but its contents (a collection of glass, faience, and carnelian beads, a bronze ring, and fragments of iron and glass bracelets) are typical of those found in graves containing artifacts. Other major collections are described in Appendix 3 in connection with Burials I.4.007, I.4.020, I.12.054, I.12.059, I.21.017A, I.22.015, I.22.119, I.31.176, I.32.049, I.32.056, I.41.051, I.41.076, and I.51.013. The separate items in these collections are treated in more detail under the various artifact types.

Occurrence of Artifacts in Relation to Grave Structure

If the single instance of an infant burial in a pottery jar (I.41.019) is disregarded, eighty-five typed burials had artifacts. As Fig. 24 shows, artifacts occurred less frequently than expected in Type I (simple earth) graves, and more frequently than expected in Type II (capped but not lined) graves. On the face of it, the group which customarily used the Type II cists (see p. 72) seems to have been more inclined to deposit jewelry and other objects with the dead than the groups using the other grave forms. However, this slight difference is accounted for by the fact that the group which used Type II graves predominantly buried some of their infants in simple earth graves (Type I). Since infants are the age group least likely to be buried with artifacts, this practice increased the incidence of artifacts in Type II graves.

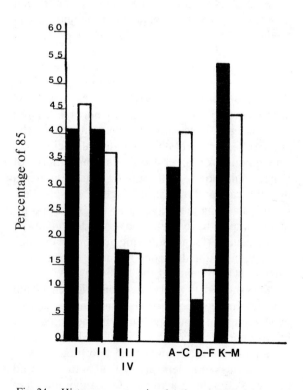

Fig. 24.   Histogram comparing the observed (black bars) and expected (white bars) values for the occurrence of artifacts in the various types of grave structures and among the various age groups. Juveniles (G-J) have been omitted. Drawn by L. E. Toombs.

On pages 41-43 is a study of the distribution of graves containing artifacts in the Field I cemetery. The study shows that graves with artifacts were not concentrated in any particular part of the cemetery.

The combined result of these two lines of investigation is that the presence of artifacts in a grave is not an indicator of the social or economic status of the family. Burials in any type of cist or in any part of the cemetery were equally likely to contain artifacts.

Occurrence of Artifacts in Relation to Age and Sex

Artifacts occurred less frequently than expected in the burials of infants and children but more frequently than expected in adult burials (Fig. 24). The number of juvenile burials was too small to permit reliable conclusions. The burial practices favored the placing of artifacts in the graves of adults but did not exclude the custom in the case of younger burials.

Fig. 25 reveals a striking difference in the occurrence of artifacts between adult male burials and adult female burials. The presence of artifacts in the burials of adult males is notably less than would be expected on the basis of chance. Their presence in the burials of adult females is correspondingly greater. This result could have been predicted, since the types of jewelry found in the Stratum II cemetery are those usually associated with women. The burial of an adult male might be expected to contain finger rings or arm bands, but the surprising feature of the cemetery is that adult male burials frequently contained beads and glass bracelets of precisely the same types as found in the graves of women. Burials I.11.004, I.12.054, I.51.067, and I.51.133 contained beads, and I.31.176 yielded several glass bracelets as well as a large collection of beads (see Appendix 3).

The problem is compounded by the presence in infant burials of bracelets clearly too large for the individual and of necklaces which could hardly have been worn by an infant in life. The most obvious illustration is the fragments of an adult's bracelet in the burial jar containing the bones of a newborn infant (I.41.019). Other burials show similar phenomena (see Appendix 3). Burial I.12.127, an infant of eighteen months to three years of age, had four large glass bracelets. Burial I.32.032A, an infant of six to eighteen months, contained an adult's necklace of glass beads. A mother-of-pearl object, probably a hair fastener, was found along with an adult's necklace in Burial I.41.051, an infant of six to eighteen months.

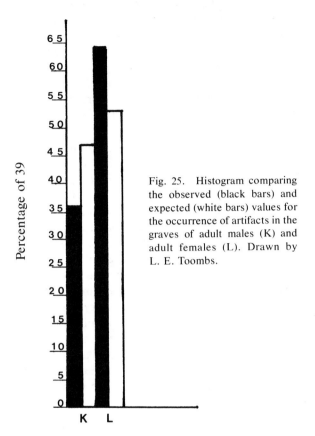

Fig. 25. Histogram comparing the observed (black bars) and expected (white bars) values for the occurrence of artifacts in the graves of adult males (K) and adult females (L). Drawn by L. E. Toombs.

The rather puzzling presence of women's jewelry in the graves of infants, children, and men may mean that bereaved women sometimes placed their jewelry in the graves of their husbands or children. In his treatment of Bedouin burial customs in Kuwait and Saudi Arabia, H. R. P. Dickson mentioned just such a practice (1951, 209-10). The bereaved wife, loudly proclaiming her loss, would approach the grave and, ripping off her adornments, throw them away (probably into the cist with the body of her husband). A parallel practice in the case of infants and children is not described but, in the light of the Hesi evidence, may be presumed.

The presence of jewelry in the graves of women causes no difficulty. Jaussen (1908, 95-105) states that, among the Arabs of the territory of Moab, if a woman wore jewelry at the time of death, she was buried wearing it. A mirror and a comb were often included in the burial, and the woman's necklace was left around her neck. Lane (1860, 516), describing Muslim burial customs in Egypt, particu-larly as he observed them in Cairo, noted that the jewelry of a dead woman was often carried to the grave attached to the *shaahid*, an upright piece of wood affixed to the head of the bier, and was subsequently placed in the grave. These two practices, taken together, may account for the fact that the jewelry was sometimes found in place on the fingers, arms, or neck of the skeleton, and sometimes scattered at random in the cist.

Beads

Forty-six of the burials contained beads, sometimes a single bead, but more often a considerable number that might have formed a necklace. For forty-one of these burials the age or sex or both are known. Sixteen are burials of infants, five of children, eight of adult males, nine of adult females, and three of adults for whom the sex is unknown.

Classification

Four bases for the classification of the beads from the Hesi cemetery suggest themselves: material, size, color, and form. In the presentation which follows, the beads are described under the headings of the various forms which have been isolated in the total collection. A few words should be said in explanation of this decision. Until the beads are broken and studied in detail, the material of which they are composed cannot always be determined with certainty. For example, the second largest category of material is faience or ceramic, covered originally with a brightly colored glaze. On the basis of the beads found in a broken condition, both ceramic and faience were used as a base for the glaze. However, in complete beads the decayed remains of the glaze covers the surface and masks the nature of the underlying material. Glass beads, the most common category, are easier to recognize, but there are still many cases of doubt as to whether the surface is a glaze laid over another material or the surface of a genuine glass bead. Carnelian is the only frequently used stone in the production of beads, although rough limestone discs, bored to be strung as beads, are occasionally found. Other materials are of infrequent occurrence.

Because the surface colors of beads were often produced by glazing, and the glaze has deteriorated badly in the earth, the original color is often difficult to determine. Moreover, the original colors of glass beads are frequently masked by a patina. For these reasons, bead colors are not coded in the Munsel color system but are given in general terms. Recognizable surface colors include: white, cream, brown, purple, gray, black, and various shades of red, green, and blue. Blue is a common color on large beads, probably because blue was traditionally considered effective in warding off evil. Multi-colored beads were sometimes found. The effect of two or three colors was produced by laying thin bands of glaze over the original surface glazing. The patterns are usually horizontal or vertical stripes, or chevrons circling the girth of the bead. Except in the case of carnelian, dentalium, and cowrie-shell beads, where the natural color of the material gives the surface color of the bead, color does not seem to have been co-ordinated with the material from which the beads were made.

Bead sizes vary widely and seem to be related in a rather imprecise way to the form and possibly also to the function of the individual beads.

On the whole, then, the most convenient starting point for a systematic description of the Stratum II beads is their form. The other characteristics may readily be subsumed under the formal classification.

Bead Forms

Sixteen basic bead forms have been identified. These are illustrated, and the relative size of typical beads in each form is indicated in Pl. 57. The basis of the classification and of the terminology used is the general shape of the bead when seen in cross-section, described in terms of a geometric form. This yields seven basic forms: flat, flattened-rounded, ovoid, spheroid (including spherical), cylindrical, biconical, and faceted. Each of these forms may be subdivided into two or more divisions on the basis of an additional characteristic, such as size, shape when seen from above, or surface treatment. The photographic illustrations (Pls. 59-67) are arranged roughly in the order of the forms as given in Pl. 57. However, since the reader may wish to see how the forms are related to one another in individual burials, the collection of beads from each grave has been kept together. This involves some jumping to and fro among the plates in the description of the bead forms.

A complete listing of the beads found in the Field I cemetery is given in Appendix 3. If the beads are shown in the published photographs,

the plate reference is given in column 5 of Appendix 3 (e.g., Pl. 59a, nos. 1, 5, 42). If the beads do not appear on the plates, reference is made in column 5 to the plate where the form to which they belong is best illustrated (e.g., cf. Pl. 59a, nos. 1, 5, 42).

In order to avoid loss or misplacement, the beads were strung in the field laboratory. The stringing arrangement has been retained in the photographs, but does not necessarily represent the disposition of the beads in the original necklaces.

It should be pointed out that the impression of sixteen discrete forms, created by Pl. 57, may be misleading. The forms tend to merge into one another by gradual degrees. For example, there is no clear line of distinction between Form 5 (flattened-rounded, large) and Form 7 (spheroid), or between Form 7 (spheroid) and Form 10 (cylindrical, squat). In both cases the distinction depends on the degree to which the sides of the beads have been rounded. The workmanship, particularly of faceted beads, is often crude, so that Form 13 (biconical), Form 14 (biconical, double-faceted), Form 15 (simple-faceted), and Form 16 (double-faceted) tend to merge, and a single bead may carry the characteristics of more than one form. The final classification is a convenient and sometimes arbitrary device for ordering the discussion of the beads.

Form 1: Flat Disc Beads

Form 1 beads are illustrated on Pl. 59a, nos. 2-4, 7-9, 11, 13, 15, 17, 19, 21-23, 25, 27, 29, 31, 33, 35-37, 40, 41; Pl. 62c, no. 7; Pl. 66a, nos. 7, 14, 21, 22; Pl. 66b, no. 8; Pl. 67a, nos. 6, 7.

Beads belonging to this form are thin in cross-section with the edges vertical, or nearly so, and are round when viewed from above. A necklace in which Form 1 beads are numerous is shown in Pl. 59a. Most of the beads belonging to Form 1 (nos. 2, 4, 7, 9, 11, 13, 15, 17, 19, 21-23, 25, 27, 29, 31, 33, 35, 37, 40, 41) are made of glass, although some may be of faience. They are now dull brown in color, but traces of bright red glaze appear on some of the beads. They vary in size from 0.8 to 1.7cm in diameter. The workmanship is crude, and the beads show irregularities in both thickness and shape. The best-made bead is a large specimen (1.7cm thick) of highly polished red glass (Pl. 59a, no. 41). A similar disk of red glass, more crudely made than usual, appears in Pl. 62c, no. 7, and other examples of somewhat better workmanship are shown in Pl. 66a, nos. 7, 14, and Pl. 67a, nos. 6, 7.

One carnelian bead (Pl. 66b, no. 8) belongs rather uncomfortably in Form 1. It is a handsome, well-cut stone which, although disc-like, is not flat and does not have vertical edges. The craftsman cut the stone on a bias from both the top and bottom of the stone to produce a pointed ridge around the girth. The end result is a very squat biconical form (between Form 1 and Form 13).

Two types of flat disc beads are made of metal. Pl. 59a, no. 3, is a silver disc, 0.8cm in diameter, scalloped on the edges to produce a rosette effect. Two very thin, coin-like copper discs are shown on Pl. 66a, nos. 21, 22. They are classified as Form 1 beads because they are bored near the center as if to be strung like disc beads. The copper discs are badly corroded, but surface examination revealed no trace of inscription. They were probably not coins, therefore, but were manufactured for inclusion in a necklace.

Form 2: Flat, Diamond

Only two beads belonging to this form were found (Pl. 60a; Pl. 60b, no. 1). Both are cut to a regular diamond shape and are bored longitudinally. The carnelian bead, shown in Pl. 60a, is only 0.4cm in thickness, and the string hole has a diameter only slightly smaller than the thickness of the bead. The stone is beveled on the long edges and is highly polished. The bead illustrated in Pl. 60b, no. 1, is coarser and thicker (0.5cm), and has a similar beveling of the long edges. The material is quartz or possibly clear glass. The string hole was bored from opposite ends of the bead with the intention of meeting in the middle. One of the borings wandered off center, however, and in the attempt to correct the defect, the stone cracked. These Form 2 beads were probably used as centerpieces for necklaces.

Form 3: Flat, Irregular

The flat, irregular form is found only in one bead collection from the simple earth grave of an adult female (I.41.085A). The four beads of this form (two of which are shown in Pl. 59b, nos. 2, 5) are made of bone and are roughly five-sided. They vary in length from 1.0cm to 1.5cm in the longest dimension, and are very thin (about 0.1cm). The bone is polished, and the string hole is bored near the center. The animal source of the bone has not been determined. The bone beads may be a cheaper version of the copper discs described above.

Form 4: Flattened-rounded, Small

Form 4 beads are illustrated on Pl. 60b, nos. 2-6, 8-10, 17-19, 21-25; Pl. 61a, nos. 1-6, 9-10, 12-14, 17-25, 27-31, 33-37; Pl. 61b, nos. 1-37, 40-59, 69-85, 87-91, 93-116; Pl. 61c, nos. 1-20, 22-25, 29-42, 46-54; Pl. 67b, nos. 6, 9, 11.

This form introduces a type of bead called "seed beads" in the field laboratory. They are small in size, averaging 0.1-0.3cm in height, and occur frequently. Their forms are: Form 4 (flattened-rounded, small); Form 9 (cylindrical, small); and a tiny variety of Form 7 (spheroid). In some burials seed beads occurred by themselves (Pls. 61a and b), and sometimes they were found along with larger beads (Pls. 60b, 61c, 67b). This suggests that seed beads were sometimes used by themselves in multiple strands to form a wide band of beads and sometimes either grouped in clusters to separate larger beads in a necklace or arranged to form the upper, less visible part of a necklace whose more eye-catching beads were displayed on the chest.

In Pl. 60b, nos. 2-6, 8-10, 17-19, and 21-25, are typical seed beads of Form 4. All are of glass with a dark grey or black patina which usually masks an original purple, dark blue, or dark green color. Another example of these very small beads may be seen in Pl. 61a, no. 23. Most of the beads shown in Pl. 61a (nos. 1-6, 9-10, 12-14, 17-25, 27-31, 33-37) are slightly larger in size, however, at the upper end of the seed-bead range. The material of these beads is glass. The form is predominantly Form 4, although no absolute distinction can be made between this form and a tiny variety of Form 7 (spheroid). Indeed, in all probability no such distinction was intended by the beadmaker. He simply set out to make small beads in a roughly ovoid shape, and some turned out flatter than others. The beads of this chain have a rather drab appearance. The surfaces are patinated to a grey or white color. Where the original color can be detected, it is pale blue or light green.

The necklace shown in Pl. 61b is much gayer in appearance. The small beads of Form 4 (nos. 1-37, 40-59, 69-85, 87-91, 93-116) are all of green, blue, or red glass. Nos. 1, 31, 58, 73, and 74 are deep red in color, evidently in imitation of carnelian. Nos. 12 and 78 have the green color of bottle glass.

Nos. 3 and 56 are dark red in color and are decorated with two pairs of parallel white stripes. The stripes are placed vertically, one pair on each side of the bead.

The necklace illustrated in Pl. 61c has numerous beads of Form 4. Some of these (nos. 4, 5, 7, 10, 13-20, 30-31, 33, 36, 39, 42, 48, 51, 54) are of glass, patinated to a grey, sometimes almost black, color. Others (nos. 1-3, 6, 8-9, 11-12, 22-25, 29, 32, 34-35, 37-38, 40-41, 46-47, 49-50, 52-53) are cream-colored and appear to have no patina. They are probably made of faience, although this could not be established for certain without breaking the beads.

Pl. 67b, no. 6, is a Form 4 bead in a glossy black glass. Nos. 9 and 11 are slightly larger specimens, the first patinated to a mottled grey and the second to a white color.

Form 5: Flattened-Rounded, Large

Beads of this form are illustrated in Pl. 60b, nos. 13-14; Pl. 61b, nos. 61, 67-68; Pl. 61c, nos. 26-27; Pl. 62a, no. 1; Pl. 63b, nos. 5-6, 8, 10, 15-16, 22, 24-25, 33, 38-44, 46-55; Pl. 66a, nos. 2, 11; Pl. 67a, no. 3; Pl. 68a, no. 1.

Form 5 beads, called "doughnut beads" in the field laboratory, are a larger version of Form 4, evidently intended to take a more prominent place in the necklaces. Their nickname is neatly descriptive of their shape, which tends to merge into spheroid (Form 7) or cylindrical, squat (Form 10).

The largest collection of Form 5 beads is shown in Pl. 63b, nos. 5-6, 8, 10, 15-16, 22, 24-25, 33, 38-44, 46-55. These are small beads (0.6cm in diameter), covered by a thick black patina. The underlying colors are rich, deep reds, blues, and greens. Similar beads appear in Pl. 61b, nos. 61, 67, and 68. No. 61 is of black glass decorated with three vertical white stripes placed at equal intervals around the circumference. Nos. 67 and 68 are of bright blue glass. Pl. 66a, no. 2, shows a bead of the same size (0.6cm in diameter), heavily patinated, but apparently of transparent glass. A slightly smaller bead (0.5cm in diameter) appears in Pl. 61c, no. 26. It is of pale blue glass. The two glass beads shown in Pl. 60b, nos. 13, 14, are similar in color and size to the flat disc beads on Pl. 59a, of which they appear to be thickened and more rounded variants.

Slightly larger beads of Form 5 are also found. Pl. 60b, nos. 13, 14, are of glass or faience in a bright red color and are 0.9cm in diameter. The

beads shown in Pl. 67a, no. 3, and Pl. 68a, no. 1, are poorly made of red glass and have a diameter of 1.0cm. Pl. 62a, no. 1, and Pl. 66a, no. 11, illustrate the largest beads of Form 5. They are 1.2cm in diameter. The former is clear amber and the latter bright blue glass.

Form 5 thus constitutes a small but attractive class of brightly colored, medium-sized beads, almost all of which are made of glass. The one notable exception is a bead 0.7cm in diameter, made of highly polished bone (Pl. 61c, no. 27).

Form 6: Ovoid

Beads belonging to this form are elongated with the side of the bead notably curved, rather than almost straight, as in the cylindrical forms. Form 6 beads are illustrated in Pl. 60b, nos. 12, 15; Pl. 62b, in toto.

A small collection of these beads was found together in Grave I.41.212 (Pl. 62b). These beads, 0.9cm in height, have a dark grey surface patina. All except no. 3 are decorated with three vertical white stripes at equal intervals around the circumference, and their string holes are somewhat off center, giving the beads a lop-sided appearance. No. 3 is similar in shape, size, and color, but is more accurately bored and lacks decoration. A bead similar to those in the collection from Grave I.41.212 appears in Pl. 60b, no. 15, but it is undecorated. No. 12 in the same plate is smaller and much elongated (0.3cm in diameter and 0.6cm high). It has the dark grey surface coloration characteristic of beads of this form, but lacks decoration.

Forms 7 and 8: Spheroid and Spherical

Form 7 beads are illustrated in Pl. 59a, nos. 10, 12, 14, 16, 18, 20, 24, 26, 28, 30, 32, 34; Pl. 59b, nos. 1, 3-4; Pl. 60b, no. 16; Pl. 61a, nos. 7, 11, 16; Pl. 61c, no. 28; Pl. 62a, no. 6; Pl. 62c, nos. 10-11; Pl. 62d, nos. 2-4; Pl. 64a, no. 2; Pl. 65b, nos. 1-3; Pl. 66a, nos. 1, 4, 8, 12; Pl. 66b, nos. 5, 7, 13; Pl. 67b, nos. 4, 7. Form 8 beads are illustrated in Pl. 62a, nos. 2-3, 5; Pl. 62c, nos. 3-4, 14; Pl. 66a, no. 9; Pl. 66b, no. 12.

Form 7 beads approach the truly spherical form but are more or less flattened in the region of the string holes. The fully spherical form (Form 8) curves regularly up to the string hole. Since the two forms are so closely related, and since so few spherical beads occur, the two forms may conveniently be treated together.

A striking feature of Form 7 beads is the wide range of sizes in which they occur. A large number of them fall within the "seed bead" range (height less than 0.3cm). For a discussion of these tiny beads see pp. 95-96. Examples of seed beads in Form 7 may be seen in Pl. 61a, nos. 7, 11, 16; Pl. 61b, nos. 44, 71; Pl. 65b, nos. 1-3; Pl. 67b, nos. 4, 7. The majority of these beads are of glass or faience with the surface colors cream or pink, but those shown in Pl. 67b, nos. 4, 7, 9, are of black glass. In the case of these very small beads the formal classification is often difficult to determine and somewhat arbitrary.

Pl. 62d indicates that not all "seed beads" were used in necklaces. The photograph shows a heavily corroded oval band of copper/bronze (3.0-3.7 cm in diameter). The band is open and is flattened at its widest part, opposite the opening. From the wide portion it appears to taper to a point on either side of the opening. The left side comes to a simple point. The right side, however, consists of a cylinder of copper/bronze (Pl. 62d, no. 1), formed by wrapping a thin copper/bronze wire around the band 1.5-2.0cm from the point. Between this cylinder and the point, two small beads of Form 7 (diameter 0.4cm. height 0.2cm) are skewered on the band (Pl. 62d, nos. 2-3). A third bead of the same form (Pl. 62d, no. 4) was found loose but closely contiguous to the band. The beads are of glass, patinated to a dull orange color, but showing traces of bright red beneath. The object was most likely an earring to be worn in a pierced ear lobe. The earring was decorated, presumably on the outside of the lobe, with the twisted cylinder of copper/bronze and three bright red beads.

Medium-sized Form 7 beads include specimens from 0.5cm to 0.9cm high. A collection of Form 7 beads from the bottom of the medium-sized range is illustrated in Pl. 59a, nos. 10, 12, 14, 16, 18, 20, 24, 26, 28, 30, 32, 34. All are glass or faience, patinated to a pale pink or cream color. Similar beads, also with a cream-colored patina, appear in Pl. 60b, no. 16; Pl. 66a, nos. 4, 8, 12. Form 7 beads from the upper part of the medium-sized range are illustrated in Pl. 59b, nos. 1, 3-4; Pl. 61c, no. 28; Pl. 62a, no. 6; Pl. 62c, nos. 10-11; Pl. 64a, no. 2; Pl. 66a, no. 1; Pl. 66b, nos. 5, 7, 13. The colors of these larger beads vary more widely than do those of the smaller Form 7 beads. In two specimens (Pl. 61c, no. 28; Pl. 66a, no. 1) a dark grey patina covers deep blue glass. In Pl. 62a, no. 6, a creamy white patina probably covers pale blue or green glass. Pl. 59b, nos. 1, 3-4, and

Pl. 64a, no. 2, have a creamy patina over amber-colored glass. In Pl. 66b, nos. 5, 7, 13, are glossy black glass.

One medium-sized Form 7 bead is made of carnelian (Pl. 62c, no. 11). The other carnelian beads within this size range (Pl. 62c, nos. 3-4, 14; Pl. 66b, no. 12) are spherical in shape and belong to Form 8.

The Form 8 beads in glass are all of large size (over 1.0cm high). The three shown in Pl. 62a, nos. 2-3, 5, are of white or very pale blue glass. The one illustrated in Pl. 66a, no. 9, is of bright blue glass.

Form 9: Cylindrical, Small

Beads of this form are illustrated in Pl. 60b, nos. 7, 20; Pl. 61a, nos. 8, 15, 26, 32; Pl. 61b, nos. 38-39, 86, 92; Pl. 61c, nos. 21, 43-45; Pl. 63a, *in toto*; Pl. 67b, no. 2.

The small cylindrical form belongs to the category of beads less than 0.3cm high, referred to above (pp. 95-97) as "seed beads." Small cylindrical seed beads, less frequent in occurrence than the small flattened-rounded (Form 5) and the tiny spheroid (Form 7) varieties, are illustrated in Pl. 60b, nos. 7, 20; Pl. 61b, nos. 38-39, 86, 92; Pl. 61c, nos. 21, 43-45; Pl. 67b, no. 2. The two beads in Pl. 67b are of glossy black glass. All the other specimens are of glass with a heavy white, cream, or amber patina, completely masking the underlying colors. The beads shown in Pl. 61a, nos. 8, 15, 26, 32, are at the top of the seed-bead size range. They are also glass beads patinated to white or grey. The underlying colors are masked by the patina.

An unusual collection of small cylindrical (Form 9) beads is shown in Pl. 63a. These beads are tiny rings of copper/bronze, only 0.2-0.3cm high. The walls of the cylinders are thin, so that the string holes are relatively large. These copper/bronze objects may not have been intended for use in a necklace but for some other adornment of the body or garments.

Form 10: Cylindrical, Squat

Form 10 beads are illustrated in Pl. 59a, nos. 1, 5, 42; Pl. 61b, nos. 60, 62-66; Pl. 62c, no. 8; Pl. 63b, nos. 1-4, 7, 9, 11-14, 17-21, 23, 26-32, 34-37, 45; Pl. 64a, nos. 3, 5, 7, 9; Pl. 64b; Pl. 66a, nos. 5-6, 10, 13, 15, 20; Pl. 67a, no. 4; Pl. 67b, no. 1.

The majority of the squat cylindrical beads are relatively small (0.3-0.5cm high), just above the seed-bead range. The largest collection is shown in Pl. 63b, nos. 2-4, 7, 9, 11, 13-14, 17-21, 26-32, 35-37. They are intermingled with similarly colored Form 5 beads, described on page 96. The beads are of glass, patinated to a dull black, covering greens, blues, and reds. Pl. 61b, nos. 60, 62-66, illustrate an interesting decorated version of small Form 10 beads. They are of red glass with three vertical stripes placed at equal intervals around the circumference. The stripes consist of a single band of black glass, bordered on each side by a narrower band of white glass. A third grouping of small Form 10 beads is seen in Pl. 63b, no. 29; Pl. 64a, nos. 3, 5, 7, 9; Pl. 66a, nos. 5-6, 13, 15, 20. These glass beads are patinated to white or light grey. The original colors are, in most cases, completely masked. Where observation can be made, the creamy white patina seems to cover pale green, and the grey patina darker green, blue, or red.

One of the squat cylindrical beads of small size was evidently not strung directly in a necklace but was a decorative element on a copper/bronze object of uncertain use (Pl. 64b). The bead itself is 0.4cm high with a white patina, through which the underlying pale green glass can be detected. This bead is strung on a copper/bronze wire which has a closed loop at the top. Below the loop is a cylinder formed of twisted copper/bronze wire. The object may have been a straight pin with an ornamental head, of which the bead was one element, and with a point that was subsequently broken off. Alternatively, the copper/bronze wire may have had several beads strung on it, and may have functioned as a pendant or as the centerpiece for a necklace.

A smaller number of Form 10 beads range in size from 1.0 to 1.3cm high. The most common beads of this size range are made of dull red faience or frit (Pl. 59a, nos. 1, 5, 42; Pl. 63b, nos. 1, 12, 23, 34, 45). The grave (I.4.007) from which the beads shown in Pl. 63b came contained numerous broken beads of the same kind (not shown on the photograph). The only other undecorated bead of Form 10 in this range appears in Pl. 66a, no. 10. It is of clear white glass under a thin white patina.

The three remaining examples of large Form 10 beads are decorated. The specimen shown in Pl. 62c, no. 8, is of dull grey frit or faience. A blotchy scalloped design in pale green paint runs around the circumference of the bead. The example shown in Pl. 67b, no. 1, is of black glass or

faience. A wavy white line runs around the center of the bead, with three horizontal white lines on one side and two on the other. The decoration is of applied glass. An unusual, large, Form 10 bead appears on Pl. 67a, no. 4. It is made of stone, probably travertine, and the decoration is the natural grain of the stone. The white, brown, and orange grain gives a handsome effect of horizontal striping. A loop of copper wire runs through the string hole, so that the bead could be used as a pendant or as the centerpiece of a necklace.

Form 11: Cylindrical, Elongated

Beads of this form are illustrated in Pl. 62c, nos. 6, 9, 12, and Pl. 64a, no. 4. Form 11 beads differ from Form 10 in that they are relatively long in proportion to their width. Beads of this form are few in number and occur in three different materials.

Pl. 64a, no. 4, shows the only glass bead in Form 11. It is 1.3cm long and 0.4cm in diameter. The material is bright red glass with a blotchy grey patina.

Pl. 62c, nos. 6, 9, 12, are Form 11 beads made from the long bones of sheep, smoothed and polished. Their color is the natural color of the bone. They are about 2.1cm long and 0.9cm in diameter. Because of the material of which they are made, the walls are thin and the string hole large.

Pl. 67b, nos. 3, 5, 8, 10, are technically Form 11 beads, but the form is incidental to the material. They are made from the thin and delicate shells of the genus of mollusks called *Dentalium*. In nature the shell is tusk-shaped, tapering to a point. The beads were made by breaking or cutting off the curved portion so as to leave about 0.9cm of shell, tapering from about 0.3 to 0.15cm in diameter. Dentalium beads have the ivory-white color of the shell.

Form 12: Cylindrical, Faceted

These beads appear to have been made by trimming the sides of squat cylindrical beads so as to produce a roughly square cross-section when the bead is viewed from above. The rarity of the form and the crudeness of the manufacture may mean that the beads were unsuccessful attempts to produce Form 14 (biconical, double-faceted). Only two examples are illustrated (Pl. 60b, no. 11, and Pl. 67a, no. 2). Both are crudely made of very brittle red glass, which has a dull pink patina. The first bead is 0.4cm high and the second is 0.6cm high.

Form 13: Biconical

The form is illustrated in Pl. 59a, no. 39; Pl. 65a; Pl. 65b, no. 4; Pl. 66b, no. 19.

Biconical beads are elongated and slope gradually toward the string holes from a maximum diameter at the center of the bead, giving the impression of two truncated cones joined at the base. The best example of the form is shown in Pl. 65a. This bead, 1.1cm long, is made of silver. The ripple effect on the surface is caused by the fact that the bead was made by coiling silver wire. Pl. 59a, no. 39, is a red glass bead of Form 13, patinated to a dull pink. It is 0.7cm high, and has a white band of applied glass near each extremity of the bead. Pl. 65b, no. 4, appears to be a crude attempt to make a biconical bead in red glass which resulted in a roughly pear-shaped product. An unusual bead of this form appears in Pl. 66b, no. 19. It is of green frit, squat in shape with a ridge at the point of maximum diameter. It is decorated with incisions along the ridge.

Form 14: Biconical, Double-faceted

Beads of this form are illustrated in Pl. 59a, no. 6; Pl. 62c, no. 2; Pl. 64a, nos. 1, 8; Pl. 65c, *in toto*; Pl. 66a, nos. 3, 16-19; Pl. 66b, no. 1; Pl. 67a, no. 1.

Form 14 beads have the general structure of biconical beads (Form 13), except that the upper and lower segments of the bead are both given four flat surfaces, so that the bead has the appearance of two irregular pyramids joined at their bases.

Form 14 beads fall into two groups. The first consists of squat, rather crudely made beads in red glass, 0.6-0.8cm high, with a dull pink patina. Examples may be seen in Pl. 59a, no. 6; Pl. 65c, nos. 1-3; Pl. 66a, nos. 3, 16-19; Pl. 66b, no. 1. This group is more numerous than the illustrations indicate. The glass of which they are made is very brittle, and numerous broken beads, not shown in the photographs, were found in association with the beads illustrated in Pls. 65c and 66a.

Form 14 beads of the second group (Pl. 64a, no. 8; Pl. 65c, nos. 4-23; Pl. 67a, no. 1) are of brittle black glass. Numerous broken specimens are shown in Pl. 64a, no. 1. The beads are 0.6-0.8cm high, but are smaller in diameter than the beads of the first group and hence have a more elongated appearance.

One bead (Pl. 62c, no. 2) stands outside the two main groups. It is a carefully made carnelian bead 0.9cm in diameter and 0.6cm high. The gemcutter left a sharp ridge around the center of the bead and cut six triangular facets above and below the ridge. The end result is a very squat, biconical, double-faceted bead.

Form 15: Simple-faceted

Simple-faceted beads are cut from a cube or near cube. The gemcutter worked from both the top and bottom of the bead, cutting from both ends toward a line around the bead at its mid-point. In the cutting process the craftsman worked across the corners of the cube. This left large diamond-shaped facets on all four sides of the bead (see Pl. 57). Although beads of this form are rare, they are large and attractive. Pl. 62a, no. 4, is a Form 15 bead, 1.3cm × 1.3cm, made of copper/bronze. Pl. 66a, no. 24, is a bead of amber glass, 1.9cm × 1.3cm, cut with great precision. In the string hole is a piece of iron wire, flattened at one end of the bead to form a head and broken off at the other. If the broken end of the wire was originally looped, this splendid bead could have served as a pendant or centerpiece of a necklace. If the wire was pointed, it might have been a pin with the bead as its ornamental head.

Form 16: Double-faceted

This form is illustrated in Pl. 59a, no. 38; Pl. 62c, nos. 5, 13; Pl. 64a, no. 6; Pl. 66b, nos. 2-4, 6, 9-11, 15-18.

Double-faceted beads, like the simple-faceted form, are cut from a cube or near cube. In this case, however, the cutting process is more complex. From the top of the bead the gemcutter worked parallel to the face of the cube, and from the bottom he worked across the corners. The result is four approximately triangular faces in the top half and four on the bottom half of the bead. The triangles interlock around the circumference of the bead. Five large, well-made beads of this form are illustrated. Those shown in Pl. 62c, nos. 5, 13, are made of amber glass. The first is 1.9cm high × 1.9cm wide, the second 1.5cm high × 1.5cm wide. Three large and carefully cut beads in purple glass appear in Pl. 66b, nos. 9-11. Less care was taken in the fashioning of the smaller, but relatively more numerous, Form 16 beads in amber and transparent glass (Pl. 59a, no. 38; Pl. 64a, no. 6; Pl. 66b, nos. 2-4, 6, 15-18). These beads vary considerably in size. The norm is about 0.7cm high, but one specimen (Pl. 66b, no. 16) is almost 1.0cm in height. They also show irregularities in cutting, so that some approach the biconical, double-faceted form (Form 14). Pl. 66b, no. 14, looks like a faceted bead, but is really a chip of carnelian broken off a larger ornament and re-bored for use as a bead.

Shell Beads

Dentalium shell beads have been discussed (p. 98). Agate cowrie (*C. achatidea Sby.*) shells of the Mediterranean were occasionally used in necklaces (Pl. 67a, nos. 8-9). The shells used were apparently picked up on the beach, since they are bleached white, and the upper side of the shell is worn away. Because of the resemblance of the aperture of the shell to the female vulva, the cowrie was regarded from antiquity as a fertility charm. It is possible that it had the same symbolic value in the community which used the Hesi cemetery. One badly water-worn marine mollusk shell, probably belonging to the *Triton* family, was found in association with beads (Pl. 67a, no. 5). It appears to have been deliberately bored through the spire of the shell near the apex, perhaps so that it could be strung as a bead. A fragment from the thick portion of a marine bivalve shell near the umbone had been smoothed to a round outline and bored with a large string hole, forming a deeply concave disc bead. This bead (not illustrated) came from Burial I.21.072B.

Double-bored Objects

A disc of soft green frit, 1.0cm in diameter, is shown in Pl. 68a, no. 2. Two holes have been bored side by side but somewhat off center through the disc. It was tentatively identified in the field laboratory as a button, but the fragility of the material makes this doubtful. It is more probable that the object was strung in a necklace or used as a pendant. At least three other specimens of similar objects have been found in the cemetery.

The copper/bronze disc illustrated in Pl. 68b has two holes near the edge. Since the disc is very thin, it could not have served as a button. Traces of Arabic lettering showing through the corrosion on the disc indicate that it was probably a coin. It is a well-known practice of Bedouin women to string coins together to form a band which is worn as a fringe around the front of the headdress. The double-bored copper/bronze disc may have been used in this way.

Pl. 68c shows an elongated band of mother-of-pearl, somewhat pitted and worn. It is 3.1cm long and 1.0cm wide. Neatly bored holes are located near the extremities of the band. The object was tentatively identified in the field laboratory as a "hair fastener," but this was little better than a guess. The real function of the object remains unknown.

Pendants

Pendants may be defined as objects either bored with a hole near the edge or provided with a loop or hook from which they can be suspended. Pendants may have been worn at the neck, either separately or as the centerpiece of a necklace, or they may have been attached to a headband or earring. Pendants in five different materials have been found in the Hesi cemetery: glass, mother-of-pearl, stone, silver, and copper/bronze. They are of four forms: bead-like, roughly triangular, disc-shaped, and bell-shaped.

Bead-like Pendants

These have been classified and described with the beads. The ornate travertine bead with the copper loop in its string hole (Pl. 67a, no. 4) almost certainly functioned as a pendant and probably formed the centerpiece of a necklace (see p. 98). The beads shown in Pl. 64b and in Pl. 66a, no. 24, may have been pendants or decorations on ornamented pins (see pp. 98 and 99). The flat, diamond-shaped beads, illustrated in Pls. 60a and 60b, no. 1, may just possibly have been pendants of a sort.

Triangular Pendants

These objects are made of mother-of-pearl, derived from a marine bivalve. The mother-of-pearl was removed from the shell, leaving some of the calciferous material of the shell adhering to it. The mother-of-pearl was then cut into a roughly triangular slab, and a hole was bored near the apex of the triangle. Examples of this type of pendant are shown in Pl. 59a, no. 43; Pl. 62c, no. 1; and Pl. 66a, no. 23.

Disc-shaped Pendants

All pendants of this form recovered from the Hesi cemetery, with the possible exception of the double-bored frit object shown in Pl. 68a, no. 2, are coin-like objects. The example shown in Pl. 69a is silver, the only specimen in that material found in the cemetery. Traces of lettering show through the surface corrosion and indicate that the object was actually a coin. The string hole seems to have been made by hammering a small nail through the disc. The disc pendant shown in Pl. 69b is of copper/bronze, one of several found in this material. Faint traces of lettering may be detected through the heavy corrosion. The folding back of the metal where the nail was driven through to make the string hole appears clearly in the photograph.

Bell-shaped Pendants

These ornaments, of which several whole or fragmentary examples were recovered, are made of copper/bronze. Their form varies from an elongated football shape (Pl. 69c) to almost perfectly spherical (Pl. 69d), and they have a loop fused to the surface. The spherical example shown in Pl. 69d has a hole, apparently deliberately bored, near the loop. The reason for this feature is unknown. How and where on the person the bell-shaped pendants were worn is uncertain, but they may have been strung with the pierced coins along the fringe of the headdress. This is the way modern Bedouin women wear similar ornaments. The pendant shown in Pl. 69d had fragments of the shroud or burial garments adhering to it.

Unbored Disc

One copper/bronze disc, about 1.5cm in diameter with a semi-circular protuberance on the edge, was found (Pl. 70). There may have been a string hole near the top of the protuberance which has broken off. Since the hole does not now exist, it is impossible to say whether the object was a pendant or fulfilled some other function.

Rings

Finger Rings

Simple Band

A simple band ring is one in which the ring is permanently closed, the band is of regular thick-ness, and no provision has been made for the mounting of a gem stone. Rings of this type occur most frequently in iron, badly corroded, and often in fragments. Several simple bands of copper/bronze have also been recovered, as well as two simple band rings in bone. The illustrations show representative examples in iron (Pl. 71a) and in copper/bronze (Pl. 71b). The two bone rings are shown in Pl. 71c, nos. 1, 2.

The iron ring in Pl. 71a has an outside diameter of 1.9cm. It shows the heavy corrosion suffered by all iron objects from the cemetery. A similar iron ring, fused to one of copper/bronze, appears in Pl. 72c.

The copper/bronze band in Pl. 71b is almost circular in cross-section. Broken specimens of bands in the same material are often flatter and thinner in cross-section. If the ring shown in Pl. 75c is a finger ring, rather than an earring, it would provide a good illustration of the flatter type. The ring in Pl. 71b is distinctive in having traces of silverplating over the copper/bronze base. Pl. 72b, no. 1, illustrates a copper/bronze ring made by squeezing together the ends of a loop of copper/bronze wire.

The bone band, illustrated in Pl. 71c, no. 1, was made from a sheep/goat vertebra. The interior of the ring was scraped out and smoothed. The exterior was also polished, so that only a suggestion of the configuration of the bone remains. The ring shown in Pl. 71c, no. 2, was cut from a sheep/goat scapula and polished to a smooth surface.

Rings with Center-discs

The bands of these rings are usually thin and flat in cross-section. The band is fused to a disc which would have appeared on the outside center of the ring finger. The disc is generally ovoid in shape, frequently approaching the circular. All but one of these rings are copper/bronze. The exception is the iron ring illustrated in Pl. 73b, no. 2.

Sometimes more than one ring was found in the same burial, and presumably the living woman often wore several rings. Pl. 72a shows three center-disc rings from the same burial. Unexpectedly this is the interment of a juvenile male in a capped and lined grave (I.41.058). The rings may have been worn by the teenage boy, or they may have been deposited in the grave by a bereaved mother (see p. 93). The latter alternative is supported by the presence in the grave of fragments of bronze bracelets. Pl. 72b, no. 2, shows a center-disc ring found in association with a plain band of copper/bronze (no. 1). The burial was that of an adult female in a simple earth grave (I.11.026). The most interesting combination of rings appears in Pl. 72c. A plain iron band was found fused to a center-disc ring of copper/bronze. The fusing together of the rings is best explained if they were worn on the same finger.

The center-discs on these rings have three forms. (1) Most frequently they are thin and flat (Pl. 72a, nos. 1-2; Pl. 72b, no. 2; Pl. 72c; Pl. 73a; Pl. 73b, no. 2). When the corrosion on one ring (Pl. 72a, no. 1) was subsequently cleaned away, the disc was seen to be decorated with impressed circles, each with a dot in the center. Tiny pieces of colored glass could have been set in the circles, in the manner still practiced by Arab jewelers. At least some of the thin, flat discs might thus have been designed to carry their own decoration. (2) Sometimes (Pl. 72a, no. 3; Pl. 73b, no. 1) the discs are thicker and have a deep groove around the edge. The groove may have provided a means by which the setting for a stone could have been attached to the ring. Near the find spot of the ring shown in Pl. 73b, no. 1, a carnelian gemstone was recovered. It would have fit well on the center disc of the ring. (3) The most elaborate of the center-disc rings (Pl. 73b, no. 3) has both the setting and the "stone" intact. The setting is cylindrical in shape, and the "stone" is held in place by four pointed prongs projecting upward from the cylinder. The "stone" itself is half a sphere of blue-green glass.

The iron center-disc ring (Pl. 73b, no. 2) is unusual in that the centerpiece is rectangular in shape. It awaits cleaning in order to determine whether a design was engraved on it. This ring was found in throw-out from gravedigging and cannot be associated with a specific burial. Indeed, it may belong to the Hellenistic or late Persian period.

The diameter of center-disc rings varies from 1.8cm to 2.2cm.

Toe Rings

Pl. 74a shows a badly corroded iron band, 2.8cm in diameter. Part of the band has been broken away and lost, but the ring may well have been originally continuous. It was found on the right great toe of an adult of unknown sex (Burial I.51.135). Two other continuous bands, both of copper/bronze (Pl. 74b, c) may also have been toe

rings. They are thicker and heavier than simple-band finger rings and have a slightly larger diameter (2.3cm). The ring illustrated in Pl. 74b was found in the burial of an infant. It is too small to be an infant's bracelet (if, indeed, infants wore such ornaments) and too large to be an infant's ring. Probably the infant's mother deposited the ring in the grave. It was the only object found in the burial. The ring shown in Pl. 74c came from the burial of an adult female, where it was found in association with the earring shown in Pls. 62d and 75a.

Earrings

Only one object can be identified with certainty as an earring. It is illustrated in Pls. 62d and 75a, and is fully described on page 97. As Pl. 75a shows, fragments of cloth were found adhering to the ring. The thin copper/bronze band illustrated on Pl. 75b may be an earring, somewhat distorted in shape, but is more likely a plain band of the type shown in Pl. 72b, no. 1, which has come apart at the point of fusion. A wide, thin copper/bronze band, 1.5cm in diameter and open on one side (Pl. 75c), may also be an earring, although the width of the band at the opening would make it difficult to attach the object to the ears. Alternatively, it may be an open finger ring of an unusual type (cf. p. 101).

Bracelets

Bracelets occur in three materials: glass, copper/bronze, and iron. They take one of two main forms: continuous closed bands and open bands. The open-band form is found only in copper/bronze bracelets.

Glass Bracelets

Glass bracelets, which are all of the closed type, may be classified as decorated and undecorated.

Undecorated Glass Bracelets

Almost all the undecorated glass bracelets are simple closed bands in various shades of blue, especially bright blue. The choice of blue is probably because that color was considered to be effective in warding off the evil eye. Pl. 76a shows four glass bracelets found in the same grave. Nos. 1-3 are undecorated bands of bright blue glass. No. 4 is of amber glass. Unfortunately, this selection does not prove that more than one bracelet was worn by a single individual. They were found in the grave of an infant (I.12.127), and their diameter (5.0cm) is too large for an infant's arm. They probably constitute yet another case of jewelry deposited by the mother (or sister) in an infant's grave.

Undecorated bracelets often show evidence of veining in the glass. Streaks of lighter or darker color run round the band (see Pl. 76a, nos. 2-3). These may have been produced by heating rods of various shades of glass together and drawing the hot glass out to form the bracelet. Pl. 76a, nos. 2-3, are bright blue with darker blue veining. No. 4 in the same plate is amber glass with blue and brown veining.

Pl. 76b shows a rather large (7.0cm in diameter) bracelet in bright blue glass. The surface is patinated in places to a light grey, and traces of iron rust can be seen on the surface. There is little or no veining in the glass. The presence of the rust indicates that this bracelet was worn on the same arm as an iron bracelet. The specimen comes from the burial of an adult female (I.32.056).

The bracelet illustrated in Pl. 76c came from the grave of an adult of unknown sex (I.21.026A), but is unexpectedly small. The diameter (4.0cm) is too large for a ring and, as a bracelet, would only fit the arm of a very small-boned woman. It may have had some other function, such as the drop for an earring, or it may have been a child's bracelet treasured by the mother even in death. The glass is light blue in color with prominent veins of bright blue.

Decorated Glass Bracelets

Bracelets classified as decorated have designs in glass applied to the surface of the band.

Pl. 77a shows a small (4.5cm in diameter) bracelet of pale blue glass. Six lozenge-shaped decorative elements, evenly spaced around the circumference, have been applied to the surface. These consist of angled strips of black, red, yellow, and bright blue glass. The technique was apparently to fuse thin rods of colored glass to the surface of the bracelet under sufficient heat to flatten the rods into strips. The bracelet was the only object found in the burial of an infant (I.41.065), and may have belonged to the infant's mother.

The bracelet illustrated in Pl. 77b is larger (about 6.0cm in diameter) and more elaborately decorated than the previous example. Its basic color is blue, now heavily patinated. A rod of red

glass was fused to the center of the band all the way round the circumference but under a low enough heat to allow it to remain round in section. Presumably above this rod, in a position where it would show to best advantage when the bracelet was on the arm, a continuous decorative pattern of angled black, red, and white stripes was applied. Below the rod the bracelet is undecorated. The grave from which this object came (I.22.119) was that of a child, and the bracelet may have been the possession of the mother.

Copper/Bronze Bracelets

Bracelets in this material fall into three categories: continuous bands, simple open bands, and snake-decorated bands.

Continuous Bands

An example of this form of bracelet is illustrated in Pl. 78. It is 5.8cm in diameter and is relatively thick and heavy. It may have been an anklet, rather than a bracelet.

Simple Open Bands

Pl. 79a and b illustrate simple open bracelets in copper/bronze. The bands are flattened and thin in cross-section, and are fairly wide. Pl. 79a has a diameter of 5.0cm and a width of 1.0cm. Pl. 79b is 5.5cm in diameter and 1.0cm wide. The thickness of the bracelets is only 0.1-0.2cm. At the opening the ends of the bracelets are gently rounded. As the photographs show, both examples have fragments of cloth adhering to them. One open-band bracelet in iron (not illustrated) came from Burial I.22.015 (see Appendix 3).

Open, Snake-Decorated Bands

This type of bracelet is circular in cross-section, and the edges of the opening have been specially worked to give the bracelet its distinctive characteristics. On one side of the opening the band has been thickened to represent the head of a serpent. In Pl. 80a the head is stylized, but in Pl. 80b it is more realistic. The serpent's eyes and mouth are clearly depicted. On the other side of the opening the band is flattened to represent the serpent's tail. The bracelet shown in Pl. 80b is twisted all along its length. The rippling effect gives a dramatic suggestion of the serpent in motion. This attractive bracelet came from the burial of an adult female in the most elaborate type of cist (Type

III). The same burial (I.32.048) contained the unusual copper/bronze beads described on page 97, as well as other jewelry (see Appendix 3). It was evidently the burial of a well-to-do woman. The bracelet shown in Pl. 80a (diameter 4.5cm) was found in place around the lower arm bones of a child of unknown sex (I.21.017A).

Iron Bracelets

Iron bracelets are invariably found in a badly corroded condition. The surfaces are covered with a thick, flaky deposit of rust which masks the surface features and distorts the shape and dimensions of the object. The rust has cut so deeply into the metal that the bracelets are easily broken and usually found in fragments. For these reasons little can be said about them until they are cleaned and studied by specialists.

Pl. 81a illustrates one of the few intact iron bracelets recovered. Its small size (diameter 4.5cm) and its relatively great thickness apparently preserved it from breakage. The bracelet in Pl. 81b is more typical in size and thickness. It has an approximate diameter of 6.5cm and, like so many iron bracelets, was uncovered in fragments. It appears to have been originally a continuous band, however.

By contrast, the object shown on Pl. 81c may have been an open iron band with special working of the edges of the opening. Cleaning should determine whether this suggestion is correct.

Pins

A piece of copper wire, looped at one end and with a squat cylindrical bead (Form 10) mounted on it (Pl. 64b), may have functioned as a straight pin for securing a garment (see p. 98). The only other object which could possibly be a pin is a straight rod of copper/bronze, 4.2cm long and 0.1cm thick (not illustrated). The object (from Burial I.22.034, see Appendix 3) is badly corroded, but appears to have a point at one end and a small knob at the other. It is not a needle, since it has no hole for the thread, but is most likely a straight pin used for fastening the garments or shroud of the deceased.

Studded Leather Band

The burial of an adult male in a capped grave (I.51.067) contained many fragments of decayed leather. Imbedded in these fragments were four intact spheroids of copper/bronze and fragments of several others. The best suggestion is that these objects are the remains of a leather wrist band, set with copper/bronze studs. This would seem to be an ornament appropriate to an adult male.

General Remarks on Jewelry

The community which used the Hesi cemetery, particularly its women members, displayed a marked fondness for jewelry. Not only is its occurrence in burials frequent, but an individual often wore several pieces of jewelry of different types. The woman buried in Grave I.22.207, for example, had at least two iron and two glass bracelets, a copper/bronze finger ring, and a string of beads (Pl. 58, and cf. Appendix 3). More than one bracelet might be worn on the same arm, and more than one ring on the same finger.

By and large, the jewelry is of inexpensive materials and unimpressive workmanship. Gold is absent and silver rare. With few exceptions, the craftsmanship in copper/bronze and iron is simple. No precious stones are found, and carnelian, though present, occurs infrequently. The glass jewelry is sometimes quite attractive, but the styles are almost always simple, and the workmanship is frequently shoddy. Natural materials, such as bone, shell, and mother-of-pearl, are used, but with only the simplest modification of the material. These phenomena indicate that the community was a poor one, lacking the wealth to use costly materials or skilled craftsmanship in satisfying its penchant for ornamentation.

The most difficult question raised by the survey of the jewelry is, "What age and sex groups wore it?" On page 93 it was suggested that the occurrence of jewelry in the graves of infants, children, and adult males might be explained by a mourning custom in which women deposited their jewelry in the graves of loved ones. This tentative conclusion now requires re-examination.

Burial I.12.054, the interment of an adult male in a capped grave (Type II.K.4.f), provides a good basis on which to raise the relevant questions. An iron bracelet of the open-band type (Pl. 81c) was found *in situ* on the arm of the skeleton. A copper/bronze ring with silver plating (Pl. 71b) was on the right hand, and an open-style copper/bronze bracelet (Pl. 79b) was on the right arm. The beads shown in Pl. 62b were also found in the cist. There is little doubt that the ring and bracelets were in place on the body at the time of burial. This burial strongly suggests that the men of the community, as well as its women, wore jewelry.

In addition to I.12.054, three burials of adult males contained iron bracelets (I.2.020, I.4.020, I.32.037). Of these, one (I.4.020) also contained an iron ring. Beads occurred in four adult male burials besides I.12.054 (I.11.004/096, I.31.176, I.51.067, and I.51.133), although in the last of these burials only a single bead was found, and its presence may have been accidental. In I.51.067, the beads were identified (see p. 104) as part of a studded leather wrist band.

At first consideration it might seem to be stretching credulity to include glass beads among male ornaments, but Arab men often carry a string of spheroid or spherical beads which they stroke and pass through their fingers while standing or walking. Such beads, the authentic possession of the adult male, may have been placed in the grave with the body, perhaps held in the hand. This explanation would cover the spheroid beads found in Burials I.11.004/096 and I.12.054, but not the seed beads of Burial I.31.176.

The possibility exists, though it is somewhat remote, that the men did not wear jewelry in life, but that the women sometimes placed their jewelry on the bodies of dead male relatives during the preparation for burial. No parallel to this presumed practice can be found among the Bedouin. A second alternative, painful to contemplate, is that the skeletons were incorrectly sexed in the field, or that the sex was incorrectly recorded on the code forms. All in all, the most likely explanation is that two factors are at work in the appearance of jewelry in the graves of adult males. Some of the jewelry found in these contexts was worn by the men in life, notably bracelets of metal, finger rings, and wrist bands. Some was deposited in the grave by grieving female members of the family.

In the main the jewelry found in the graves of children is of a size and form suitable to that age group. Among the present-day Bedouin, children receive and wear jewelry at a very early age. However, as in the case of adult males, some of the jewelry found in the graves of children may have been put there by women.

Almost all the jewelry recovered from infant burials is of a size and type more appropriate to adults. Most, if not all, of it was probably deposited in the graves by adults.

The jewelry provides slight, but definite, evidence of an element of superstition in the beliefs of the community. The widespread use of blue colors was probably to ward off the evil eye. The snake motif, occasionally found on bracelets, may have been insurance against snake bite. In any event, the serpent is an ancient amuletic symbol. The cowrie shell beads were probably fertility charms, as they have been from antiquity.

Copper/Bronze Discs

Nine specimens of these discs were recovered from Burial I.21.017A, the interment of a child in a simple earth grave (Type I.F.0.1). They are approximately 1.8cm in diameter and 0.4cm thick. They are not bored, and their surfaces are not worked in any way. Large cloth fragments were found adhering to them. Indeed, they seem to be associated with the *same* piece of cloth (cf. the two specimens shown in Pl. 80a). The field laboratory immediately identified them as weights, but did not speculate as to their function.

An idea of how these discs were used may be gained from present-day Bedouin practice. The Bedouin, children as well as adults, are outdoors a great deal, tending the flocks of sheep and goats. The long headdresses of the women would flap uncontrollably in the high winds prevalent in the area unless the edges were weighted down. Accordingly, weights are sewn into the hem of the headdress. The nine copper/bronze discs found in Burial I.21.017A were probably weights used for this purpose. The position of the arms of the skeleton was not reported, but a Bedouin headdress is long enough to bring the hem level with the forearm in the manner shown in Pl. 80a. Unfortunately, no other grave produced similar weights.

Cloth

Numerous cloth fragments were found, in every case either adhering to or in intimate association with copper/bronze objects. Instances are shown in Pls. 69d, 75a, 79a and b, 80a. Of this phenomenon Plenderleith and Werner stated, "It is common ... to find fragments of textile surviving when they are in contact with corroding copper, the corrosion products having acted as sterilizing agents" (1971, 100).

Drs. R. J. Kominar and M. Krech of the Wilfrid Laurier University Department of Chemistry performed a partial qualitative analysis on the salt encrustation from Ob. Reg. No. 64 (1973) from Burial I.22.079 (see Pl. 75a). "Tests for carbonate

($CO_3^=$), chloride (Cl^-), and phosphate (PO_4^{3-}) showed positive results. Tests for nitrate (NO_3^-) and sulphate ($SO_4^=$) were negative. The sample appears to be mainly carbonate with some chloride and phosphate, but little or no nitrate or sulphate.'' The poisonous salts, released by the corrosion of the copper, permeated the fabric and impeded its deterioration.

Examination of the position of the cloth in relation to the objects to which it adheres might be expected to cast some light on the question of whether the body was buried naked in a shroud or clothed in the garments worn in life. In the case of the earring illustrated in Pl. 75a, the cloth was detached when found and hence contributes nothing to the question. The cloth shown in Pl. 79a and b adhered to only one side of the object, but could equally come from garments or a shroud. As Pl. 69d shows, the cloth adhering to a bell-shaped object is attached to one side only, and does not touch the loop of the bell. Again, it may have come from either garments or a shroud. However, if, as was argued on page 101, the bells were strung along the fringes of headdresses, they would not have been present in the graves unless the headdress was being worn by the deceased. The most convincing evidence is illustrated in Pl. 80a. Here the cloth is seen adhering to two copper/bronze discs. If these were weights used to hold down the headdress, their presence in the grave cannot be explained unless the headdress was, in fact, on the body. We may conclude, with a fair degree of probability, that the dead were buried in their ordinary garments. This does not eliminate the possibility that the body, fully clothed, was also wrapped in a shroud.

No analysis of the cloth from the Field I cemetery has as yet been carried out, but a sample of cloth recovered from the Field VI cemetery in 1977 was studied by Dr. Chaja Frydman of the Israel Fibre Institute. Microscopic analysis by transmitted and polarized light revealed that the fibres had the characteristic structure of flax, so that the garment or shroud in question was linen.

Pottery

Side-spouted Water Pitchers

Burial I.4.020 was the grave of an adult male, buried in an extended position on the back, looking southeast (Type II.K.2.f). The grave was capped with large field stones, and the spaces between them were chinked with smaller, rounded stones. As the first of the cappers began to appear in the excavation, three side-spouted water pitchers, called by the Arabs *ibrīq* (plu. *abārīq*), were found partially imbedded in the capstones of the grave. The position of these three *abārīq* is shown in Pl. 82, where A and B are capstones of the grave and C, D, and E are the *abārīq*. Subsequent excavation revealed three more of these vessels. The area supervisor assigned all six to the soft fill in the grave shaft and associated them with the grave cappers on which they were lying.

The six *abārīq* are illustrated in Pl. 83. No drawings are provided, because the photographs give all the essential features of the vessels in sufficient detail. Nos. 1-3 and 5-6 are in ''black'' ware (Munsell 5YR 3/0 to 5YR 2/0, ''very dark gray'' to ''black''). The broken specimen (no. 4) is Munsell 2.5YR 3/6, ''dark red.'' The vessel form closely resembles that of the *abārīq* sold today in Arab marketplaces. *Abārīq* are purchased by the Hesi expedition for use by the volunteers to take their daily water supply into the field. They are very efficient for this purpose. The porous sides allow the vessel to sweat and thus keep its contents pleasantly cool. No cups are necessary, since the user drinks directly from the side spout, and because the side spout does not touch the lips of the drinker the vessels are sanitary.

The Hesi *abārīq* have the characteristic long neck with slightly outflaring rim, the short conical spout, the two vertical loop handles and the low disc base of the present-day vessels. They differ from their contemporary counterparts in the ridging around the upper neck, sometimes terminating at the bottom in a particularly sharp ridge (nos. 1, 3-5), and in the shallow ridging which appears on the bodies of some of the vessels (nos. 1-3, 6). All have two handles. Present-day *abārīq* frequently have only one, on the side opposite the spout. The most conspicuous difference is the prevailing dark grey color of the vessels. *Abārīq* now available in the area range from red to buff, but are rarely black.

Since the longevity of the type and the history of changes in its form have not been studied, Theodore A. Rosen, the expedition's photographer in 1970 and 1971, undertook to inquire about the vessels from potters in the area. Since ''black Gaza ware'' is a virtual cliché at the pottery-reading table, and since Gaza is nearby and is a famous pottery-making center, Rosen showed vessel no. 3 to a number of Gaza potters. They denied that it belonged to their pottery-making tradition. The vessel was, they claimed, "antique," and when pressed they suggested that it was thirty to forty years old and originated in "the north." One Gaza potter thought that the pitcher came from Jeba', but a potter from Jeba' denied that the vessel was in the Jeba' tradition. He remembered, however, that his grandfather had acquired a similar *ibrīq* in Haifa before the 1948 war, but the Hesi *ibrīq* seemed to him to be older than his grandfather's purchase. "Probably about forty years old" was his estimate.

The inquiry, reported by Rosen in an unpublished paper, is not very satisfactory in establishing the date of the *abārīq* from Hesi. It demonstrates that the style belongs to an earlier period than the present, but the forty-year estimate is probably a guess rather than a statement of fact. The vessels are therefore of little value in dating the grave in which they were found, except to indicate that it was before living memory.

Why *abārīq* were deposited in this grave (and this grave alone) is something of a mystery. The occupant of the grave may have been a potter, but Bedouin communities normally purchase their pottery vessels, rather than manufacture them. A long-shot guess is that the deceased engaged in small-time trading and was the supplier of *abārīq* for the community. Some of his wares may have been buried with him.

Burial Jar

Grave I.41.019 contained the body of a newly born or prematurely born infant in a pottery jar (Type V.C.0.0) whose earth fill contained a fragment of an adult's glass bracelet. The burial jar is seen *in situ* in Pls. 26 and 27, and the jar after removal is shown in Pl. 84. The photograph adequately illustrates the main features of the vessel, and no drawing is provided.

The jar is dark grey to black in color (5YR 3/0 to 5YR 2/0), with a flattened, slightly convex base. Since the rim and neck have been broken off, presumably to accommodate the body more readily, the rim form is unknown, and it is impossible to determine whether or not the vessel had handles. The jar has shallow ridging on the upper body and on the lower body near the base. Between the two zones of ridging are five irregular bands of combing, each containing three to seven parallel indentations.

Four jars found at Tel Mevorakh contained the skeletons of infants (Stern, 1978). These are discussed on page 5 and illustrated by drawings in Fig. 1:1-4 and by photographs in Pls. 6:4-5; 21 of the official publication. Two of the vessels (Pl. 21:1, 4; Fig. 1:2, 4) have body forms similar to that of the Hesi jar. The Tel Mevorakh jars have narrow mouths, well-defined necks, and two handles set high on the shoulder. The corresponding features have been lost from the Hesi jar. In both Tel Mevorakh jars the bottom has been broken off or cut through, but neither seems to have had a formed base like that of the Hesi jar. The body of the infant was inserted into the Tel Mevorakh jars from the bottom, whereas at Hesi the body was introduced from the top.

Tel Mevorakh Fig. 1:2 has combed decoration on the body, but the decoration is more precisely patterned than is that of the Hesi jar. It consists of two registers of combed design, each composed of two parallel bands of combing with a wavy band between. Fig. 1:4 has ridging on the upper body only, and no combing.

On the basis of modern parallels, Dr. Stern dated the burial jars from Tel Mevorakh "to the mid-nineteenth century onward" (Stern, 1978, 5) and pointed out that a jar similar to the Tel Mevorakh vessels was found at Tel Zeror (Stern, 1978, 8, note 10). The excavators of Tel Zeror dated the cemetery there to the twelfth to fourteenth centuries A.D. (see above, p. 17). In view of the ambiguity of the dating evidence and the differences in style among the burial jars, no chronological conclusions are warranted.

Small Side-spouted Jar

A very interesting small vessel was found in Field VI in the simple earth grave of an infant (VI.P-1a.001, Type I.C.0.0). A photograph of the jar is given in Pl. 85 and a drawing in Pl. 88b. The rim and part of the neck and shoulder are missing. A spout very much like that of an *ibrīq* was attached to the shoulder after the body had been formed. The opening into the vessel was made by thrusting a rod down the spout and through the side of the jar, leaving irregular globs of clay around the opening. The remains of handle attachments show that a vertical loop handle ran from the center of the body to the neck on the side opposite the spout. The jar stands on a well-formed and fairly high ring base. Its squat, globular body is decorated with six bands of shallow ridging around the girth. The exterior color is light grey (10YR 7/1) with patches of darker grey (2.5YR 4/0). The core is grey (2.5YR 5/0) with numerous small and a few medium-sized grits.

No parallels have been found for this vessel, but it seems to be a small version of an *ibrīq*, and may have been a small child's toy or drinking vessel. Since the grave was that of an infant from six to eighteen months of age, the intriguing possibility exists that the vessel was the baby's feeding bottle. The author has not had the opportunity to ask whether miniature *abārīq* are or were used in the area as babies' feeding bottles. The dark patches on the surface of the vessel appear to be smoke blackening, and it is tempting to conjecture that the baby's milk was heated in the little *ibrīq*.

Piriform Juglet

Grave I.51.013, the burial of an infant in a simple earth grave (Type I.C.2.e), yielded a juglet with a piriform body and a small flat base. The juglet appears in a photograph in Pl. 86, *in situ* in the bottom of the grave shaft in Pl. 87, and in a drawing in Pl. 88a. The rim and the upper part of the neck are broken off. One vertical lug handle survives at the junction of the neck and body, and the attachment for a similar handle is found on the opposite side of the neck. The surface is covered with a thick cream slip (5YR 8/2), and the underlying color is light reddish brown (5YR 6/4).

The vessel could be an Early Bronze Age object, accidentally included in the fill of the grave, or a juglet of the Arabic period accidentally or deliberately placed in the burial. Lug-handled juglets are common in Early Bronze Age contexts, but their bodies are more globular and their bases wider than those of the vessel under discussion. Therefore, the juglet is probably an Arabic vessel, although no parallels from the period were found. Its narrow neck suggests a container for perfume or oil, but its purpose in relation to the burial is unclear.

Objects Possibly Associated with Burials

Copper Wire

Burial I.12.054, the interment of an adult male in a capped grave (Type II.K.4.f), contained numerous fragments of copper/bronze wire. The filaments were folded together as if in a tight coil or bundle. Wire of this type was used to string beads or pendants, probably for use as decoration on headdresses or for the centerpieces of necklaces.

In this case, however, nothing is mounted on the wire, and the reason for its being in the grave is unknown.

Glass Fragments

Burial V.P-1e.005, the capped grave of an adult male (Type II.K.0.g), produced the only fragment of glass on which definite features were preserved. It is a portion, about 4.0cm long, broken off the strap handle of a glass vessel. The flared, elliptical handle-attachment is preserved at one end (Pl. 89). The glass is pale blue and heavily patinated.

An irregularly shaped fragment of pale green glass, 2.9cm long, 2.2cm wide, and 0.1-0.2cm thick, came from the simple earth grave of an adult male (I.1.016, Type I.K.0.0). It is slightly curved, as if it had formed part of the body of a thin-walled, glass vessel. A triangular sliver of pale green glass, also slightly curved, was found in Burial I.32.039, the capped and lined grave of an adult male (Type III.K.6.0). It is 1.6cm long, 0.6cm wide at the base, and 0.1-0.2cm thick. An irregular fragment of pale green glass, heavily patinated, was recovered from the capped grave of a child of unknown sex (I.32.070, Type II.F.2.f). It has a slight double curvature as if it came from the base of the neck of a vessel. The fragment is 1.7cm long, 1.6cm wide, and 0.3cm thick.

These few glass fragments are too slight a body of evidence to warrant the conclusion that glass vessels were buried with the dead in the Hesi cemetery. Of the cemeteries reviewed in Chapter 3, only that at Tel Gat, a near neighbor of Tell el-Hesi, contained glass vessels. These were described as "small perfume bottles" (Yeivin, 1961, 30 and Pl. 1). None of the glass fragments recovered in the Hesi cemetery have the shape or thickness appropriate to such bottles.

Iron Fragments

The largest iron object is 5.5cm in length and shaped like a spear point. Its function cannot be determined until it is cleared of its heavy layer of rust. It came from the capped burial of an adult of unknown sex (I.41.217B, Type II.M.0.0).

Burial I.41.012, the lined, uncapped grave of an infant (Type IV.C.8.f), produced a badly rusted circlet of iron with an outside diameter of 1.4cm and an inside diameter of 0.7cm. It was tentatively identified in the field laboratory as an "eyelet," but it could also be a small finger ring of the type illustrated in Pl. 71a.

The remaining iron fragments, all heavily oxidized and with a flaky encrustation, resemble small nails or brads. This identification is by no means certain. Cleaning may reveal that they are broken pins or needles. Two of the objects, each about 1.5cm long, came from Burial I.41.106, the capped grave of an adult female (Type II.L.2.f). The third, 3.3cm in length, came from the burial of an infant in a simple earth grave (I.41.213, Type I.C.4.f).

Pebble (?)

A tiny dark brown sphere (0.4cm in diameter) of a very hard substance, identified in the field laboratory simply as "stone," came from the capped and lined grave of an adult male (I.32.039, Type III.K.6.0). The object, possibly formed by natural forces, may be an accidental inclusion in the grave fill.

Inclusions Probably Accidental

Included here are objects whose deposition in the graves along with the earth fill was almost certainly accidental.

Stone Objects

The most common artifacts in this grouping are chert blades made from the rich reddish brown chert common in the Hesi area. Five of them (from Burials I.11.029, I.11.045, I.12.019B, I.31.051/53, I.32.024A, B) are double-edged blades, triangular in cross-section, with a pointed ridge running longitudinally up the center of the blade. These fragments vary in length from 2.5cm to 5.0cm in length. One double-edged blade fragment, 2.5cm long, has a wide, flat ridge along the center of the blade (I.12.018A, Type I.C.8.f). No complete blades were found.

Burial I.2.008, the interment of an adult female in a simple earth grave (Type I.L.0.g), contained two roughly elliptical limestone flakes. The larger of these is 12.0cm by 7.0cm, the smaller 3.5cm by 2.0cm. The edges of both flakes are sharp and crudely notched. They are probably not man-made tools, but stone fragments, shaped and notched by natural processes.

Loom Weight

An almost certainly accidental inclusion in Burial I.4.020, the capped grave of an adult male (Type II.K.2.f), was a crudely made ceramic loom weight of biconical form, 3.0cm in diameter and 2.3cm high. This type of loom weight occurs frequently in the Hellenistic and Late Persian levels into which the graves were dug.

Bone Fragments

A 2.6cm-long bone sliver, found in the simple earth grave of an infant (I.32.009, Type I.C.2.g), and the head of a sheep/goat long bone from an adult female burial in a capped and lined grave (I.22.015, Type III.L.8.f) were undoubtedly both accidental inclusions.

Harness (?)

Two puzzling objects came from Burial I.4.007, the burial of an adult female in a capped grave (Type II.L.2.f). One is a short bronze bar, elliptical in cross-section (length 6.6cm, width 1.5cm, height 0.8cm), with two upright rings 1.3cm high welded to one side of the bar. The rings are 2.3cm apart and 1.5cm from the ends of the bar. The bar has a very slight curvature with the rings on the upper part of the curve. The second object is a hook-shaped piece of copper/bronze, broken at both ends, with an apparent diameter of approximately 7.0cm.

The identity of these objects is obscure. It has been conjectured that they are part of a horse's harness, possibly from the bridle, but this identification is highly speculative. If the objects are not accidental inclusions in the grave fill, no reason for their presence in the burial can be given.

CHAPTER 11

Conclusions and Dating Evidence

The preceding chapters have attempted both to present the archaeological data relating to the Hesi cemetery and to offer suggestions as to their cultural significance. Some of the avenues explored in the examination of the evidence have proved to be blind alleys. Others have led to conjectures, to possibilities, or to probabilities. These occur as isolated statements in the text in a rather undigested form. This final chapter will draw together the principal conclusions of the analysis and combine them in such a way as to present a composite picture of the community which used the cemetery and of its funerary practices.

References scattered throughout the chapter direct the reader to the places in the text where the primary evidence for the conclusions may be found. To avoid fragmenting the text unduly these have been kept to a minimum.

The chapter concludes with a discussion of the date of the cemetery.

The Community

Religion

The most obvious characteristic of the community which used the cemetery is that it was Muslim in religion. The most consistent features of the burials are that the heads are in the western ends of the graves and that the eyes are directed toward the Holy City of Mecca. The eye direction is certainly religiously motivated; the orientation of the body is less obviously so. The position may have been adopted so that the individual would be properly oriented when he or she rose from the grave at the Last Day. The meticulous care with which bones displaced during gravedigging were reburied shows a respect for the dead which is an integral part of Muslim and particularly Bedouin tradition.

The community's adherence to Islam seems to have been strict and orthodox. The simple burials reflect the Koranic injunction against building elaborate tombs for the dead, and stand in sharp contrast to the above-ground cement structures common in the cemeteries of city Arabs. The arrangement of the cemetery in relation to the tomb of the Holy Man also suggests the determinative effect of religion on the community in death, as well as in life.

Orthodoxy in religion does not preclude superstition. The snake motif, found on several bracelets, and the fondness for blue, the color which wards off the evil eye, create the impression that the Islamic traditionalism of the community was at least tinged with superstition.

Hand in hand with devotion to Islam went a stern morality, particularly in sexual matters. The decapitated woman found in the cemetery was probably an adultress who had received summary and violent justice (p. 90). The practice of covering the pelvis with the hands, particularly in the burial of women, indicates a reticence about sex which was probably religiously motivated (pp. 83-84, 84-85).

Economic Basis

The nature of the Hesi burials was such that they gave little direct evidence as to the economic basis of the community. The use of animal bone in the jewelry (pp. 95, 98, 101) suggests stockraising, which could have been combined with seasonal agricultural activity. It is clear that, whatever its economic basis, the community had not the means to acquire much surplus wealth to be spent on luxuries. Though the grave construction and the grave goods show that some members of the community were better off than others, the degree of difference in economic status was small. Extremes of wealth and poverty did not exist, and the members of the community all stood on the same, relatively low, economic level.

Although poor, the community was not isolated. There was some form of access to the coast from which sea shells and mother-of-pearl were obtained. Since it is doubtful that the glass, metal, and pottery found in the graves were manufactured by the community, contact with larger centers of population, where these things were available, must be assumed. A likely model for this contact is the Bedouin market, such as the one still held weekly in Beersheba. Such a market provides an opportunity for the sale of animals and their products, such as wool. In return, trinkets of jewelry and household necessities may be obtained. Some members of the community may have been small-time traders, keeping a stock of articles frequently required for sale within the community (pp. 106-107).

Social Stratification

In other respects as well, the community seems to have been homogeneous and egalitarian. There were no zones in the cemetery with distinctive burial customs, grave types, or grave goods. No stratum of the society appears to have isolated itself from the rest of the community in death, although there was a tendency for better-constructed and better-furnished burials to be concentrated near the south end of the cemetery in closer proximity to the tomb of the Holy Man. This was merely a tendency, not a consistent pattern. All types of grave construction and grave goods occurred in all parts of the cemetery. It may be concluded that some members of the community, because of religious motivation, prestige, or financial means, could claim the preferred places in the burial ground, but this slight differentiation need not imply strong or deeply rooted social stratification.

Sub-groups

While most anomalies in the burials can be explained as the result of carelessness in carrying out the burial practices, two appear significant enough to indicate the presence of small sub-groups within the general framework of the community.

The first consists of four individuals with relatively long skulls, two of whom had the bones stained with what was probably red ochre. On page 90 it was argued that these may have been the burials of women of a different tribal group, introduced into the community by marriage, who retained the custom of staining the skin with red dye. In this case, the first sub-group would be composed of "foreign" wives, presumably Muslim in religion, brought into the community as wives of some of its members.

The practice, found in three graves, of burying the body with the eyes directed to the north, instead of to the southeast, is a deliberate violation of the most fundamental of the burial customs and hence probably indicates a small sub-group with divergent burial practices. The preference of this group appears to be for Jerusalem, rather than Mecca, as the Holy City. Various possible explanations for this phenomenon are offered on page 79. It should be emphasized that Jerusalem is a holy city to Muslims as well as to Christians and Jews, and the orientation of the eyes toward that city does not prove a non-Muslim element in the community.

Family Orientation

Several lines of evidence converge to show that the community was strongly family oriented. The overlapping and intersecting of the graves can best be explained as the result of a desire to keep the family together in death (pp. 22-27). While the presence of jewelry appropriate to women in the graves of infants, children, and adult males may be the result of prescribed mourning customs mechanically fulfilled, it more probably represents firm bonds of affection among family members (pp. 104-105) and reinforces the conclusion that the community was firmly centered in the family. The presence of close family bonds is further attested by those multiple burials in which infants and children who died at the same time were placed in one another's arms (pp. 23-24).

Muslim practice permits polygamy, but the preponderance of women over men in the burials would have been considerably greater than it is if polygamy had been practiced on a large scale. Indeed, the larger number of women than men in the cemetery can be explained on other grounds than polygamous marriage (pp. 65-66).

The status of women in the everyday life of the community is not necessarily indicated by the burials, but in death, at least, women were honored. Their graves were often better constructed and their bodies laid to rest with more careful attention to the burial practices than were those of adult males (pp. 69-72).

The burials of children show greater concern for grave construction and for the niceties of body position than do infant interments (pp. 70-71). Apparently, as the individual passed from babyhood to childhood his or her value in the eyes of the community increased sharply.

The families which used the Hesi cemetery were tightly knit, mainly monogamous units in which children were valued and women respected.

Medical Standards and General Health

To two groups within the community death came frequently. It struck especially at newborn infants, less often at older infants and young children, and it carried away many young women at the age of childbearing (pp. 65-66). The birth of a child was clearly a time of crisis, when the lives of the mother and her baby hung in jeopardy, and the first years of life were a time of special peril for the infant.

On the basis of this evidence, the community did not possess the facilities or trained personnel to handle cases of difficult childbirth, or the specialized knowledge and equipment required to safeguard the lives of infants with medical problems. It may be inferred that the delivery of the baby took place in the family dwelling and was in the charge of a midwife rather than a doctor. Infection and the diseases of infancy also raised problems with which the community could only inadequately cope. Multiple burials of infants and/or children in the same grave (pp. 23-24) probably indicate that such diseases could reach epidemic proportions and take the lives of more than one member of the same family.

If Burial I.41.058 is the grave of a juvenile buried alive (p. 89), the medical knowledge of the community may have fallen short of the ability to establish accurately the fact of death.

In spite of deficiencies in medical knowledge, the juvenile and adult members of the community appear to have enjoyed generally good health. The burials of juveniles are very few in number. The skeletons of some very old people have been found in the cemetery. The teeth are remarkably well preserved and show little evidence of decay. Diseases associated with malnutrition, which would have affected the bones, were exceedingly rare. The active, outdoor life and plain but wholesome diet of a nomadic or semi-nomadic community may have been responsible for the excellent health of the population.

Burial Customs

Preparation of the Body

Muslim tradition calls for burial as soon as possible after death. If death occurs in the morning, burial usually takes place the same afternoon. If it occurs in the afternoon or at night, burial is usually the following morning. The body is washed by a professional washer and wrapped in a linen shroud (Ashkenazi, 1938, 111). The literature does not say whether the body is reclothed before being placed in the shroud. The Hesi cemetery provides evidence that, in some cases at least, the body was dressed in the garments and adorned with the jewelry of everyday life (pp. 104-105). A shroud may have been used as well. The linen fabric identified in the Field VI cemetery (p. 106) may well have come from such a shroud.

Preparation of the Grave

The position of the grave in the cemetery was probably determined by the location of the family plot (pp. 22-29) and by a discussion within the family as to whose body was to be most closely contiguous to that of the deceased (p. 26). The grave party would then locate the designated place and lay out the outline of an ovoid cist in dimensions appropriate to the size of the individual. The long axis of the grave was set at right angles to the direction of Mecca. Following this outline the diggers would excavate the grave to a depth proportional to the height of the dead person (pp. 36-37).

In many cases the excavation of this simple earth grave was the only preparation required. In others, however, the base of the cist was lined with stones, usually upright stone slabs. In contrast to a practice reported by Jaussen as in vogue in the Nablus district (Jaussen, 1927, 334), the Hesi burial parties never placed a stone floor in the grave. If the grave was to be capped but not lined, the diggers would need to leave a ledge of earth about 0.30-0.50m above the bottom of the excavation to support the cappers. For all capped graves, whether lined or not, the burial party would make sure that a supply of suitable stones (flat slabs or field stones) was placed near the excavation. The excavated earth was probably heaped up nearby for convenience in filling the shaft. It could contain objects from graves disturbed by the digging process or objects present by chance in the earth, but would not contain bones. Any bones encountered in digging the grave were either reburied in a shallow pit nearby, or set aside to be interred in the shaft of the grave when it was filled in. Capstones or liners dug up in the excavation were reused in the new burial. Further details of grave construction are given in Chapter 4.

Interment of the Body

The body may have been brought to the cemetery in a wooden, coffin-like bier (Lane, 1860, 518) or wrapped in a shroud and carried on a wooden platform. The body was taken from the bier or coffin and lowered into the grave so that the head was in the western end of the cist. Someone would have had to enter the grave with the body in order to place it properly.

The one feature of the body position dictated rigidly by the burial customs was the direction of the eyes. They must look toward Mecca. If the body rested on the right side this eye direction was naturally achieved. If it lay on the back the head would have to be turned to the right. In order to insure that the head would remain properly positioned it was often wedged in place with stones.

The burial customs did not dictate whether the body was to be placed on the back or on the right side. The choice seems to have been a matter of preference or convenience. If the body was placed on the right side, then whether the legs were slightly flexed or left straight also appears to have been optional under the prevailing burial customs. As far as the disposition of the limbs is concerned, the aim seems to have been to place them in any natural or comfortable position suggestive of repose. One hand was often placed on the pelvis, so as to cover the sexual organs.

If the body were concealed by a shroud, the person responsible for adjusting the body would have had to work by touch alone. Consequently, some errors in the placement of the head, arms, or legs would have been inevitable. Most of the anomalies in burial position may be attributed to this cause.

During the interment, mourning female relatives might place some of their jewelry in the grave with the deceased.

The Filling of the Grave

If the grave was to be capped, the burial party would place the capstones in position over the body and then fill in the shaft. The burial cist below the cappers, originally hollow, would gradually fill in as earth filtered through the chinks. In the case of an uncapped grave the earth would fall directly on the corpse.

No direct evidence of how the graves were marked survives. The earth was probably heaped up in a mound to allow for settling (Jaussen, 1908, 98; 1927, 340). A stone may have been set at the head and the foot of the grave (Jaussen, 1908, 98). Perhaps these grave markers lying thick on the mound deceived Volney who visited the area in the late 1700s, but did not personally inspect the site at close quarters. He reported that the ascent to the mound was paved and that its summit contained the remains of a strong citadel (Volney, 1787, 337). Some such explanation must be true, since the mud-brick construction of the ancient cities would not leave the kind of traces which Volney reported.

The Identity of the Community

The fact that the cemetery belonged to a Muslim community is beyond doubt. What type of community this was is less certain. That it was a major village or city seems to be ruled out by the absence of the tombs built above ground which are characteristic of cemeteries in such urban centers as Jerusalem and Nablus. The community must then have been a rural one, and the choice seems to be among a pure Bedouin, a semi-nomadic, and a *fellahin* (small village farming) community.

Perhaps the best way to establish the validity of this range of possibilities is to summarize the observations of two authors who have studied the burial customs of such communities. Single asterisks indicate customs which, because of the nature of the evidence, cannot be demonstrated at Hesi. Double asterisks indicate practices which are different from those found in the Hesi cemetery.

Antonin Jaussen observed the burial practices of Arabs in the Transjordanian region. The most common form of burial was a shaft grave of a depth equal to the height of the dead person (about 1.60m) and a length sufficient to receive the body. Stone slabs were arranged at the bottom of the grave, in order to isolate the body from the earth.** Other stones were placed around the body to form a chamber containing the corpse. A vault, formed of stones (and mortar**) protected the body from all contact with the earth. The grave was filled, so that the heaped-up earth formed a hillock.* Two dressed stones, one at the head and one at the foot, marked the length of the grave and served to evoke the presence of two protecting spirits.** The head was to the west and the feet to the east of the grave. The body was inclined a little to the right side, so that the face was turned toward the south. If a woman wore bracelets or other ornaments at the time of death, she was buried with this jewelry. She frequently wore a necklace around her neck. A mirror and a comb were often placed in the grave.** For an infant the ceremonies were simpler than for an adult (Jaussen, 1908, 95-105).

Tovia Ashkenazi discussed the customs of semi-nomadic tribes in northern Palestine. Her treatment of the burial customs may be summarized as follows. The body was washed* and wrapped in a shroud. Four or five young men dug a deep excavation in the shape of a human body. The dead person was placed in the grave between two rows of stones about 0.5m in height. The head rested on a stone. The body was covered with stone slabs, and the grave was filled with earth. Many of the tribes buried their dead in the same family tomb. At each death the tomb was opened, and the body of the dead was covered by the bones of those who preceded him or her in the grave. The cemetery was located near the tomb of a saint venerated by the tribe. Many semi-nomads and most nomads did not use commemorative markers. Each grave was marked by a small heap of stones, and the cemetery resembled a field covered with scattered stones** (Ashkenazi, 1938, 110-13).

The correspondence between the burials described by Ashkenazi and those found in the Hesi cemetery is remarkably close. More divergences exist between the Hesi burials and those reported by Jaussen, which included burials of village Arabs. On this evidence the Hesi cemetery is more likely to have belonged to nomadic or semi-nomadic people than to fellahin villagers.

William Robinson identified six Bedouin tribes in the Hesi area in 1833 (the Henâdy, the Wa-haîdeh, the Jebârât, the Zeyâdât, the Sâwârikeh, and the 'Amarin). The Henâdy were harvesting the grain fields in the area and may thus be classified as semi-nomads. Robinson saw encampments of the Wahaîdeh and Jebârât, but only heard reports of the other three tribes (Robinson and Smith, 1856, 48).

Thirty-six years later in 1869 the (D)jebârât seem to have become dominant. Guérin mentioned their presence in the region without specifying other tribes (Guérin, 1888, 296). Berslovsky, who studied the Bedouin of the Negev in 1950, reported that the Djebârât was a populous tribe with forty-six families, consisting of 4,452 persons, living in 890 tents (Berslovsky, 1950, 250).

This data is presented, not to identify the tribe which founded and used the Hesi cemetery, but to make the point that at least since 1833 the region around Tell el-Hesi was the preserve of semi-nomadic tribes which engaged in agriculture as well as stock-raising. A glance at the Survey of Western Palestine map of the area shows that Hesi is remote from any village, in a territory open to the movements of the Bedouin. When Bliss worked at the site in 1891 and 1892 he found that his nearest neighbors were seminomads. He imported his fellahin workmen, with whom he was less than satisfied, from the village of Bureir, about 10km north of Tell el-Hesi (Bliss, 1894, 147).

There is no reason to assume that the distribution of the population in the Hesi region is of recent origin. Probably during most of the period of Arab domination in Palestine the villages lay to the north of Tell el-Hesi, and the banks of the wadi were occupied by seminomads who supplemented their stockraising with agriculture on the broad plains which flank the wadi. To one or more of these groups the Hesi cemetery owes its origin and use.

The Dating of the Cemetery

Terminus ante Quem

When Petrie arrived on the scene in 1890 he found crops growing on the summit of the mound, a condition which certainly would not have been permitted if any tribe in the area venerated the site as a cemetery. Bliss's excavation in the northeast quadrant of the acropolis revealed numerous graves of a type similar to those uncovered by the Joint Expedition. There can be little doubt that

Bliss's cemetery was a northward extension of the one reported in this volume. Bliss's Bedouin workmen showed no knowledge of the existence of the cemetery and no reticence in digging up the graves (above, p. 19). The period of use of the cemetery had come to an end long enough before 1890 for its existence to have been forgotten. Since Arab memory for tribal activities and traditions is long, it is a fair inference that the people who worked for Bliss had no tribal connection with the community which used the cemetery.

It is possible to carry the *terminus ante quem* of the cemetery a step further back in time. Guérin visited Hesi in 1869 and described the summit of the mound in these terms: "Quelque traces d'ancienne constructions se remarquent pareillement, mais d'une manière peu distincte, sur plusieurs points du sommet" (Guérin, 1888, 296). This observation does not sound like a description of a cemetery in active use. That Guérin recognized a Muslim cemetery when he saw one is proved by his comments on Tel Nagila, 7.5km southwest of Tell el-Hesi: "Elle est transformée actuellement en un vast cimetière musulman, où les Arabes de douars voisins viennent enterrer leur mortes" (Guérin, 1888, 295). What Guérin probably saw on the summit of Tell el-Hesi were the tops of Hellenistic stone walls. As Pocket Insert 4, layer 11, shows, these walls lie just below the present surface of the mound.

Fabri and Volney had reported walls on the summit of Tell el-Hesi (Robinson and Smith, 1856, 48, note 1; Volney, 1787, 337). In 1838 Edward Robinson visited the site with a view to describing these walls in more detail. In this he was disappointed. "We could discover nothing whatever to mark the existence of any former town or structure; there was nothing indeed but the level circular plain, which seemed never to have been occupied" (Robinson and Smith, 1856, 48). Robinson's testimony, the witness of a very careful observer, places the last use of the cemetery prior to 1838.

It was suggested above (p. 113) that Volney may have heard of the cemetery and construed what he heard as a report of the ruins of buildings. Robinson was very suspicious of Volney's assertions. He believed that they rested on "the exaggerated testimony of Arabs" (Robinson and Smith, 1856, 48, note 1), but they may indicate the existence of a cemetery on the mound in Volney's time. This suggestion is extremely tenuous, but it suggests a line of enquiry. Were there any political

events between the time of Volney (1787) and that of Robinson (1838) which could account for the abandonment of the cemetery?

In 1798 Napoleon invaded Egypt. Admiral Lord Nelson caught the invasion fleet at anchor and destroyed it in the battle of the Nile. Napoleon and his forces were left stranded in the Nile delta. At this juncture the sultan of Turkey declared war on the French. In order to extricate himself from this desperate position, Napoleon marched north through Palestine, taking el-Arish, Gaza, and Jaffo. The march was marked by the massacre of many Turkish soldiers, and the hatred of the Turks for the French was inflamed. However, many of the local sheiks along the line of march had no love for their Turkish overlords and gave their support and assistance to the French.

The tide of Napoleon's invasion broke on the fortress of Akko. Here a Turkish garrison under Djezzar Pasha and a small body of English sailors and marines commanded by Sir Sydney Smith held out against all expectations for sixty days. The half-starved army of Napoleon retreated to Cairo with the loss of 4,000 troops. The Turkish authorities set out to punish the tribes which had supported Napoleon's invasion. Many of the Bedouin chiefs were executed, and the tribesmen dispersed to other parts of the country.

While direct proof is not available, it is a reasonable hypothesis that the tribes which used the Hesi cemetery were among Napoleon's supporters and were expelled from the territory after his defeat. The cemetery would then have fallen into disuse, and its location might well have been forgotten by the new groups which moved into the area. This hypothesis would place the *terminus ante quem* of the cemetery at about A.D. 1800.

Terminus post Quem

The beginning date of the cemetery is difficult to determine. The burial customs associated with it were undoubtedly conservative and probably remained virtually unchanged from early in the Islamic period. The jewelry and pottery found in the cemetery are types which could have had a long history. However, neither the jewelry nor the *abārīq* forms seem to be particularly ancient.

The comparative evidence summarized in Chapter 2 is not particularly helpful in determining when the cemetery was established. Taking the excavators' dates at face value, the chronological range of cemeteries similar to that at Hesi would extend from the seventh century (Tel Gath) to the nineteenth century (Caesarea). If the Tel Zeror cemetery, which has close parallels to the Hesi burials, belonged to the adjacent village, then a median date between A.D. 1200 and A. D. 1400 is indicated for the Zeror cemetery and may well be plausible for the origin of the Hesi cemetery as well.

When the coins from the Field I cemetery at Hesi are cleaned and studied (if their fragile condition allows them to survive the cleaning process), some additional dating evidence may be available. Several coins recovered from the Field VI cemetery in 1977 have already been cleaned and read. The evidence was summarized in the preliminary report for the 1977 season:

> Eight coins were found in the burials. To date six of these have been cleaned. One is a coin of Constantine (A.D. 323-337) and one of Sultan Baybars I (A.D. 1260-1277). The third is a Mamluk coin of the Circassian period (A.D. 1382-1517). The fourth is also Mamluk but is too poorly preserved to be identified more closely. . . . The coins were cleaned at the Israel Museum and identified by Izhak Reiter of the L. A. Meyer Institute in Jerusalem. (O'Connell, Rose, and Toombs, 1978, 86; the fifth and sixth coins were too badly preserved to be dated.)

The Constantine and Baybars coins may be discounted as evidence since they are coins of famous persons and may have been held for a long time as heirlooms. Alternatively, they may have been picked up as surface finds and kept in the family "treasury." If the Baybars coin is contemporary with any stage of the cemetery, the Hesi burial ground is much older than has been supposed. If the Mamluk coins are regarded as contemporary with the (early) use of the cemetery, they would support a beginning date in the fifteenth or early sixteenth centuries.

On the basis of the present evidence, the most probable hypothesis is that the Hesi cemetery falls within the four centuries between A.D. 1400 and A.D. 1800.

A logical possibility is that the oldest part of the cemetery was located immediately adjacent to the weli (Field VI) and that it spread gradually during its centuries of existence to embrace, first, the neighboring dune (Field V) and, eventually, the summit of the mound (Field I). The excavation currently proceeding in Fields V and VI may shed further light on this possibility.

Appendices

APPENDIX 1

Index of Burials

The index provides a serial listing by field, area, and locus number of all recorded burials (through the 1975 season) in Fields I, V, and VI. The second column gives the type to which the grave belongs and permits ready reference to Appendix 2: Typological Catalogue, where fuller data on each burial are given. The abbreviation i.d. in this column indicates that insufficient data were available to allow the grave type to be determined. The equal sign and a grave number occur in column 2 when a single grave was excavated under two different locus numbers. Column 3 indicates the location in the text where the specific grave, or a grave of the same type, is discussed. The fourth column refers to the illustration(s) in which the burial appears; an asterisk (*) in this column indicates that the burial is listed in Table 18. Most burials appear on the General Plan (Pocket Insert 1).

Grave Number	Type	Page(s)	Illustration(s)
I.1.007	Secondary	45	
I.1.010	II.F.0.0		
I.1.011	i.d.		Pocket Insert 2
I.1.014	III.C.0.0		
I.1.015	II.H.0.0		Pocket Insert 2
I.1.016	I.K.0.0	108	
I.1.020	I.F.0.0		
I.1.021	i.d.		Pocket Insert 2
I.1.022	I.K.0.0		Pocket Insert 2
I.1.024	I.K.0.c	77, 78	*
I.1.026	i.d.		
I.1.029	Secondary	45-46	
I.1.031	II.L.0.0	90	
I.1.034	II.L.0.0		Pocket Insert 2
I.1.035	II.K.0.0		Pocket Insert 2
I.2.006	I.C.0.0		
I.2.007	I.K.0.g		
I.2.008	I.L.0.g	109	
I.2.009	I.E.0.g		
I.2.010	I.L.0.0		
I.2.011	Secondary	45-46	
I.2.012	I.C.0.0		
I.2.013	II.K.0.g	33	
I.2.014	i.d.	46	
I.2.015	i.d.	46	
I.2.017	i.d.		
I.2.018	i.d.	33	

Grave Number	Type	Page(s)	Illustration(s)
I.1.036	II.K.0.0		Pocket Insert 2
I.1.037	II.L.0.0		Pocket Insert 2
I.1.038	=I.2.090		
I.1.039	I.K.0.0	36-37	Pocket Insert 3
I.1.044	I.F.0.0	35	
I.1.045	i.d.	46	
I.1.046	III.L.0.g	35, 90	
I.1.066	II.L.0.0	37-38	
I.1.084	I.F.0.0		
I.1.109	=I.1.046		
I.1.111	I.L.1.f	77	*
I.1.150	=I.1.066		
I.1.154	=I.2.009		
I.1.157	=I.2.021		
I.1.158	=I.1.039		
I.2.019	=I.3.099		
I.2.020	II.K.0.g	38, 105	
I.2.021	II.L.0.0	38	
I.2.028	II.M.0.0		
I.2.029	i.d.		
I.2.030	I.C.0.0		
I.2.034	II.F.0.0		
I.2.052	=I.2.028		
I.2.066	Secondary	45-46	
I.2.083	=I.2.007		
I.2.084	I.C.0.0		
I.2.085	=I.2.021		

Grave Number	Type	Page(s)	Illustration(s)	Grave Number	Type	Page(s)	Illustration(s)
I.2.089	i.d.			I.2.092	=I.2.009		
I.2.090	II.C.2.g	45	Pocket Insert 3	I.2.094	=I.2.014		
I.2.091	=I.2.007			I.2.102	II.O.0.g		
I.3.010	I.C.0.0	36, 41		I.3.051	I.K.0.0	80	
I.3.017	II.C.0.0			I.3.097	I.C.2.0	80	
I.3.018	I.C.0.0			I.3.099	I.F.2.f		Pocket Insert 4
I.3.043	II.L.0.0	38, 90					
I.4.007	II.L.2.f	38, 91, 98, 109	Pl. 63b	I.4.022	i.d.		
I.4.020	II.K.2.f	38, 83-84, 89, 91, 105-6, 109	Pls. 44, 82, 83	I.4.024	i.d.		
I.11.004	I.K.0.0	92, 105	Pocket Insert 2	I.11.029	I.C.0.0	37, 45, 109	Pocket Insert 3
I.11.008	II.F.0.0			I.11.031	i.d.		
I.11.013	I.C.0.0		Pocket Insert 2	I.11.032	i.d.		
I.11.014	Secondary	34, 45-46	Pocket Insert 2	I.11.045	II.K.0.g	34, 37, 109	Pocket Insert 2
I.11.018	I.F.0.0			I.11.049	i.d.		
I.11.019	II.C.0.0			I.11.050	i.d.		Pocket Insert 2
I.11.020	I.F.0.0			I.11.058	II.F.0.0	34, 37	Pocket Insert 3
I.11.021	i.d.			I.11.062	I.C.0.0	23	
I.11.022	II.L.0.g		Pls. 67a, 69d, 71c	I.11.071	i.d.		
				I.11.077	I.F.0.0		
I.11.023	Secondary	45-46		I.11.096	=I.11.004		
I.11.024	II.M.0.g			I.11.097	=I.11.004		
I.11.025	II.C.0.g			I.11.108	=I.11.045		
I.11.026A	I.L.0.g	25, 34, 101-2	Pocket Insert 2, Pl. 72b	I.11.123	=I.1.111		
				I.11.127	II.F.2.f	23	
I.11.026B	Secondary	25, 34, 45	Pocket Insert 2	I.11.172	II.K.2.g	23	
I.11.027A	Secondary	25, 45-46		I.11.210	=I.21.017C		
I.11.027B	Secondary	25, 45-46		I.11.211	I.L.7.c	77, 79, 88	Pl. 55, *
I.11.028	Secondary	45-46					
I.12.005	Secondary	45		I.12.036	i.d.		
I.12.006	i.d.	34, 46	Pocket Insert 4	I.12.038	I.C.8.f		
I.12.009	I.C.2.f			I.12.039	II.M.2.g	93-94	
I.12.011	I.C.2.0			I.12.050	=I.12.036		
I.12.014	i.d.	46		I.12.054	II.K.4.f	38, 75-76, 84, 89, 91-92, 96, 108	Pls. 45, 62a, 71b, 79c, 81c
I.12.015	II.C.2.a	77-78	Pl. 53, *				
I.12.016	III.F.2.f						
I.12.017	III.L.8.f	39, 76, 84, 89	Pls. 23, 24	I.12.055	I.C.8.f	74-75	
I.12.018A	I.C.8.f	23-24, 109		I.12.059	I.O.0.f	91-92	Pl. 62c
I.12.018B	I.C.2.f	23-24		I.12.060	I.K.0.0		
I.12.019A	IV.L.2.f	24-25, 76, 83-84, 89	Pl. 11	I.12.066	II.C.0.0		
				I.12.093	i.d.		
I.12.019B	I.K.8.f	24-25, 109		I.12.105	i.d.		
I.12.021	I.L.8.f	34, 76	Pocket Insert 4, Pl. 47	I.12.106	i.d.		
				I.12.127	II.C.2.a	34, 77-78	Pocket Insert 3, Pl. 76a, *
I.12.023	i.d.		Pocket Insert 4				
I.12.033	I.C.8.g	74-75, 84, 89	Pls. 38, 65a	I.12.132	=I.12.039		
I.12.035	II.C.8.f	74-75, 84	Pl. 39	I.12.166	=I.11.058		
I.12.037	I.K.4.g	36, 75-76, 84, 89	Pl. 19				
I.13.007	I.F.8.g	12, 35, 75, 80		I.13.031	i.d.		
I.13.016	i.d.			I.13.033	i.d.		
I.13.022	i.d.			I.13.057	i.d.		
I.13.028	I.K.2.0	75-76		I.13.058	i.d.		
I.13.029	I.C.8.f	74-75					

Grave Number	Type	Page(s)	Illustration(s)
I.21.005A	III.C.8.g	23-24, 35-36, 74	Pl. 8
I.21.005B	III.C.8.e	23-24, 35-36, 74	Pl. 8
I.21.005C	III.F.0.0	23-24, 35-36	Pl. 8
I.21.006	=I.21.008		
I.21.007	=I.21.041		
I.21.008	II.C.0.0		Pocket Insert 3
I.21.009	Secondary	45	Pocket Insert 3
I.21.010	I.C.0.0		
I.21.012	II.M.0.0	38	Pocket Insert 2
I.21.013	II.M.0.0	38	Pl. 73a
I.21.015	II.M.0.0	23	Pl. 69a
I.21.017A	I.F.0.i	25, 77-79, 91-92, 104-5	Pocket Insert 3, Pl. 80a, *
I.21.017B	Secondary	25, 45	Pocket Insert 3
I.21.017C	Secondary	25, 35, 45	
I.21.020	I.C.0.0		Pocket Insert 3
I.21.021	I.M.0.0		
I.21.022	II.C.0.0	23	
I.21.023	I.C.2.0		
I.22.006	I.C.7.c	35, 77-79, 84, 88	*
I.22.008	I.C.2.0	35	
I.22.015	III.L.8.f	23, 36, 91, 103, 109	Pls. 49, 66b
I.22.016	I.C.2.0	23, 35, 80	
I.22.023	III.C.2.f		
I.22.024	Secondary	45-46	
I.22.029	i.d.		
I.22.034	I.L.2.g	23, 38, 104	
I.22.035	i.d.		
I.22.036	I.C.8.b	77-78, 80-81, 88	Pl. 9, *
I.22.037	II.C.4.g		
I.22.038	II.F.4.g	75, 84, 89	Pl. 42
I.22.041	I.C.8.e	36	
I.22.060	II.C.4.f	74, 84	Pls. 37, 68a, 69b
I.22.065A	II.C.4.f	24, 38, 74	Pl. 9
I.22.065B	II.C.4.f	24, 38, 74	Pl. 9
I.22.066	II.L.0.0	38	
I.22.068	I.C.4.f		
I.22.070	I.K.4.f		
I.22.076	I.C.2.f		
I.22.078	i.d.		Pocket Insert 4
I.22.079	III.L.8.f	76, 84, 89-90, 105-6	Pls. 50, 62d, 74c, 75a
I.31.014	I.F.0.0		
I.31.015	III.F.0.i	35, 38-39, 77-78	*
I.31.016	Secondary	45	
I.31.021	Secondary	36, 45	
I.31.022	III.C.0.0	37	Pocket Insert 2
I.31.023	=I.31.031		
I.31.024	i.d.		Pocket Insert 2
I.31.026	II.L.0.0		
I.31.027	II.C.0.0		
I.31.028	II.M.0.0		
I.31.029	II.C.0.0	37	Pocket Insert 2
I.31.030	i.d.		
I.31.031	II.C.0.0		Pocket Insert 2
I.31.034	i.d.		Pocket Insert 3
I.21.026A	III.C.0.0	26, 103	Pocket Insert 2, Pl. 76c
I.21.026B	III.M.0.0	26	Pocket Insert 2, Pl. 76c
I.21.027	III.M.0.0	23, 34, 37	Pocket Insert 2
I.21.031	II.C.0.0		
I.21.033	I.C.0.0		
I.21.034	i.d.		
I.21.036	II.M.0.0	23, 77	Pocket Insert 3
I.21.037	II.M.0.0		Pocket Insert 2
I.21.038	II.C.0.0		Pocket Insert 2
I.21.041	i.d.		Pocket Insert 3
I.21.056	I.M.0.0	37	
I.21.060	I.M.0.0	37	Pocket Insert 3
I.21.063	III.J.0.0	23, 34, 37	Pocket Insert 2
I.21.072A	I.C.0.0	23, 26	Pocket Insert 2
I.21.072B	I.L.4.g	23, 36	Pocket Insert 2
I.21.073	I.C.0.0		Pocket Insert 3
I.22.084	I.L.0.f	90	
I.22.090	II.F.0.0	34, 37	Pocket Insert 4
I.22.092	I.C.4.0		
I.22.094	I.L.2.f	35	
I.22.097	I.K.4.f		
I.22.100	I.K.4.g		
I.22.101	I.M.0.0		
I.22.102	III.K.2.c	77-78, 83-84, 88	Pl. 54, *
I.22.103	II.L.2.f	23, 38	
I.22.107	I.F.4.f	36, 80-81	
I.22.119	I.F.2.f	91-92, 103	Pl. 77b
I.22.122	=I.22.102		
I.22.124	i.d.		
I.22.126	II.L.2.f	38	
I.22.127	I.C.0.0	12	
I.22.133	III.C.0.2		
I.22.134A	III.C.8.0	26	
I.22.134B	II.M.2.0	26	
I.22.147	III.C.2.0		
I.22.150	I.C.3.0	77-78	*
I.22.153	III.C.2.e		
I.22.207	II.L.4.h	41, 91, 104	Pl. 58
I.31.036	Burial Pit	22, 46	
I.31.037	i.d.		Pocket Insert 3
I.31.038	II.C.0.0		
I.31.039	i.d.	77	
I.31.040	i.d.		Pocket Insert 3
I.31.043	III.M.0.0		
I.31.044	=I.32.125		
I.31.045	i.d.		
I.31.046	=I.31.038		
I.31.049	i.d.		
I.31.051	Burial Pit	22, 46, 109	Pocket Insert 2
I.31.052	I.C.0.0	45	Pocket Insert 3
I.31.053	=I.31.051	37	
I.31.072	i.d.		

Grave Number	Type	Page(s)	Illustration(s)
I.31.082	=I.31.051/53		
I.31.121	=I.31.049		
I.31.136	I.L.2.0		
I.31.138	=I.31.051		
I.31.163	I.F.4.f		
I.32.009	I.C.2.g	35, 80	
I.32.010	I.C.0.0	80	
I.32.011	I.C.2.a	77-78	*
I.32.012A	II.C.2.f	24, 74	Pl. 10
I.32.012B	II.C.2.f	24, 74, 83-84	Pl. 10
I.32.016	I.C.2.f		
I.32.018	II.M.8.0	36, 38, 89	
I.32.019A	II.C.8.f	24, 38	
I.32.019B	II.C.4.f	24, 38	
I.32.022	i.d.	46	
I.32.023	i.d.	46	
I.32.024A	II.L.2.h	25, 36, 76, 83-84, 109	Pl. 12
I.32.024B	II.K.8.g	25. 36, 76, 83-84, 89, 109	Pl. 12
I.32.027	II.M.0.0	38	Pocket Insert 4
I.32.030	i.d.		
I.32.032A	II.C.3.j	24, 77, 79, 88, 92	*
I.32.032B	II.C.2.0	24	
I.32.037	III.K.6.f	44, 77-78, 84, 89, 104-5	Pl. 52, *
I.32.038	III.L.4.h	44-46, 76, 84	Pl. 34
I.32.039	III.K.6.0	44, 77-78, 84, 89, 108-9	Pl. 29, *
I.32.040	III.C.2.a	36, 44-46, 77-78, 84, 88	Pl. 34, *
I.32.042	I.O.0.g		
I.32.046	II.L.7.g	25, 38, 77-78, 80-81, 84, 89	Pls. 13, 15, 66a, 72c, *

Grave Number	Type	Page(s)	Illustration(s)
I.31.171	i.d.		
I.31.175	I.M.2.a	77-78	*
I.31.176	II.K.4.f	91-92	
I.31.195	=I.31.051		
I.32.048	III.L.2.0	38, 103-4	Pls. 22, 80b
I.32.049	II.L.4.f	44-45, 76, 91-92	Pls. 31, 63a, 79a
I.32.053	i.d.		
I.32.056	II.L.2.g	25, 76, 83-84, 89, 91-92, 103	Pls. 14, 15, 75c, 76b, 81b
I.32.060	II.L.8.g	76, 90	Pl. 48
I.32.063	II.K.2.g		
I.32.064	II.F.2.f	44, 90	Pl. 30
I.32.067	Secondary	45-46	
I.32.070	II.F.2.f	75, 83-84, 108	Pocket Insert 4, Pl. 41
I.32.080	II.K.1.h	77, 84, 89	Pl. 51, *
I.32.081	I.K.8.0		
I.32.090	II.M.2.0		
I.32.092	II.M.2.0		
I.32.094	IV.L.2.f	39, 76, 83-84, 89	Pls. 25, 61b
I.32.096	i.d.		Pocket Insert 4
I.32.101	I.F.2.f		
I.32.110	i.d.		
I.32.111	i.d.		
I.32.121	I.C.2.f		
I.32.122	I.K.2.f	37	Pocket Insert 3
I.32.125	i.d.		Pocket Insert 3
I.32.126	=I.32.016		
I.32.127	i.d.	37	Pocket Insert 3
I.32.145	II.L.4.g	38	Pl. 73b
I.32.172	i.d.		
I.32.195	i.d.		

Grave Number	Type	Page(s)	Illustration(s)
I.41.007	i.d.		
I.41.012	IV.C.8.f	23, 39, 41, 108-9	
I.41.013	IV.F.2.e	23, 39, 41	
I.41.016	III.F.2.g	80	Pl. 71a
I.41.018	IV.C.2.f	23, 39	
I.41.019	V.C.0.0	36, 39-40, 91-92	Pls. 26, 27, 84
I.41.020	I.C.4.g		
I.41.024	I.C.0.f		
I.41.026	II.C.4.g	23, 38	
I.41.028	III.C.2.f	23, 74	Pl. 35
I.41.032	III.C.2.f		
I.41.035	II.C.8.f	90	Pl. 60a
I.41.039	i.d.		
I.41.040	I.C.0.0		
I.41.042	I.C.2.f	23	
I.41.043	I.C.2.f	23	
I.41.044	i.d.		
I.41.045	i.d.	36-37	
I.41.046	III.F.2.f		
I.41.047	i.d.		
I.41.048	i.d.		
I.41.049	III.L.4.0	23	
I.41.050	I.F.4.f		

Grave Number	Type	Page(s)	Illustration(s)
I.41.051	III.C.2.a	77-78, 88, 91-93	Pl. 64b, 68c, *
I.41.052	I.C.2.0	34	
I.41.053	i.d.	34	
I.41.054	i.d.		
I.41.056	III.F.2.f		Pl. 60b
I.41.057	IV.C.4.0	39, 80-81	Pocket Insert 3
I.41.058	III.G.2.0	89, 101-2	Pls. 56, 72a
I.41.063	IV.L.8.0	39	Pocket Insert 3
I.41.064	I.C.2.e		Pl. 74b
I.41.065	IV.C.2.0	39, 103	Pl. 77a
I.41.067	I.M.8.0		
I.41.068	III.L.2.f	45, 81	Pocket Insert 3
I.41.070	III.K.0.0	38-39	
I.41.071	Secondary	34, 45	Pocket Insert 3
I.41.072	i.d.		
I.41.076	I.F.2.f	36, 91-92	Pls. 64a, 69c
I.41.077	Burial Pit	36, 46	
I.41.081	II.K.2.0	25, 34, 37, 45	Pocket Insert 3, Pl. 16
I.41.082	I.C.4.f		
I.41.083	Secondary	45	Pocket Insert 2
I.41.084	I.K.2.0		
I.41.085A	I.L.2.f	21, 23, 95	Pls. 6, 7, 59b

Grave Number	Type	Page(s)	Illustration(s)	Grave Number	Type	Page(s)	Illustration(s)
I.41.085B	i.d.	21	Pls. 6, 7	I.41.117	III.M.0.0		Pocket Insert 3
I.41.089	I.F.2.e	21, 23	Pl. 7	I.41.120	I.M.2.0	23, 34, 37	Pocket Insert 2
I.41.090	II.E.2.h	38		I.41.121	II.K.8.0	23	
I.41.091	I.L.4.0			I.41.123	i.d.		Pocket Insert 3
I.41.092	Secondary	45		I.41.132	III.M.0.0	37	Pocket Insert 3
I.41.096	II.K.8.h	38		I.41.134	II.L.2.f	34, 37-38	Pocket Insert 2
I.41.100	III.L.2.g	38-39	Pl. 21	I.41.203	I.C.8.f		
I.41.102	Burial Pit		Pocket Insert 2	I.41.204	I.C.0.f	23, 35, 80	
I.41.103	i.d.			I.41.207	i.d.		
I.41.104	Secondary	13, 45	Pocket Insert 2	I.41.209	I.C.8.f	24	
I.41.105	i.d.	25, 34, 37	Pocket Insert 3, Pl. 16	I.41.211	i.d.	34, 37	Pocket Insert 3
				I.41.212	I.C.6.0	24, 77-78	Pl. 62b, *
I.41.106	II.L.2.f	25, 37, 76, 89, 109	Pl. 16	I.41.213	I.C.4.f	24, 108-9	
				I.41.216	i.d.		Pocket Insert 2
I.41.108	Secondary	45	Pocket Insert 3	I.41.217A	II.K.2.g	23, 25, 34, 37	Pocket Insert 3, Pl. 17
I.41.111	I.K.0.f		Pocket Insert 2				
I.41.114	II.L.4.0	37-38	Pocket Insert 3	I.41.217B	II.M.0.0	23, 25, 34, 37, 108-9	Pocket Insert 3, Pl 17
I.41.115	II.C.4.f	23, 37-38	Pocket Insert 2, Pl. 61a	I.41.218	II.L.4.h	76, 84, 89	Pl. 46
I.41.116	=I.51.106		Pocket Insert 2	I.41.223	III.K.2.g	37	Pocket Insert 2
I.51.013	I.C.2.e	45, 91-92, 108	Pls. 61c, 86-88	I.51.049	I.K.8.f		
I.51.015	Burial Pit	46		I.51.050	I.C.8.g		Pocket Insert 2
I.51.016	II.C.8.f			I.51.053	I.M.0.0		Pocket Insert 2
I.51.017	II.F.2.h		Pocket Insert 2	I.51.054	I.C.8.f		
I.51.018	i.d.	46		I.51.057	i.d.	37	Pocket Insert 3
I.51.019	I.J.2.g	75	Pl. 43	I.51.063	i.d.		
I.51.022	I.K.2.g			I.51.065	II.M.0.0	37	Pocket Insert 2
I.51.023	i.d.			I.51.067	II.K.4.g	41-42, 92, 104-5	Pl. 65c
I.51.024	II.F.2.f	23, 44, 75, 83-84	Pl. 32	I.51.080	I.C.4.0	37	Pocket Insert 3
I.51.025	i.d.			I.51.106	I.L.0.g		Pocket Insert 2
I.51.028	I.C.8.h	35-36, 41, 74-75, 80, 89	Pls. 18, 68b, 81a	I.51.121	i.d.		
				I.51.125	i.d.	37	Pocket Insert 3
I.51.032	II.F.0.g			I.51.126	i.d.		Pocket Insert 3
I.51.034	II.C.2.e			I.51.128	i.d.		
I.51.037	I.C.8.0	23		I.51.129	i.d.		
I.51.038	I.C.2.f	23, 36, 44, 74, 83-84	Pl. 33	I.51.131	III.C.2.0		Pocket Insert 3
				I.51.132	i.d.		Pocket Insert 3
I.51.039	I.M.0.0	23, 44	Pls. 32, 33	I.51.133	II.K.1.g	77, 92, 105	*
I.51.041	I.F.0.0	23		I.51.134	I.M.1.b	77, 79	Pocket Insert 2, Pl. 70, *
I.51.043	I.M.2.f	23					
I.51.044	II.C.0.0			I.51.135	I.M.0.0	102	Pl. 74a
I.51.045	III.C.8.f			I.51.136A	I.C.0.0	23, 26	
I.51.048	I.K.4.f			I.51.136B	I.L.2.g	23, 26	Pl. 59a
V.P-1a.006	I.C.2.e	35, 41-42, 74-75, 80, 83-84	Fig. 6, Pl. 28	V.P-1e.005	II.K.0.g	108	Fig. 6, Pl. 89
				V.P-1f.006	I.C.4.g	74, 84	Fig. 6, Pl. 36
V.P-1b.006	II.C.0.f	38	Fig. 6	V.P-1p.004	I.F.2.f	35, 75, 80	Fig. 6, Pl. 40
V.P-1c.008	Burial Pit	46	Fig. 6				
VI.P-1a.001	I.C.0.0	107-8	Fig. 7, Pls. 85, 88	VI.P-1a.004	I.C.0.0		Fig. 7
				VI.P-1a.005	II.L.2.g	38	Fig. 7, Pl. 20
VI.P-1a.003	i.d.		Fig. 7	VI.P-1a.006	II.L.2.g		Fig. 7

APPENDIX 2

Typological Catalogue

Throughout the catalogue the abbreviation UR (unreported) is used when for any reason the information necessary to complete an entry is not available. Sometimes, because of the burial's state of preservation or its position in relation to the balks, the observation could not be made. Sometimes the observation was possible, but was either not made or not reported.

Structure of the Catalogue

The catalogue is divided into four sections, as follows:

Section I: Typed Graves

This section contains those burials for which the grave construction and at least one other element of the four-part typology are known. In this section the burial data are tabulated in eleven columns.

Section II: Secondary Burials

These burials are described in the same eleven columns used for the typed graves. The section contains interments which may with a fair degree of certainty be regarded as having been displaced from their original location. The list of secondary burials is probably too short, since some were undoubtedly included among the typed burials. Where this possibility is strong, it has been noted in column eleven of Section I.

Section III: Burial Pits

This section contains all clear cases of multiple burials in a common grave, when the bones have been displaced from their original place of burial.

Section IV: Insufficient Data

This section lists individual graves for which insufficient data were available to make the eleven-column analysis of Sections I and II meaningful. The graves are reported by means of prose descriptions, summarizing what is known about each grave.

Notes on Grave Tabulation

The following comments apply to Sections I and II of the catalogue, where the eleven-column analysis is used.

Column One: Type

The column gives in four entries (separated by decimal points) the type to which each grave belongs. The nature and rationale of the typology is given above, pp. 60-76 (see Table 16). Its content is summarized here for the reader's convenience in interpreting the table. The presence of "0" in any of the entries indicates that the necessary information was not available.

Entry one is in Roman numerals and refers to grave construction according to the following system:

   I. Graves which are neither capped nor lined with stones;

   II. Graves which are capped but not lined;

   III. Graves which are both capped and lined;

   IV. Graves which are lined but not capped;

   V. Jar burials.

Entry two, in block capitals, gives the age and sex of the skeleton. The letter I is omitted to avoid confusion with entry one.

   A. Infant (0-3 years), male;

   B. Infant (0-3 years), female;

C. Infant (0-3 years), sex undetermined;
D. Child (3-10 years), male;
E. Child (3-10 years), female;
F. Child (3-10 years), sex undetermined;
G. Juvenile (10-17 years), male;
H. Juvenile (10-17 years), female;
J. Juvenile (10-17 years), sex undetermined;
K. Adult (over 17 years), male;
L. Adult (over 17 years), female;
M. Adult (over 17 years), sex undetermined.

Entry three, given in Arabic numerals, shows eight possible positions of the skeleton in the grave.

1. Extended on the front;
2. Extended on the back;
3. Extended on the left side;
4. Extended on the right side;
5. Flexed on the front;
6. Flexed on the back;
7. Flexed on the left side;
8. Flexed on the right side.

Entry four, in lower-case letters, gives the eye direction in ten categories.

a. Looking up;
b. Looking down;
c. Looking north;
d. Looking northeast;
e. Looking east;
f. Looking southeast;
g. Looking south;
h. Looking southwest;
i. Looking west;
j. Looking northwest.

Column Two: Field Date

This column gives in three entries (separated by decimal points) the field (Roman numeral), area (one-digit or two-digit Arabic numeral for Field I, a hyphenated probe designation for Fields V and VI), and locus (three-digit Arabic numeral) for each burial. The graves are arranged serially by field, area, and locus under the type to which they belong.

Column Three: Relationships

This column indicates the vertical relationships of the burials to one another. Since burials in vertical sequence often cut into one another, the grave outlines were not always clearly defined. Any discrepancies between this column and the general plan of the cemetery reflect divergences be-

tween the daily top plans of the areas and the information given on the locus sheets.

Column Four: Level

The level given is the bottom level of the burial in meters above mean sea level.

Column Five: Associated Artifacts

The artifacts are listed by registry number, with the year of discovery following in parentheses. Additional information about the artifacts is provided in Appendix 3: Index of Artifacts.

Column Six: Orientation

The direction of the head in relation to the axis of the burial gives the orientation of the skeleton. If, for example, the head is to the west, the axis of the grave is west-east. Only the eight major compass directions are recognized.

Column Seven: Articulation

The following abbreviations describe the degree of articulation of the skeleton.

"A" indicates a skeleton in which the bones remained substantially articulated, but often with minor displacement of the smaller bones.

"PA" is used for a burial in which part of the skeleton was missing, but the surviving bones were articulated in the sense described above.

"D" indicates a skeleton which had suffered major displacement of the bones.

A few cases of ambiguity among the categories occur, but their number is small.

Column Eight: Age

This column supplements the broad age categories given under grave type by specifying the age more closely in cases where relevant data are available.

Column Nine: Position of Arms

The column uses the general categories "extended" and "flexed." It gives the degree and location of the flexation and the position of the hands where these data are known.

Column Ten: Photograph

Column ten gives the number of any figure containing a photograph of the grave. All the grave photographs taken by the Joint Expedition are included, except for five in which the quality of the picture or the state of preservation of the remains made the photograph uninformative.

Column Eleven: Comments

The comments serve several functions: (1) to indicate points of uncertainty or to account for the absence of data in other columns, (2) to point to anomalies in the burial, (3) to supply details of grave construction, (4) to comment further on the relationship to other burials, and (5) to describe the degree of preservation of the skeleton.

Typological Catalogue
Section I: Typed Graves

TYPE	FIELD DATA	RELATIONSHIPS	LEVEL	ASSOCIATED ARTIFACTS	ORIENTATION	ARTICULATION	AGE	POSITION OF ARMS	PHOTO	COMMENTS
I.O.O.f	I.12.059	Single	142.58m	79, 93, 98 (1973)	Head to SW	D	UR	UR		Mostly in E balk
I.O.O.g	I.32.042	Single	142.83m	None	Head to SW	UR	UR	UR	None	Skull only; remainder cut off by I.32.038
I.C.O.O	I.2.006	Single	142.46m	37 (1970)	UR	A	Ca. 2 yrs.	UR	None	Partially in E balk
	I.2.012	Over I.2.034	142.35m	None	UR	UR	Ca. 2 yrs.	UR	None	Mostly in S balk
	I.2.030	Over I.2.029	142.08m	None	UR	D	Under 2 yrs	UR	None	Partially in N balk
	I.2.084	Single	142.49m	None	UR	D	UR	UR	None	Mostly in E balk
	I.3.010	Single	UR	UR	Head to SW	A	UR	UR	None	Head rested on flat stone
	I.3.018	Single	UR	See comments	Head to W	A	0-6 mos.	UR	None	Copper wire bracelet, large beads, not in registry. Partly in N balk
	I.11.013	Single	142.96m	None	UR	UR	UR	UR	None	Shallow pit very near surface
	I.11.029	Single	142.99m	None	UR	D	Newborn	UR	None	
	I.11.062	Over I.11.105	142.75m	None	UR	A	UR	UR	None	Mainly in N balk
	I.21.010	Single	142.99m	None	Head to W	A	UR	UR	None	Head disturbed by military trenching
	I.21.020	Single	142.05m	None	UR	UR	UR	UR	None	Mainly destroyed by military trenching
	I.21.033	Single	142.41m	None	UR	UR	UR	UR	None	Disturbed by military trenching
	I.21.072A	Under I.21.027	142.42m	None	UR	UR	0-3 mos.	UR	None	Mother and child in same grave? (cp. I.21.072B)
	I.21.073	Single	142.65m	None	UR	UR	UR	UR	None	Disturbed by Pit I.21.025
	I.22.127	Single	142.54m	None	Head to W	A	0-6 mos.	UR	None	Skull only; remainder destroyed by military trenching
	I.31.052	Single	142.44m	27, 28, 30 (1970)	Head to W	D	UR	UR	None	One primary burial, but evidence of two infants in same grave
	I.32.010	Single	142.43m	None	Head to NW	D	6-18 mos.	UR	None	Two skulls in grave. Head direction anomalous
	I.41.040	Over I.41.045	143.61m	None	UR	D	0-6 mos.	UR	None	Badly disturbed
	I.51.136A	Under I.41.103 Over I.51.136B	143.46m	None	UR	A	0-3 yrs.	Rt. extended Lt. UR	None	On top of skeleton I.51.136B
	VI.P-1a.001	Single	138.90m	384, 388 (1975)	UR	A	6-18 mos.	UR	None	Side-spouted jar in grave
I.C.O.f	VI.P-1a.004	Single	138.55m	None	UR	PA	6-18 mos.	UR	None	Partial skeleton only
	I.41.024	Over I.41.134 and I.41.206	143.67m	None	UR	PA	UR	UR	None	
	I.41.204	UR	143.44m	None	Head to NW	A	6-18 mos.	Rt. extended Lt. UR	None	Head direction anomalous. Partly removed as I.31.028

Section I: Typed Graves—Continued

TYPE	FIELD DATA	RELATIONSHIPS	LEVEL	ASSOCIATED ARTIFACTS	ORIENTATION	ARTICULATION	AGE	POSITION OF ARMS	PHOTO	COMMENTS
I.C.2.0	I.3.097	Single	141.93m	89 (1971)	Head to S	D	6-18 mos.	Rt. extended Lt. UR	None	Crushed in bottom of military trench
	I.12.011	Single	142.54m	None	Head to W	A	UR	UR	None	Categorized as 'infant' because of size of cist and bones. Skull destroyed by military trench.
	I.21.023	Single	142.94m	None	Head to W	A	UR	UR	None	
	I.22.008	Single	UR	None	Head to W	D	0-6 mos.	UR	None	Grave orientation N-S. May be a secondary burial
	I.22.016	Over I.22.103	142.84m	None	Head to SE	D	0-6 mos.	UR	None	Grave orientation N-S. May be a secondary burial
	I.41.052	Single	143.47m	None	UR	A	6-18 mos.	Rt. extended Lt. across pelvis	None	Grave not clearly defined
I.C.2.a	I.32.011	Over I.32.018 and I.32.081	143.32m	None	Head to W	D	UR	Rt. extended Lt. UR	None	
I.C.2.e	I.41.064	Over I.41.096	143.34m	7 (1973)	Head to W	A	18 mos. to 3 yrs.	Rt. across abdomen Lt. extended	None	Cut into I.41.067
	I.51.013	Single	143.27m	72, 106, 108, 111 (1973)	Head to W	A	0-6 mos.	Both extended	None	Adult bones in grave
	V.P-1a.006	Single	141.82m	None	Head to S	A	UR	Rt. extended Lt. across chest	Pl. 28	Beneath round stone on W. side. Anomalous head direction. Head rested on stone
I.C.2.f	I.12.009	Single	142.59m	None	Head to W	A	6-18 mos.	Rt. extended Lt. flexed at elbow	None	No pelvis or femur found; otherwise articulated
	I.12.018B	Under I.12.018A	142.45m	None	Head to W	A	6-18 mos.	Both extended	None	
	I.22.076	Single	142.94m	None	Head to SW	A	6-18 mos.	Both extended	None	
	I.32.016	Single	143.22m	None	Head to W	A	18 mos. to 3 yrs.	Both extended	None	Partly in S and E balks
	I.32.121	Over I.32.127	143.30m	None	Head to SW	A	18 mos. to 3 yrs.	Both extended	None	Mostly in S and E balks
	I.41.042	Over I.41.085 and I.41.089	143.42m	None	Head to W	A	18 mos. to 3 yrs.	Both extended	None	
	I.41.043	Single	143.35m	None	Head to W	A	18 mos. to 3 yrs.	Rt. extended Lt. UR	None	
	I.51.038	Under I.51.024 Over I.51.039	142.94m	None	Head to W	A	0-6 mos.	Rt. extended Lt. hand in pelvis	Pl. 33	Cut into S edge of I.51.039
I.C.2.g	I.32.009	Over I.32.081	143.42m	33 (1971)	Head to NW	D	0-3 yrs.	Rt. extended Lt. across pelvis	None	Head direction anomalous
I.C.3.0	I.22.150	Single	142.50m	None	Head to E	D	UR	UR	None	Head direction anomalous

Section I: Typed Graves—Continued

TYPE	FIELD DATA	RELATIONSHIPS	LEVEL	ASSOCIATED ARTIFACTS	ORIENTATION	ARTICULATION	AGE	POSITION OF ARMS	PHOTO	COMMENTS
I.C.4.0	I.22.092	Single	142.59m	None	UR	D	0-6 mos.	UR	None	
	I.51.080	Single	142.60m	None	Head to W	A	6-18 mos.	Rt. extended Lt. UR	None	Skull in W. balk
I.C.4.f	I.22.068	Single	142.73m	None	Head to W	A	0-6 mos.	Rt. extended Lt. hand in pelvis	None	
	I.41.082	Over I.41.168 and I.41.100	143.23m	None	Head to W	A	0-6 mos.	Rt. extended Lt. hand in pelvis	None	
	I.41.213	Under I.41.209 and I.41.212	143.34m	246 (1973)	Head to SW	A	18 mos. to 3 yrs.	Rt. extended Lt. UR	None	In same grave with I.41.209, I.41.212; immediately below I.41.212
I.C.4.g	I.41.020	Single	143.72m	None	Head to W	A	18 mos. to 3 yrs.	Rt. flexed at elbow Lt. extended	None	
	V.P-1f.006	Single	142.25m	None	Head to SW	A	Ca. 10 mos.	Rt. extended Lt. hand in pelvis	Pl. 36	
I.C.6.0	I.41.212	Under I.41.209 Over I.41.213	143.34m	253 (1973)	Head to SW	A	18 mos. to 3 yrs.	Rt. extended Lt. hand in pelvis	None	In same cist with I.41.209, I.41.213, and intermediate between them
I.C.7.c	I.22.006	Single	143.06m	None	Head to W	A	UR	Both flexed at elbow with arm across chest	None	Identified as infant by size of grave. Grave oriented NW-SE. Eye direction anomalous
I.C.8.0	I.51.037	Over I.51.038	143.07m	None	Head to SW	A	6-18 mos.	Rt. hand on femur Lt. arm across abdomen	None	Grave outline not determined
I.C.8.b	I.22.036	Single	142.87m	None	Head to E?	A	18 mos. to 3 yrs.	Rt. extended Lt. across chest	None	Head direction possibly wrongly reported
I.C.8.e	I.22.041	Over I.22.070	143.03m	None	Head to SW	A	18 mos. to 3 yrs.	Rt. extended Lt. hand in pelvis	None	Grave shape anomalous
I.C.8.f	I.12.018A	Over I.12.218B	142.70m	294, 423, 424 (1971)	Head to W	A	18 mos. to 3 yrs.	Both extended	None	Beads in situ around infant's neck
	I.12.038	Single	142.30m	None	Head to SW	A	18 mos. to 3 yrs.	Rt. extended Lt. hand on pelvis	None	
	I.12.055	Single	142.63m	None	Head to SW	A	6-18 mos.	Rt. extended Lt. hand on pelvis	None	
	I.13.029	Single	141.81m	None	Head to W	A	18 mos. to 3 yrs.	Lt. across chest	None	Grave partially lined
	I.41.203	Over I.41.218	143.52m	None	Head to SW	A	0-6 mos.	Both extended	None	Cist ill defined. Head lost in winter of 1971/72

Section I: Typed Graves—Continued

TYPE	FIELD DATA	RELATIONSHIPS	LEVEL	ASSOCIATED ARTIFACTS	ORIENTATION	ARTICULATION	AGE	POSITION OF ARMS	PHOTO	COMMENTS
I.C.8.f (cont'd)	I.41.209	Over I.41.212	143.34m	None	Head to SW	A	0-6 mos.	Rt. extended Lt. hand in pelvis	None	In same cist with I.41.212, I.41.213; immediately above I.41.212
	I.51.054	Single	142.72m	None	Head to W	A	0-6 mos.	Both across abdomen	None	
I.C.8.g	I.12.033	Single	142.83m	9 (1973)	Head to SW	A	6-18 mos.	Rt. extended Lt. across chest	Pl. 38	One crumbly yellow sandstone slab that may be a surviving capstone
	I.51.050	Single	142.75m	168, 199 (1973)	Head to W	A	6-18 mos.	Rt. UR Lt. hand in pelvis	None	
I.C.8.h	I.51.028	Single	143.02m	78, 90 (1973)	Head to NW	A	6-18 mos.	Both across abdomen	Pl. 18	Rock pillow under head. Head direction is anomalous
I.E.O.q	I.2.009	Single	142.16m	None	Head to W	PA	Ca. 8 yrs.	UR	None	
I.F.O.O	I.1.020	Over I.1.034	UR	None	UR	A	Ca. 5 yrs.	UR	None	
	I.1.044	Single	142.18m	None	UR	A	UR	UR	None	Grave oriented NW-SE
	I.1.084	Single	142.14m	None	UR	UR	UR	UR	None	Mostly in N balk
	I.1.018	Under I.11.004	UR	None	Head to W	A	UR	UR	None	
	I.11.020	Single	UR	None	UR	A	UR	UR	None	
	I.11.077	UR	UR	None	UR	UR	Ca. 5 yrs.	UR	None	In N balk; not on top plan
	I.31.014	Over I.31.037	143.41m	None	UR	UR	2-5 yrs.	UR	None	This burial destroyed an earlier capped burial. Mixed with animal bones
	I.51.041	Under I.51.024	142.83m	None	UR	D	UR	UR	None	Destroyed by I.51.024
I.F.O.i	I.21.017A	Over I.21.017C	143.18m	11, 14 (1970)	Head to W	PA	3-8 yrs.	UR	None	See I.21.017B and C
I.F.2.e	I.41.089	Under I.41.042 Over I.41.085	143.10m	None	Head to W	A	3-4 yrs.	Rt. hand in pelvis Lt. UR	Pl. 7	Cut into I.41.085A
I.F.2.f	I.3.099	Single	UR	None	Head to W	A	3-4 yrs.	Both extended	None	Same as I.2.019
	I.22.119	Under I.22.102	142.61m	236, 237, 240, 245, 258 (1973)	Head to SW	A	3-4 yrs.	Rt. extended Lt. hand in pelvis	None	
	I.32.101	Under I.32.032	142.53m	None	Head to SW	A	6-8 yrs.	Rt. extended Lt. UR	None	
	I.41.076	Under I.41.063 Over I.41.132	143.18m	23, 24, 25, 26 (1973)	Head to SW	A	3-4 yrs.	Rt. extended Lt. UR	None	Cut into I.41.063
	V.P-1p.004	Single	142.21m	None	Head to S	A	3-4 yrs.	Rt. extended Lt. hand on femur	Pl. 40	
I.F.4.f	I.22.107	Under I.22.035	142.24m	None	Head to E	D	3-4 yrs.	Both extended	None	Head direction anomalous; possibly wrongly reported
	I.31.163	Single	143.11m	None	Head to W	D	3-4 yrs.	Rt. extended Lt. UR	None	
	I.41.050	Single	143.40m	367, 376 (1971)	Head to W	A	3-4 yrs.	Rt. UR Lt. extended	None	

Section I: Typed Graves—Continued

TYPE	FIELD DATA	RELATIONSHIPS	LEVEL	ASSOCIATED ARTIFACTS	ORIENTATION	ARTICULATION	AGE	POSITION OF ARMS	PHOTO	COMMENTS
I.F.8.g	I.13.007	Single	142.12m	None	Head to NW	A	3-4 yrs.	Elbows flexed	None	Head direction anomalous. Grave may once have been capped. Apparently in military trench
I.J.2.g	I.51.019	Over I.51.067	143.18m	None	Head to SW	A	11-15 yrs.	Rt. UR Lt. across abdomen	Pl. 43	Lower part of body cut away by military trench
I.K.O.0	I.1.016	Under I.1.014	UR	2 (1970)	UR	A	UR	UR	None	
	I.1.022	Over I.1.034	142.41m	None	UR	A	UR	UR	None	Partially in E balk
	I.1.039	Under I.1.066	141.70m	None	UR	PA	UR	UR	None	Disturbed by I.1.066. Very tall individual, ca. 6'6". Cist unusually large and deep
	I.3.051	Single	140.53m	None	Head to NW	D	Ca. 24 yrs.	UR	None	Partly in E balk
	I.11.004	Over I.11.018	142.65m	88 (1971)	Head to W	A	Over 24 yrs.	UR	None	Disturbed by military trenching. Original description supplemented from I.11.096 and I.11.097
	I.12.060	Single	142.05m	None	Head to W	A	Over 24 yrs.	UR	None	Partially in W balk
I.K.O.c	I.1.024	Over I.1.034	UR	None	Head to W	A	Ca. 30 yrs.	UR	None	Partially in E balk
I.K.O.f	I.41.111	Single	142.99m	None	Head to W	A	40-45 yrs.	UR	None	Most of body in E balk
I.K.O.g	I.2.007	Over I.2.021	UR	None	Head to W	A	27-30 yrs.	UR	None	Same as I.2.083 and I.2.091
I.K.2.0	I.13.028	Single	142.02m	None	UR	A	Over 24 yrs.	UR	None	Head and upper body in S balk
	I.41.084	Single	143.49m	None	Head to W	A	Over 17 yrs.	Rt. extended Lt. hand in pelvis	None	Partially in E balk; associated with the bones of a child of 3-4 yrs.
I.K.2.f	I.32.122	Single	142.99m	None	Head to SW	A	Over 24 yrs.	Rt. extended Lt. hand in pelvis	None	
I.K.2.g	I.51.022	Over I.51.067	142.99m	None	Head to W	D	Over 24 yrs.	Rt. extended Lt. UR	None	Cut by I.51.023
I.K.4.f	I.22.070	Under I.22.041	142.65m	None	Head to W	PA	Ca. 50 yrs.	Rt. extended Lt. hand in pelvis	None	
	I.22.097	Single	142.16m	None	Head to SW	A	Ca. 25 yrs.	Rt. extended Lt. across chest	None	
	I.51.048	Single	142.47m	None	Head to SW	A	Over 24 yrs.	Rt. extended Lt. across chest	None	
I.K.4.g	I.12.037	Single	142.15m	None	Head to W	A	Over 24 yrs.	Rt. extended Lt. across abdomen	Pl. 19	Grave shape anomalous
	I.22.100	Over I.22.101	142.40m	None	Head to W	A	55-60 yrs.	Rt. extended Lt. across abdomen	None	Cut off part of I.22.101

Section I: Typed Graves—Continued

TYPE	FIELD DATA	RELATIONSHIPS	LEVEL	ASSOCIATED ARTIFACTS	ORIENTATION	ARTICULATION	AGE	POSITION OF ARMS	PHOTO	COMMENTS
I.K.8.0	I.32.081	Under I.32.009, I.32.011 and I.32.018. Over I.32.048	142.77m	None	Head to SW	A	Over 24 yrs.	Both across pelvis	None	
I.K.8.f	I.12.019B	Under I.12.005 and I.12.019A	142.35m	352 (1971)	Head to W	A	Over 24 yrs.	Rt. flexed at elbow Lt. across abdomen	None	Possibly disrupted by I.12.019A
	I.51.049	Single	142.52m	None	Head to SW	A	16-20 yrs.	Rt. extended Lt. across abdomen	None	
I.L.0.0	I.2.010	Over I.2.015	141.99m	None	UR	D	Over 50 yrs.	UR	None	Skull and a few bones partially in N balk. Shaft merged with that of I.2.029. May be a secondary burial
I.L.0.f	I.22.084	Single	142.43m	None	Head to SW	A	30-35 yrs.	Rt. extended Lt. across chest	None	Elongated skull; red coloration on bones
I.L.0.g	I.2.008	Single	142.33m	40 (1970)	Head to W	A	Ca. 30 yrs.	UR	None	Flint scraper found under skull, probably intrusive
	I.11.026A	Over I.11.045	142.82m	45A, 45B (1970)	Head to W	PA	Over 17 yrs.	UR	None	Two fragmentary skeletons in shaft, immediately above body. Cf. I.11.026B under "Secondary Burials"
	I.51.106	Over I.51.134	142.92m	None	Head to W	A	Over 24 yrs.	Rt. extended Lt. UR	None	Same as I.41.116
I.L.1.f	I.1.111	Over I.1.046	UR	431, 438, 445 (1971)	Head to W	A	17-24 yrs.	Both arms extended	None	Not drawn on top plan
I.L.2.0	I.31.136	Single	142.90m	345 (1971)	Head to W	A	Over 24 yrs.	Rt. extended Lt. hand in pelvis	None	Skull missing
I.L.2.f	I.22.094	Under I.22.035	142.42m	None	Head to SW	A	30-35 yrs.	Rt. extended -hand on pelvis Lt. flexed at elbow	None	
	I.41.085A	Under I.41.042 and I.41.089	143.09m	127, 207 (1973)	Head to W	A	17-24 yrs.	Rt. extended Lt. across chest	Pls. 6, 7	Cut through I.42.085B. Cut through by I.41.089
I.L.2.g	I.22.034	Under I.22.015	142.31m	349 (1971)	Head to W	A	Over 17 yrs.	UR	None	Probably once capped, and cappers removed by excavation for I.22.015
	I.51.136B	Under I.41.103	UR	304, 305, 310 (1975)	Head to W	A	17-24 yrs.	UR	None	Cut off at waist by military trenching
I.L.4.0	I.41.091	Under I.41.019, I.41.032 and I.41.092	143.15m	None	UR	A	25-30 yrs.	Rt. UR Lt. across pelvis	None	Cut by I.41.090

Section I: Typed Graves—Continued

TYPE	FIELD DATA	RELATIONSHIPS	LEVEL	ASSOCIATED ARTIFACTS	ORIENTATION	ARTICULATION	AGE	POSITION OF ARMS	PHOTO	COMMENTS
I.L.4.g	I.21.072B	Under I.21.027	142.42m	95, 100 (1970)	Head to W	A	Over 24 yrs.	UR	None	Mother and child in same grave. Cp. I.21.072A
I.L.7.c	I.11.211	Single	142.20m	None	Head to W	A	Over 24 yrs.	Rt. across chest Lt. extended	Pl. 55	Sea shells found with skeleton. Eye direction anomalous
I.L.8.f	I.12.021	Under I.12.006	142.35m	None	Head to W	A	Over 24 yrs.	UR	Pl. 47	Partially in W balk; very tightly flexed
I.M.0.0	I.21.021	Single	UR	None	UR	A	Over 24 yrs.	UR	None	Virtually destroyed by I.21.012
	I.21.056	Single	142.59m	None	UR	UR	Over 24 yrs.	UR	None	Mostly in S balk
	I.21.060	Under I.21.041	UR	None	UR	UR	Over 24 yrs.	UR	None	Partially destroyed by I.21.041
	I.22.101	Single	142.41m	None	UR	UR	Over 24 yrs.	UR	None	All but pelvis and legs cut away by I.22.100 and I.22.103
	I.51.039	Under I.51.024 and I.51.038 Over I.51.043	142.87m	None	UR	PA	UR	UR	Pls. 32, 33	Legs and feet only; upper skeleton cut away by I.51.043
	I.51.053	Over I.51.065	142.73m	None (1975)	UR	UR	UR	UR	None	Mostly in E. balk
	I.51.135	Under I.51.063	142.64m	297 (1975)	UR	A	UR	UR	None	
I.M.1.b	I.51.134	Over I.51.106	142.97m	295 (1975)	Head to SW	A	UR	Rt. extended Lt. UR	None	Excavated from rib cage up; rest in E balk
I.M.2.0	I.41.120	Under I.41.115	142.56m	123 (1973)	UR	A	Over 17 yrs.	Both extended	None	Skull missing. Cut off by I.41.115
I.M.2.a	I.31.175	Under I.31.136 and I.31.163	142.79m	None	Head to W	A	Over 24 yrs.	Rt. extended Lt. UR	None	Part of feet missing
I.M.2.f	I.51.043	Under I.51.024, I.51.039 and I.51.041	142.83m	None	Head to SW	A	Over 24 yrs.	Both extended	None	Skull, ribs and arms only. Cut through and destroyed by I.51.039
I.M.8.0	I.41.067	Under I.41.064	143.25m	None	Head to W	PA	Over 24 yrs.	UR	None	Cut into and partially destroyed by I.41.064. Grave outline not determined
II.O.0.g	I.2.102	Single	UR	None	Head to W	D	UR	UR	None	
II.C.0.0	I.3.017	Single	UR	UR	Head to W	A	UR	UR	None	
	I.11.019	Under I.11.008	142.61m	None	UR	D	UR	UR	None	
	I.12.066	Single	142.53m	None	UR	D	0-6 mos.	UR	None	Legs missing. Cappers were cobble size
	I.21.008	Over I.21.009	142.65m	None	UR	D	UR	UR	None	
	I.21.022	Under I.21.005	143.04m	None	UR	D	UR	UR	None	Virtually destroyed by I.21.005
	I.21.031	Single	UR	None	UR	UR	UR	UR	None	Badly disturbed by military trenching; may be a child
	I.21.038	Single	UR	None	UR	UR	UR	UR	None	Mostly in E balk
	I.31.027	Single	142.56m	None	UR	D	UR	UR	None	

Section I: Typed Graves—Continued

TYPE	FIELD DATA	RELATIONSHIPS	LEVEL	ASSOCIATED ARTIFACTS	ORIENTATION	ARTICULATION	AGE	POSITION OF ARMS	PHOTO	COMMENTS
II.C.00 (cont'd)	I.31.029	Under I.31.022	143.10m	None	UR	D	UR	UR	None	A few other bones in shaft, possibly from I.31.029. Some non-human bones
	I.31.031	Single	142.68m	None	Head to W	PA	UR	UR	None	Head cut off by military trenching
	I.31.038	Over I.31.051 and I.31.053	142.90m	None	UR	UR	UR	UR	None	
II.C.0.f	I.51.044	Single	143.16m	None	UR	D	UR	UR	None	
	V.P-1b.006	Single	141.93m	None	Head to SW	A	6-18 mos.	UR	None	Covering of field stones
II.C.0.g	I.11.025	Single	142.61m	None	Head to W	A	UR	UR	None	Skeleton crushed in place
II.C.2.0	I.32.032B	Over I.32.101	143.31m	327, 397, 428 (1971)	Head to SW	A	0-6 mos.	Both hands on pelvis	None	Covering stone slabs. Apparently in same grave with I.32.032A, but cist outline not determined. Partly in S balk
II.C.2.a	I.12.015	Single	142.56m	None	Head to W	A	0-6 mos.	Both arms extended	Pl. 53	Many shells in grave
	I.12.127	Under I.12.039	142.24m	293 (1975)	Head to SW	A	18 mos. to 3 yrs.	Rt. extended Lt. flexed at elbow	None	
II.C.2.e	I.51.034	Single	142.80m		Head to W	A	6-18 mos.	Both extended	None	A few bones of an adult male were associated with this grave
II.C.2.f	I.32.012A	Over I.32.080	143.29m	None	Head to W	A	18 mos. to 3 yrs.	Rt. UR Lt. extended	Pl. 10	Holding younger infant (I.32.012B) in arms
	I.32.012B	Over I.32.080	143.29m	None	Head to W	A	0-6 mos.	Both hands in pelvis	Pl. 10	In arms of older infant (I.32.012A)
II.C.2.g	I.2.090	Single	142.34 m	None	Head to W	PA	6 mos. to 3 yrs.	Both arms extended	None	Same I.1.038. Two skulls in grave
II.C.3.j	I.32.032A	Over I.32.101	143.31m	327, 397, 428 (1971)	Head to SW	A	6-18 mos.	Rt. extended Lt. flexed at elbow	None	Covered by six field-stones. Apparently in same grave with I.32.032B, but cist outline not established. Partly in S balk
II.C.4.f	I.22.060	Single	143.02m	15, 16 (1973)	Head to SW	A	6-18 mos.	Rt. extended Lt. hand in pelvis	Pl. 37	Obj. reg. #16 (1973) may be a coin
	I.22.065A	Single	142.81m	89 (1973)	Head to SW	A	6-18 mos.	Both extended	Pl. 9	Covering of small stones arranged in two parallel rows. Two infants in same grave. Rt. arm under head of I.22.065B

Section I: Typed Graves—Continued

TYPE	FIELD DATA	RELATIONSHIPS	LEVEL	ASSOCIATED ARTIFACTS	ORIENTATION	ARTICULATION	AGE	POSITION OF ARMS	PHOTO	COMMENTS
II.C.4.f (cont'd)	I.22.065B	Single	142.81m	89 (1973)	Head to SW	A	0-6 mos.	Rt. UR Lt. extended	Pl. 13	As above in I.22.065A. Head rested on rt. arm of I.22.065A
	I.32.019B	Single	142.23m	632 (1971)	Head to W	A	18 mos. to 3 yrs.	Rt. UR Lt. extended	None	Covering is of small field stones. Beneath I.32.019A.
	I.41.115	Under I.41.018, I.41.026 and I.41.083 Over I.41.120	142.80m	121 (1973)	Head to SW	A	18 mos. to 3 yrs.	Rt. flexed at elbow Lt. extended	None	Capstones scattered. Adult bones in grave. Probably cut through an adult burial
II.C.4.g	I.22.037	Single	143.17m	None	Head to SW	A	6-18 mos.	UR	None	
	I.41.026	Over I.41.104 and I.41.115	143.50m	None	Head to W	A	18 mos. to 3 yrs.	Rt. extended Lt. hand on pelvis	None	Covered with small field stones
II.C.8.f	I.12.035	Single	142.68m	None	Head to SW	A	0-6 mos.	Rt. flexed at elbow Lt. across abdomen	Pl. 39	
	I.32.019A	Over I.32.019B	143.41m	632 (1971)	Head to W	A	18 mos. to 3 yrs.	Both extended	None	Covered with small field stones
	I.41.035	Single	143.45m	263 (1971)	Head to W	A	18 mos. to 3 yrs.	Rt. extended Lt. flexed at elbow	None	Skull rested on its base
	I.51.016	Single	142.86m	142, 198 (1973)	Head to SW	A	18 mos. to 3 yrs.	Rt. extended Lt. across abdomen	None	
II.E.2.h	I.41.090	Under I.41.067 and I.41.091	143.08m	None	Head to W	A	4-6 yrs.	Rt. extended Lt. UR	None	Primary Burial I.41.091 was an adult, cut in half by I.41.090. Flat capstones
II.F.0.0	I.1.010	Over I.1.035	142.67m	None	Head to W	D	UR	UR	None	Mostly in S balk
	I.2.034	Under I.2.012	142.25m	None	UR	D	UR	UR	None	Grave oriented SW-NE; dug into shaft of I.11.019
	I.11.008	Over I.11.019	142.65m	None	Head to SW	A	UR	UR	None	
	I.11.058	Single	UR	None	Head to SW	D	UR	UR	None	Mainly in W balk
	I.22.090	Single	142.40m	None	UR	UR	UR	UR	None	Mostly in W balk
II.F.0.g	I.51.032	Over I.51.133	143.02m	None	Head to SW	UR	6-8 yrs.	UR	None	Skull only; rest in N balk and lost during winter rains
II.F.2.f	I.11.127	Under I.11.062	142.50m	None	Head to SW	A	4-8 yrs.	UR	None	Locus no. I.11.105 was given to the capstones of this burial
	I.32.064	Single	142.97m	None	Head to SW	A	4-6 yrs.	Rt. extended Lt. hand on pelvis	Pl. 30	Skull and upper torso only. Longer skull than normal
	I.32.070	Under I.32.022 Over I.32.046, and I.32.056	142.61m	116 (1973)	Head to SW	A	4-6 yrs.	Both extended	Pl. 41	Skull in W balk
	I.51.024	Over I.51.038, I.51.039 and I.51.043	142.92m	None	Head to W	A	4-6 yrs.	Rt. extended Lt. hand in pelvis	Pl. 32	Cut off upper part of I.51.039

Section I: Typed Graves—Continued

TYPE	FIELD DATA	RELATIONSHIPS	LEVEL	ASSOCIATED ARTIFACTS	ORIENTATION	ARTICULATION	AGE	POSITION OF ARMS	PHOTO	COMMENTS
II.F.2.h	I.51.017	Over I.51.031	143.28m	None	Head to W	A	4–6 yrs.	Both across pelvis	None	Lower limbs in E balk
II.F.4.g	I.22.038	Under I.22.029	142.78m	None	Head to SW	A	3–4 yrs.	Rt. extended Lt. hand in pelvis	Pl. 42	
II.H.0.0	I.1.015	Over I.1.036	142.80m	None	UR	A	Ca. 12 yrs.	UR	None	
II.K.0.0	I.1.035	Under I.1.010	142.36m	None	UR	A	UR	UR	None	Partially in E balk
	I.1.036	Under I.1.015	142.16m	None	UR	A	UR	UR	None	Partially in E balk
II.K.0.g	I.2.013	Single	141.71m	None	Head to W	A	UR	UR	None	0.50 m of shaft identified. Charred sheet/goat bone in mouth of skeleton
	I.2.020	Single	142.00m	42 (1970)	Head to W	A	Ca. 25 yrs.	UR	None	Five large flat capstones
	I.11.045	Under I.11.026A and I.11.026B	142.07m	87 (1970)	Head to W	D	UR	UR	None	Apparently two individuals, a young male and a mature male (over 24 yrs.). Bones of adult male removed as I.11.108
	V.P-1e.005	Single	141.83m	338 (1975)	Head to SW	UR	Over 24 yrs.	UR	None	Skull only; body in N balk
II.K.1.g	I.51.133	Under I.51.032 and I.51.128 Over I.51.129	143.00m	316 (1975)	Head to W	A	Over 24 yrs.	UR	None	Arms and pelvis were missing
II.K.1.h	I.32.080	Under I.32.012A and I.32.012B	142.78m	None	Head to W	A	25–30 yrs.	Rt. hand in pelvis Lt. arm extended	Pl. 51	Capped and partially lined with slabs
II.K.2.0	I.41.081	Over I.41.105 and I.41.106	142.84m	None	Head to SW	A	21–25 yrs.	Rt. extended Lt. UR	Pl. 16	Cut into and partly destroyed I.41.105. Shaft contained disarticulated bones
II.K.2.f	I.4.020	Single	140.63m	390, 401, 418, 444, 457, 473 (1971)	Head to W	A	Over 24 yrs.	Both hands on femur	Pl. 44	Cappers consisted of fieldstones with one a reused grindstone. Three whole and three broken 'abariq associated with the burial
II.K.2.g	I.11.172	Under I.11.062 and I.11.125	142.39m	None	Head to SW	A	Over 24 yrs.	Both hands on femur	None	Rt. arm crossed over abdomen
	I.32.063	Under I.32.023 and I.32.037 Over I.32.094	142.65m	None	Head to W	A	30–35 yrs.	Rt. extended Lt. UR	None	Lower part of skeleton cut away by overlying graves
	I.41.217A	Under I.41.207 and I.41.211	142.73m	None	Head to W	A	Over 24 yrs.	Both hands on femur	Pl. 17	Apparently in same grave as I.41.217B, but cut that body
II.K.4.f	I.12.054	Under I.12.017	141.83m	76, 88, 91, 94, 95, 96 (1973)	Head to SW	A	Over 17 yrs.	Rt. extended Lt. hand on pelvis	Pl. 45	Obj. #76 on right hand; obj. #94 fused to arm bone. One yellow sandstone capper survived

Section I: Typed Graves—Continued

TYPE	FIELD DATA	RELATIONSHIPS	LEVEL	ASSOCIATED ARTIFACTS	ORIENTATION	ARTICULATION	AGE	POSITION OF ARMS	PHOTO	COMMENTS
II.K.4.f (cont'd)	I.31.176	Single	142.43m	433, 434, 435, 436, 474, 484, 487, 491, 495, 617 (1971)	Head to W	A	Over 24 yrs.	Rt. extended Lt. across pelvis, hand on femur	None	
II.K.4.g	I.51.067	Under I.51.018, I.51.019, I.51.022, and I.51.023 Over I.51.115	142.49m	159, 160, 163 (1973)	Head to W	A	Over 24 yrs.	Rt. extended Lt. hand in pelvis	None	Two layers of cappers. Stone pillow
II.K.8.0	I.41.121	Under I.41.028, I.41.039 and I.41.103	142.85m	None	Head to W	PA	Ca. 65 yrs.	UR	None	Pelvis mostly missing, cut off by I.41.103
II.K.8.g	I.32.024B	Single	143.07m	292, 481 (1971)	Head to W	A	Over 24 yrs.	Rt. extended Lt. across chest	Pl. 12	In same grave with younger female, I.32.024A
II.K.8.h	I.41.096	Under I.41.051, I.41.064 and I.41.067	142.74m	None	Head to W	A	56-60 yrs.	Rt. flexed at elbow Lt. hand on femur	None	Covering of small field stones with one slab
II.L.0.0	I.1.031	Single	UR	None	UR	A	UR	UR	None	Head not attached to spinal column. Not drawn on top plan
	I.1.034	Under I.1.020, I.1.022 and I.1.024	142.07m	None	UR	A	Over 30 yrs.	UR	None	Partially in E balk
	I.1.037	UR	UR	None	UR	A	UR	UR	None	Not drawn on top plan. Near I.1.036
	I.1.066	Over I.1.039	142.13m	None	UR	D	Ca. 19 yrs.	UR	None	Capping uncertain; only one stone survived
	I.2.021	Under I.2.007	141.83m	222 (1971)	UR	D	40-45 yrs.	UR	None	Only one large capstone recovered. Same as I.1.157 and I.2.085.
	I.3.043	Single	141.47m	64, 65 (1970)	Head to SW	A	UR	UR	None	Cappers stone slabs. Individual had curvature of the spine
	I.22.066	Single	142.41m	None	UR	UR	16-20 yrs.	UR	None	Mostly in N balk. Cappers slabs, one a reused worked stone
II.L.0.g	I.31.026	Under I.31.016	142.64m	10 (1970)	Head to SW	A	UR	UR	None	Partially in S balk
	I.11.022	Single	142.67m	43A-D (1970)	Head to SW	A	UR	UR	None	Grave oriented SW-NE
II.L.2.f	I.4.007	Single	140.84m	262, 273, 282, 291, 420 (1971)	Head to W	A	Over 24 yrs.	Rt. extended Lt. hand in pelvis	None	Capped with stone slabs
	I.22.103	Under I.22.015 and I.22.016	142.16m	None	Head to SW	A	Over 24 yrs.	Rt. extended Lt. hand in pelvis	None	Covering small field-stones. Cut through I.22.101

Section I: Typed Graves—Continued

TYPE	FIELD DATA	RELATIONSHIPS	LEVEL	ASSOCIATED ARTIFACTS	ORIENTATION	ARTICULATION	AGE	POSITION OF ARMS	PHOTO	COMMENTS
II.L.2.f (cont'd)	I.22.126	Single	142.53m	273 (1973)	Head to SW	A	17-24 yrs.	Both extended	None	Covering small field-stones
	I.41.106	Under I.41.072 and I.41.081	142.93m	87, 117 (1973)	Head to SW	A	21-25 yrs.	Rt. extended Lt. UR	Pl. 16	Cut by I.41.081
	I.41.134	Under I.41.102	142.66m	None	Head to SW	A	25-30 yrs.	Both extended	None	Only partially capped
II.L.2.g	I.32.056	Under I.32.022 and I.32.046	142.44m	48, 51, 54, 55 (1973)	Head to W	A	25-30 yrs.	Both across pelvis	Pls. 14, 15	Cappers robbed by I.32.046 which was in the cist originally prepared for I.32.056. Obj. ## 48 and 55 were on right arm of skeleton
	VI.P-1a.005	Single	138.23m	None	Head to SW	A	Over 24 yrs.	Both extended Rt. hand on femur Lt. hand in pelvis	Pl. 20	Grave empty of soil
	VI.P-1a.006	Under VI.P-1a.003	138.49m	None	Head to W	PA	Over 24 yrs.	UR	None	
II.L.2.h	I.32.024A	Single	143.07m	292, 481 (1971)	Head to NW	A	Over 24 yrs.	Both extended	Pl. 12	In same grave with I.32.024B, a somewhat older male skull in W balk
II.L.4.0	I.41.114	Under I.41.077	143.00m	None	UR	A	25-30 yrs.	UR	None	
II.L.4.f	I.32.049	Under I.32.037 and I.32.039	142.69m	28, 47, 66 (1973)	Head to SW	A	Over 24 yrs.	Rt. across pelvis Lt. UR	Pl. 31	Disarticulated bones of infant 1-3 yrs. in fill of grave
II.L.4.g	I.32.145	Single	142.30m	320 (1975)	Head to W	A	17-24 yrs.	UR	None	Capped with slabs
II.L.4.h	I.22.207	Single	142.32m	451 (1975)	Head to W	A	Over 30 yrs.	Rt. extended Lt. across chest	None	Stone under head
	I.41.218	Under I.41.203	142.97m	None	Head to W	A	Over 24 yrs.	Rt. extended Lt. hand in pelvis	Pl. 46	Almost face down
II.L.7.g	I.32.046	Under I.32.022 and I.32.070 Over I.32.056	142.52m	36, 38 (1973)	Head to E	A	17-24 yrs.	Rt. flexed at elbow Lt. extended	Pls. 13, 15	Cappers flat slabs. Head direction opposite to normal
II.L.8.g	I.32.060	Single	142.66m	None	Head to W	A	16-25 yrs.	Rt. extended Lt. across abdomen	Pl. 48	Elongated skull
II.M.0.0	I.2.028	Under I.2.014	141.95m	None	UR	A	UR	UR	None	Almost entirely in E and S balks
	I.21.012	Single	142.94m	None	Head to W	A	UR	UR	None	Many flat capstones
	I.21.013	Single	142.90m	13 (1970)	Head to W	D	UR		None	Only one capstone found. Only skull intact. Burial cut by military trenching
	I.21.015	Under I.21.005	142.70m	8 (1970)	UR	UR	Over 24 yrs.	UR	None	
	I.21.036	Under I.21.005	UR	None	UR	A	UR	UR		
	I.21.037	Single	UR	None	UR	A	UR	UR		Partially in E balk

Section I: Typed Graves—Continued

TYPE	FIELD DATA	RELATIONSHIPS	LEVEL	ASSOCIATED ARTIFACTS	ORIENTATION	ARTICULATION	AGE	POSITION OF ARMS	PHOTO	COMMENTS
II.M.0.0 (cont'd)	I.31.028	Under I.31.021	142.06m	None	UR	PA	UR	UR	None	Other bones in grave, intrusive from I.31.021
	I.32.027	Single	142.88m	None	UR	A	Over 24 yrs.	UR	None	Capped by stone slabs. Mostly in W balk
	I.41.217B	Under I.41.207 and I.41.211	142.73m	271, 272 (1973)	UR	D	Ca. 30 yrs.	UR	Pl. 17	Apparently in same grave as I.41.217A, but cut by it
	I.51.065	Under I.51.053	142.65m	None	UR	A	25-30 yrs.	UR	None	Skull and torso only; remainder in E balk
II.M.0.g	I.11.024	Single	142.56m	44 (1970)	Head to W	A	UR	UR	None	
II.M.2.0	I.22.134B	Under I.22.134B	142.77m	None	UR	A	Over 24 yrs.	Rt. UR Lt. across pelvis	None	
	I.32.090	Single	142.60m	None	Head to SW	A	Over 24 yrs.	UR	None	Feet and legs only; rest in S balk
	I.32.092	Single	142.61m	None	Head to SW	A	Over 24 yrs.	UR	None	Feet and legs only; rest in S balk
II.M.2.g	I.12.039	Over I.12.127	142.27m	None	Head to W	A	Over 24 yrs.	Rt. UR Lt. hand on pelvis	None	Same as I.12.132
II.M.8.0	I.32.018	Under I.32.011 Over I.32.048	143.27m	None	UR	A	Over 27 yrs.	UR	None	Stone covering disturbed. Upper half of skeleton cut off by I.32.048. Lower half articulated. Extreme flexation
III.C.0.0	I.1.014	Over I.1.016	UR	None	UR	A	Newborn	UR	None	
	I.21.026A	Single	142.98m	71 (1970)	Head to W	PA	UR	UR	None	Shared cappers with I.21.026B
III.C.2.0	I.31.022	Over I.31.029	143.30m	None	UR	D	UR	UR	None	
	I.22.133	Single	143.17m	None	Head to NW	A	0-6 mos.	Both hands in pelvis	None	
	I.22.147	Single	142.66m	None	Head to SW	A	UR	UR	None	
	I.51.131	Over I.41.117	143.43m	None	Head to W	A	18 mos. to 3 yrs.	UR	None	One worked stone capper. Preserved from pelvis down; rest in W balk
III.C.2.a	I.32.040	See Comments	142.68m	None	Head to W	A	0-6 mos.	Rt. across pelvis Lt. flexed at elbow	Pl. 34	Cut off legs of I.32.038. Probably reused cappers from same grave
	I.41.051	Over I.41.056, I.41.085 and I.41.096	143.46m	394, 395, 407, 449 (1971)	Head to W	A	6-18 mos.	Both extended	None	Capped and lined with large fieldstones
III.C.2.e	I.22.153	Single	143.07m	None	Head to SW	A	18 mos. to 3 yrs.	Rt. extended -hand on pelvis Lt. UR	None	Capped and lined with large fieldstones

Section I: Typed Graves—Continued

TYPE	FIELD DATA	RELATIONSHIPS	LEVEL	ASSOCIATED ARTIFACTS	ORIENTATION	ARTICULATION	AGE	POSITION OF ARMS	PHOTO	COMMENTS
III.C.2.f	I.22.023	Single	142.94m	None	Head to W	D	18 mos. to 3 yrs.	Rt. flexed at elbow, hand on pelvis Lt. across chest	None	Degree of articulation probably not correctly reported
	I.41.028	Over I.41.039, I.41.103 and I.41.121	143.52m	None	Head to W	A	18 mos. to 3 yrs.	Rt. UR Lt. extended	Pl. 35	Large stone cappers; fieldstone liners
	I.41.032	Over I.41.091	143.64m	None	Head to W	A	6-18 mos.	Rt. extended Lt. flexed at elbow	None	Capped and lined with slabs
III.C.8.0	I.22.134A	Over I.22.134B	142.95m	None	Head to SW	A	UR	Both extended Lt. hand in pelvis	None	Capped and lined with fieldstones
III.C.8.e	I.21.005B	Over I.21.015, I.21.022 and I.21.036	143.30m	None	Head to W	A	Ca. 3 yrs.	UR	Pl. 8	Middle of three burials in a common pit; see also I.21.005A, C. Mud-plaster dividers separated burials. Feet crossed at ankles. Skull probably disturbed by military trenching
III.C.8.f	I.51.045	Single	142.81m	None	Head to SW	A	6-18 mos.	Rt. extended Lt. across chest	None	
III.C.8.g	I.21.005A	Over I.21.015, I.21.022 and I.21.036	143.34m	None	Head to W	A	Ca. 2 yrs.	UR	Pl. 8	Southernmost of three burials in a common pit; see also I.21.005B, C. Mud-plaster dividers separated burials. Feet crossed at ankles
III.F.0.0	I.21.005C	Over I.21.015, I.21.022 and I.21.036	142.96m	None	Head to W	A	Ca. 4 yrs.	UR	Pl. 8	Northernmost of three bodies in a common pit; see also I.21.005A, B. Mud-plaster dividers separated burials. Only skull and shoulder bones
III.F.0.i	I.31.015	Over I.31.040	143.38m	None	Head to S	UR	6-9 yrs.	UR	None	Orientation and eye direction anomalous. Cappers and liners roughly placed
III.F.2.f	I.12.016	Single	142.56m	None	Head to SW	A	3-4 yrs.	Both extended	None	
	I.41.046	Single	143.38m	None	Head to W	A	3-4 yrs.	Both extended	None	
	I.41.056	Under I.41.051	143.38m	500 (1971)	Head to W	A	3-4 yrs.	Rt. extended Lt. UR	None	Capped and lined with large stones. In same grave with I.41.051, but at a lower level. Reused grave

Section I: Typed Graves—Continued

TYPE	FIELD DATA	RELATIONSHIPS	LEVEL	ASSOCIATED ARTIFACTS	ORIENTATION	ARTICULATION	AGE	POSITION OF ARMS	PHOTO	COMMENTS
III.F.2.g	I.41.016	Single	143.65m	210 (1971)	Head to NW	A	3-4 yrs.	Rt. hand in pelvis Lt. across abdomen	None	Partially in E balk. Lined with field-stones; capped with slabs
III.G.2.0	I.41.058	Under I.41.028, and I.41.039 Over I.41.070 and I.41.108	143.07m	570, 573 (1971)	Head to W	A	12-17 yrs.	Rt. extended Lt. across abdomen	Pl. 56	
III.J.0.0	I.21.063	Under I.21.027	UR	None	Head to W	A	Adolescent	UR	None	Both capstones and liners large slabs. Partially in E balk
III.K.0.0	I.41.070	Under I.41.058 and I.41.077	143.02m	None	UR	A	Over 17 yrs.	UR	None	Lined with small fieldstones
III.K.2.c	I.22.102	See Comments	142.55m	None	Head to W	A	Over 24 yrs.	Rt. extended Lt. hand in pelvis	Pl. 54	Feet of primary burial cut off by I.22.079. Two sets of leg bones in grave. Partially lined with field-stones. Direction of eyes anomalous
III.K.2.g	I.41.223	Under I.41.216	142.55m	None	Head to SW	A	Over 24 yrs.	Both extended	None	Preserved only from waist up. Rest in E balk
III.K.6.0	I.32.039	Over I.32.049 See Comments	143.11m	468, 502 (1971)	Head to W	A	Over 24 yrs.	Both hands on femur	Pl. 29	Skull missing, cut off by I.32.037. Cappers slabs, liners field-stones
III.K.6.f	I.32.037	Under I.32.023 and I.32.039 Over I.32.049 and I.32.063	142.83m	459, 485, 493 (1971)	Head to SW	A	Over 24 yrs.	Both hands in pelvis	Pl. 52	Cappers flat slabs; liners fieldstones
III.L.0.g	I.1.046	Under I.1.111	141.71m	None	Head to SW	PA	Ca. 19 yrs.	UR	None	Only hands and feet articulated. Skull on vault. Two layers cf cappers with six stones in each. Cist oriented SW-NE
III.L.2.0	I.32.048	Under I.32.018 Over I.32.081 and I.32.094	142.53m	37, 40 (1973)	UR	A	UR	UR	Pl. 22	Liners flat slabs
III.L.2.f	I.41.068	Under I.41.019, I.41.065 and I.41.082	143.09m	None	Head to E	A	17-24 yrs.	Rt. hand on femur Lt. hand in pelvis	None	Head direction anoma-lous. Some fragments of child burial in grave, possibly from I.41.065
III.L.2.g	I.41.100	Under I.41.012, I.41.013, I.41.018, I.41.082 and I.41.083	143.07m	None	Head to W	A	16-25 yrs.	Rt. extended Lt. hand in pelvis	Pl. 21	Only partially capped

Section I: Typed Graves—Continued

TYPE	FIELD DATA	RELATIONSHIPS	LEVEL	ASSOCIATED ARTIFACTS	ORIENTATION	ARTICULATION	AGE	POSITION OF ARMS	PHOTO	COMMENTS
III.L.4.0	I.41.049	Under I.41.012 and I.41.013	143.19m	None	Head to W	A	Over 24 yrs.	Rt. extended Lt. across chest	None	Capped and lined with large fieldstones. Skull missing
III.L.4.h	I.32.038	See Comments	142.78m	475 (1971)	Head to NW	A	Over 24 yrs.	Rt. extended Lt. hand in pelvis	Pl. 34	Legs missing; removed by Infant Burial I.32.040. Capped and lined with fieldstones
III.L.8.f	I.12.017	Over I.12.054	142.10m	None	Head to W	A	17-24 yrs.	Rt. extended Lt. flexed at elbow	Pls. 23, 24	Lining cobble-sized stones found only along sides of grave
	I.22.015	Over I.22.034 and I.22.103	142.65m	275, 276, 278, 325, 328, 421, 422, 629 (1971)	Head to W	A	17-24 yrs.	Rt. extended Lt. flexed at elbow, hand in pelvis	Pl. 49	Grave of irregular shape
	I.22.079	Under I.22.029 and I.22.038	142.54m	63, 64, 67 (1973)	Head to SW	A	25-30 yrs.	Rt. extended Lt. across chest	Pl. 50	Capstones 45x40 and 45x45 cm. Skull elongated. Reddish color on bones
III.M.0.0	I.21.026B	Single	142.71m	None	Head to W	A	Over 17 yrs.	UR	None	Partially in E balk. Apparently not associated with I.21.026A, although the capstones were continuous for both graves, and there was an earth separation between the graves
	I.21.027	Over I.21.063, and I.21.072A,B	UR	None	UR	UR	Over 17 yrs.	UR	None	
	I.31.043	Single	142.17m	None	Head to W	A	Over 17 yrs.	UR	None	Legs cut off by military trenching
	I.41.117	Under I.41.108	142.70m	None	UR	UR	Over 17 yrs.	UR	None	Mostly in S balk
	I.41.132	Under I.41.054, I.41.057, I.41.076 and I.41.123	142.61m	None	UR	A	Over 24 yrs.	UR	None	Only legs exposed; rest in W balk
IV.C.2.0	I.41.065	Over I.41.068	143.36m	6 (1973)	Head to SW	A	6-18 mos.	Rt. UR Lt. extended	None	Lined with small fieldstones
IV.C.2.f	I.41.018	Over I.41.100 and I.41.104	143.66m	None	Head to W	A	18 mos. to 3 yrs.	Both extended	None	Lined with fieldstones
IV.C.4.0	I.41.05?	Over I.41.132	143.38m	497 (1971)	Head to E	A	6-18 mos.	UR	None	One fieldstone capper in place. Head direction anomalous
IV.C.8.f	I.41.012	Over I.41.049 and I.41.100	143.50m	17 (1971)	Head to W	A	18 mos. to 3 yrs.	Rt. UR Lt. flexed at elbow	None	Lined with fieldstones. Feet cut off by I.41.013. Stone pillow under head

Section I: Typed Graves—Continued

TYPE	FIELD DATA	RELATIONSHIPS	LEVEL	ASSOCIATED ARTIFACTS	ORIENTATION	ARTICULATION	AGE	POSITION OF ARMS	PHOTO	COMMENTS
IV.F.2.e	I.41.013	Over I.41.049 and I.41.100	143.56m	None	Head to SW	A	3-4 yrs.	Both across chest	None	Fieldstone lining. Feet missing. Head on stone pillow
IV.L.2.f	I.12.019A	Under I.12.005 Over I.12.019B	142.44m	None	Head to W	A	Over 24 yrs.	Rt. extended hand on femur Lt. hand on pelvis	Pl. 11	Lining on N side missing, due to military trenching. Grave shape anomalous
	I.32.094	Under I.32.023, I.32.037 and I.32.063 Over I.32.048	142.55m	165, 176, 181 (1973)	Head to SW	A	30-35 yrs.	Both hands on femur	Pl. 25	A few slabs around body
IV.L.8.0	I.41.063	Under I.41.052 and I.41.053 Over I.41.123	143.24m	None	Head to SW	A	Ca. 25 yrs.	Rt. flexed at elbow Lt. hand in pelvis	None	Lined with field-stones. Cut into by I.41.076
V.C.0.0	I.41.019	Over I.41.068 and I.41.091	143.53m	322 (1971)	UR	A	0-6 mos.	UR	Pls. 26, 27, 84	Storage jar, broken in place

Section II: Secondary Burials

TYPE	FIELD DATA	RELATIONSHIPS	LEVEL	ASSOCIATED ARTIFACTS	ORIENTATION	ARTICULATION	AGE	POSITION OF ARMS	PHOTO	COMMENTS
	I.1.007	Over I.1.011	Just below surface	None	UR	D	Probably young child	UR	None	Skull and disarticulated bones in the shaft of I.1.011
	I.1.029	Single	UR	None	UR	UR	UR	UR	None	Secondary burial of animal bones, probably made in the excavation of grave I.1.044
	I.2.011	Single	142.09m	None	Head to E	D	Probably an infant	UR	None	Possibly displaced in digging of I.2.009
	I.2.066	Single	141.55m	None	UR	D	UR	UR	None	No cist; mixture of human and animal bones in shallow pit
	I.11.014	Over I.11.023 and I.11.032	UR	None	UR	D	See Comments	UR	None	Mixture of human and animal bones. More than one individual, including an adult and an infant
	I.11.023	Over I.11.031 and I.11.032 Under I.11.014	142.50m	46 (1970)	UR	UR	See Comments	UR	None	Irregular shaped pit, containing the disarticulated remains of three individuals--two infants and one adult
	I.11.026B	Over I.11.045	142.82m	None	See Comments	D	UR	UR	None	Two individuals--an adult male and an infant, buried in the shaft of I.11.026A. Pelvis of infant crushed into skull of adult; long bones cut and deliberately laid in.

Section II: Secondary Burials—Continued

FIELD DATA	RELATIONSHIPS	LEVEL	ASSOCIATED ARTIFACTS	ORIENTATION	ARTICULATION	AGE	POSITION OF ARMS	PHOTO	COMMENTS
I.11.027A and B	I.11.027A is over I.11.049	UR	None	UR	D	UR	UR	None	Single skeleton in two adjacent pits. Skull in SE of northern pit, facing north. Scattered bones in southern pit. Both pits of irregular shape
I.11.028	Single	142.43m	None	UR	D	See Comments	UR	None	Round pit containing the disarticulated remains of two skeletons—a young male and an infant of 6 mos.-2 yrs. Many stones around edge of pit
I.12.005	Over I.12.019 A and B	142.80m	None	UR	D	UR	UR	None	
I.21.009	Under I.21.008	142.44m	4 (1970)	UR	D	9-12 yrs.	UR	None	No skull found; sex male. Legs pointing in different directions. Vertebrae in pelvis
I.21.017B	Single	UR	None	UR	D	UR	UR	None	Adult. Evidence of at least two diggings of cist
I.21.017C	Over I.21.017A	143.18m	None	UR	D	UR	UR	None	Adult. Evidence of at least two diggings of pit
I.22.024	Single	142.61m	None	UR	D	UR	UR	None	Only a few bone fragments, mostly sheep/goat
I.31.016	Over I.31.026	143.32m	None	UR	D	UR	UR	None	In shaft of I.31.026. Partially in S balk
I.31.021	Over I.31.028	143.29m	None	UR	D	UR	UR	None	Capped secondary burial in shaft of I.31.028
I.32.067	Single	142.80m	None	UR	D	UR	UR	None	Feet only, thrust into Hellenistic wall. Probably the feet of I.32.038
I.41.071	Over I.41.063	143.37m	None	UR	UR	UR	UR	None	Fragments of adult skeleton in the shaft of I.41.063
I.41.083	Over I.41.100 I.41.115 and I.41.120	143.16m	None	UR	UR	3-4 yrs.	UR	None	Disarticulated infant burial in the shaft of I.41.115
I.41.092	Over I.41.091	143.20m	None	UR	D	Ca. 25 yrs.	UR	None	Disarticulated bones in the shaft of I.41.091

Section II: Secondary Burials—Continued

FIELD DATA	RELATIONSHIPS	LEVEL	ASSOCIATED ARTIFACTS	ORIENTATION	ARTICULATION	AGE	POSITION OF ARMS	PHOTO	COMMENTS
I.41.104	Under I.41.018 and I.41.026 Over I.41.115 and I.41.120	142.93m	None	UR	D	Adult	UR	None	Scattered bones in the shafts of I.41.114 and I.41.120
I.41.108	Over I.41.117	143.21m	None	UR	D	Adult	UR	None	Disarticulated bones probably from I.41.117

Section III: Burial Pits

I.31.036:   A deep pit with bottom at 141.98m dug from base of military trenching. Contained 15 skulls and many disarticulated bones. One child and one infant recognizable.

I.31.051 and I.31.053:   Under I.31.038 at 142.57m. The burial pit was stone-lined and had a stone-vaulted roof roughly constructed. Within it were the disarticulated bones of at least eight individuals: four mature females; two mature humans of undetermined sex; one infant; and one child. I.31.053 seemed to be an eastward extension of the original pit. It contained only a few disarticulated bones. Objects registry 55,118 (1970).

I.41.077:   At 143.17m. A jumble of disarticulated bones in a stone-lined pit. Child, adult, and animal bones recognized.

I.41.102:   At 142.77m. Over I.41.134. Contained infant, juvenile, and adult bones, all disarticulated.

I.51.015:   At 143.18m. Disarticulated bones of two infants, together with some adult bones.

V.P-1c.008:   At 141.12m. Smashed and broken bones, human and animal, covered by a large chalk stone.

Section IV: Insufficient Data

I.1.011:   142.82m. Under I.1.007. Capped but not lined. Two cappers were worked stones.

I.1.021:   Capped but not lined. Head to W. Most of skeleton in E balk.

I.1.026:   142.42m. Almost entirely in N balk. Only edge of grave excavated.

I.1.045:   Empty grave. Not drawn on plan.

I.1.014:   142.32m. Empty grave.

I.2.015:   Empty grave.

I.2.017:   Capped but not lined. Skeleton in E balk.

I.2.018:   141.63m. Capped but not lined. Five large cappers. Skeleton in S balk.

I.2.029:   142.00m. Almost entirely in N balk.

I.2.089:   142.51m. Disarticulated burial in E balk.

I.4.022:   141.15m. Burial of a child or infant. Capped but not lined. Mostly in S balk.

I.4.024:   141.29m. Burial of a child or infant. Mostly in E balk.

I.11.021:   Almost completely destroyed by military trenching.

I.11.031:   142.72m. Under I.11.023. Only a few bone fragments.

I.11.032:   Under I.11.014, I.11.023. Over I.11.050. Capped but not lined. Mostly in E and S balks.

I.11.049:   142.09m. Under I.11.027A. Capped but not lined. Head to W. Grave oriented SW-NE.

I.11.050:   Fragmentary bones in pit near S balk.

I.11.071:   142.44m. No data available. Near S balk.

I.12.006:   142.44m. Capped but not lined. Cappers tipped over. Grave empty.

I.12.014:   142.58m. Capped and lined. Grave found empty.

I.12.023:   Capped but not lined. All but the legs in W balk.

I.12.036:   142.73m. All but the skull in E balk. Probably an infant with head to W.

I.12.093:   142.40m. Bones visible in W balk but not excavated. Perhaps part of I.12.023.

I.12.105:   Capped but not lined. Cranium visible in N balk.

I.12.106:   142.39m. Almost entirely in S balk.

I.13.016:   142.13m. Disarticulated bones of a child or infant, disturbed by military trenching.

I.13.022:   141.50m. Disarticulated bones of child or infant, disturbed by military trenching and mostly in N balk.

I.13.031:   141.82m. Skull only, rest of grave destroyed by military trenching.

I.13.033:   142.20m. Capped but not lined. Cappers 0.25m × 0.50m. Grave not excavated.

I.13.057:   Neither capped nor lined. Skull exposed, but grave not excavated.

I.13.058:   Three cappers and part of skull exposed, but grave not excavated.

I.21.034:   Disarticulated bones with remains of two skulls. Probably burials displaced in the excavation of I.21.017A. Objects registry 16 (1970).

I.21.041:   143.14m. Over I.21.060. Two children in same grave. Details of burial not reported.

Section IV: Insufficient Data—Continued

I.22.029:   142.79m. No details reported.

I.22.035:   142.85m. Lined but not capped. Partially in N balk. Skull and a few bones recovered.

I.22.078:   142.70m. Lined but not capped. Partially in W balk. Feet and legs only recovered.

I.22.124:   142.37m. Neither capped nor lined. Bones too badly disturbed for analysis.

I.31.024:   142.56m. Mixture of bones, including mature and immature human, disturbed by military trenching.

I.31.030:   143.25m. Two graves in the N balk, intersecting one another. Two skulls, one in each end of burial. East end of grave cut off by I.31.029. At least one of the burials was capped.

I.31.034:   142.16m. No other information available.

I.31.037:   142.30m. Under I.31.014, which almost totally destroyed it.

I.31.039:   142.56m. Described only as "pit" and "child burial." No other data available.

I.31.040:   142.09m. Under I.31.015, which almost totally destroyed it.

I.31.045:   142.03m. Under I.31.039, which almost totally destroyed it.

I.31.049:   142.16m. Almost totally destroyed by military trenching. Objects registry 21 (1970).

I.31.072:   141.54m. Under I.31.036, which almost totally destroyed it.

I.31.171:   142.65m. Mostly in E balk.

I.32.022:   143.10m. At first identified as capstones, but no burial found beneath.

I.32.023:   Identified at first as a burial, but no bones found. Probably the shaft of I.32.063.

I.32.030:   143.14m. Badly disarticulated burial in E balk.

I.32.053:   143.25m. Disarticulated and disturbed child burial, partially in E balk.

I.32.096:   142.91m. Loose soil with a few disarticulated bones.

I.32.110:   142.67m. Disarticulated bones with stones roughly ranged around them. Over I.32.145, and possibly a secondary burial in its shaft.

I.32.111:   142.67m. Disarticulated bones over I.32.145, but outside the stones of I.32.110.

I.32.125:   142.90m. A few disarticulated bones in loose soil.

I.32.127:   142.91m. Under I.32.121. Skull only in west of grave, looking south.

I.32.172:   142.95m. Disarticulated bones from N and E balks, including part of skull.

I.32.195:   142.70m. Disarticulated bones from E balk.

I.41.007:   143.50m. Broken bones and parts of two skulls in loose soil.

I.41.039:   143.43m. Under I.41.028. Over I.41.103 and I.41.121. Badly disturbed and disarticulated. No grave outline discernible.

I.41.044:   143.39m. A few disarticulated bones in loose soil.

I.41.045:   143.57m. Disarticulated remains of a skeleton. Objects registry 338, 340 (1971). An eggshell was found with the burial.

I.41.047:   143.58m. A few disarticulated bones in loose soil.

I.41.048:   143.43m. A few disarticulated bones in loose soil. Objects registry 368 (1971).

I.41.053:   143.42m. A few disarticulated bones in loose soil.

I.41.054:   143.39m. A few disarticulated bones in loose soil.

I.41.072:   143.25m. Over I.41.106. Disarticulated bones of mature and immature humans in shaft of I.41.106. Red stains on bones.

I.41.085B: Leg bones only. Rest cut off by I.41.085A. Pls. 6, 7.

I.41.103:   143.12m. Disarticulated bones probably from underlying burial of I.41.121.

I.41.105:   142.84m. Leg bones only. Rest cut off by I.41.081 and I.41.106. Objects registry 82 (1973). Pl. 16.

I.41.123:   142.93m. Over I.41.132. Many smashed and disarticulated bones in the shaft of I.41.132. Perhaps a secondary burial.

I.41.207:   143.46m. Skull fragments in loose soil.

I.41.211:   Shaft of I.41.204.

I.41.216:   142.97m. Skull and disarticulated bones of female over 45 years. Perhaps a secondary burial in the shaft of I.41.223.

I.51.018:   143.30m. Over I.51.067. Disarticulated bones of a child or infant. Perhaps a secondary burial in the shaft of I.51.067.

Section IV: Insufficient Data—Continued

I.51.023: 143.22m. Pit with no bones. Probably the shaft of I.51.067.

I.51.025: 143.05m. Disarticulated bones of a juvenile (10-12 years) and of an infant. Disturbed in the digging of Grave I.51.024.

I.51.057: 142.87m. Legs only. Rest in W balk.

I.51.063: 143.00m. Partial skeleton of female about 35 years. Skull cut off by I.51.067. Legs in N balk.

I.51.121: Disarticulated bones. Skeleton disturbed by I.51.106.

I.51.125: 142.50m. Mostly in W balk.

I.51.126: 143.09m. Mostly in W balk. Probably a child or infant burial.

I.51.128: 143.10m. Mostly in N balk.

I.51.129: 142.93m. Mostly in N balk.

I.51.132: 143.19m. Over I.51.057. A capped and lined burial. Skeleton entirely in W balk.

VI.P-1a.003: Capped but not lined. Pelvis and legs only in excavated area. Legs extended. Over VI.P-1a.006.

APPENDIX 3

Index of Artifacts

Graves containing artifacts are listed in column one serially by field, area, and locus number. The second column gives the type to which the grave belongs and allows the reader to refer to Appendix 2: Typological Catalogue for additional information concerning the burial; "i.d." indicates that insufficient data were preserved for accurate typing of the grave. Column three gives the objects registry numbers assigned to the artifacts in the expedition's files. Each number is followed by the year in which the grave was excavated. This practice is necessary because objects were not numbered sequentially from season to season until 1973. Consequently, for the seasons covered by this report the objects registry numbers duplicate one another. Column four gives a brief identification of the object. Column five indicates the page or pages in the text where the object itself, or an artifact of a similar type, is discussed. Column six provides the number of the text figure on which the object is illustrated. If the figure number is preceded by "cf.," the illustration is not of the object itself but of a similar artifact. The abbreviation NR, used only twice, indicates that the object was reported on a locus sheet but was not registered.

Field Data	Burial Type	Nos.	Ob. Reg. Identification	Page(s)	Illustration(s)
I.1.016	I.K.0.0	2 (1970)	Glass fragment	108	None
I.1.111	I.L.1.f	431 (1971)	Fragments of iron bracelet	104	cf. Pl. 81b
		438 (1971)	Bronze pin	104	None
		445 (1971)	Fragments of iron bracelet	104	cf. Pl. 81b
I.2.006	I.C.0.0	37 (1970)	18 Form 4 glass beads	95-96	cf. Pl. 61a
			1 Form 5 faience bead	96	cf. Pl. 62a
			1 Form 11 glass bead	98	cf. Pl. 64a
			1 Form 13 glass bead	99	cf. Pl. 65b, no. 4
I.2.008	I.L.0.g	40 (1970)	Limestone flakes	109	None
I.2.020	II.K.0.g	42 (1970)	Iron bracelet	104	cf. Pl. 81b
			Fragments of iron bracelet	104	cf. Pl. 81b
I.3.018	I.C.0.0	NR	Copper/bronze bracelet		
			Several glass beads		
I.3.043	II.L.0.0	64 (1970)	Fragments of iron bracelets	104	cf. Pl. 81b
		65 (1970)	Fragments of iron bracelets	104	cf. Pl. 81b
			Fragments of glass bracelets	102-3	cf. Pl. 76a, no. 2
I.3.097	I.C.2.0	89 (1971)	5 Form 4 glass beads	95-96	cf. Pl. 61c, nos. 1-3

Field Data	Burial Type	Nos.	Ob. Reg. Identification	Page(s)	Illustration(s)
I.4.007	II.L.2.f	262 (1971)	Bronze finger ring	101	cf. Pl. 71b
		273 (1971)	Forms 5 and 10 glass beads	96-98	Pl. 63b
		282 (1971)	Bronze fragment (harness?)	109	None
		291 (1971)	Bronze fragment (harness?)	109	None
		420 (1971)	Combined with 273 (1971)	96-98	Pl. 63b
I.4.020	II.K.2.f	390 (1971)	Ceramic loom weight	109	None
		401 (1971)	Iron finger ring	101	cf. Pl. 71a
		418 (1971)	Stone capper of grave	38	None
		444 (1971)	Fragments of iron bracelets	104	cf. Pl. 81b
		457 (1971)	Fragments of iron bracelets	104	cf. Pl. 81b
		473 (1971)	Fragments of iron bracelets	104	cf. Pl. 81b
		NR	6 side-spouted ceramic jars	106-7	Pls. 82, 83
I.11.004/.096	I.K.0.0	88 (1971)	3 Form 10 glass beads	97-98	cf. Pl. 64a, no. 3
I.11.022	II.L.0.g	43A (1970)	Bone ring	101	Pl. 71c, no. 1
		43B (1970)	Bone ring	101	Pl. 71c, no. 2
		43C (1970)	Bronze bell with cloth	101, 105-6	Pl. 69d
		43D (1970)	Forms 1, 5, 10, 12, and 14 glass beads and 3 shell beads	96-100	Pl. 67a
I.11.023	Secondary	46 (1970)	1 Form 10 glass bead	97-98	cf. Pl. 63b, no. 4
I.11.024	II.M.0.g	44 (1970)	1 Form 14 carnelian bead	99	None
I.11.026A	I.L.0.g	45A (1970)	Bronze finger ring	101-2	Pl. 72b, no. 1
		45B (1970)	Bronze finger ring	101-2	Pl. 72b, no. 2
I.11.029	I.C.0.0	47 (1970)	Chert blade	109	None
I.11.045	II.K.0.g	87 (1970)	Chert blade	109	None
I.12.018A	I.C.8.f	294 (1971)	Chert blade	109	None
		423 (1971)	29 Form 9 glass beads	97	cf. Pl. 63b
		424 (1971)	Combined with 423 (1971)	97	cf. Pl. 63b
I.12.019B	I.K.8.f	352 (1971)	Chert blade	109	None
I.12.033	I.C.8.g	9 (1973)	1 silver Form 13 bead	99	Pl. 65a
I.12.054	II.K.4.f	76 (1973)	Silver-plated bronze ring	101	Pl. 71b
		88 (1973)	Forms 5, 7, 8, and 15 glass beads	96-97	Pl. 62a
		91 (1973)	Bronze bracelet with cloth	103, 105-6	Pl. 79b
		94 (1973)	Iron bracelet	104	Pl. 81c
		95 (1973)	Filaments of copper wire	108	None
		96 (1973)	Detached cloth fragments	105-6	Pl. 79b
I.12.059	I.O.0.f	79 (1973)	Combined with 93 (1973)	98	Pl. 62c
		93 (1973)	Forms 1, 7, 8, 10, 11, 14, and 16 glass beads and mother-of-pearl pendant	97-100	Pl. 62c
		98 (1973)	1 Form 11 bone bead, combined with 93 (1973)	98	Pl. 62c
I.12.127	II.C.2.a	293 (1975)	4 glass bracelets	102-3	Pl. 76a
I.21.009	Secondary	4 (1970)	2 Form 7 glass beads	96-97	cf. Pl. 62c, no. 11
I.21.013	II.M.0.0	13 (1970)	Bronze finger ring	101-2	Pl. 73a
I.21.015	II.M.0.0	8 (1970)	Silver-plated coin	101	Pl. 69a
			Double-bored "button"	100	cf. Pl. 68a, no. 2

Field Data	Burial Type	Nos.	Ob. Reg. Identification	Page(s)	Illustration(s)
I.21.017A	I.F.0.1	11A (1970)	Bronze bracelet with bones and cloth	103-6	Pl. 80a
		11B (1970)	Fragments of iron ring	101	cf. Pl. 71a
		11C (1970)	2 bronze discs	105	Pl. 80a
		14A (1970)	7 bronze discs	105	Pl. 80a
		14B (1970)	Detached cloth	105-6	None
I.21.026A	III.C.0.0	71 (1970)	Glass bracelet	103	Pl. 76c
I.21.034	i.d.	16 (1970)	1 Form 16 glass bead	99-100	cf. Pl. 64a, no. 6
I.21.072B	I.L.4.g	95 (1970)	1 marine shell bead	100	None
			1 Form 7 bead	96-97	cf. Pl. 62a, no. 6
			Fragments of Form 14 beads	99	cf. Pl. 65b, no. 4
		100 (1970)	Bronze ring	101	cf. Pl. 71
			Bored stone disc	None	None
I.22.015	III.L.8.f	275 (1971)	Fragments of iron bracelets	104	cf. Pl. 81b
		276 (1971)	Combined with 422 (1971)	see 422 (1971)	Pl. 66b
		278 (1971)	Combined with 422 (1971)	see 422 (1971)	Pl. 66b
		325 (1971)	Fragments of iron bracelets	104	cf. Pl. 81b
		328 (1971)	Combined with 422 (1971)	see 422 (1971)	Pl. 66b
		421 (1971)	Iron bracelet	104	cf. Pl. 81c
		422 (1971)	Forms 1, 7, 8, 13, 14, and 16 glass beads	94, 96, 99-100	Pl. 66b
		629 (1971)	Bone fragment	109	None
I.22.034	I.L.2.g	349 (1971)	Bronze needle or pin	104	None
I.22.060	II.C.4.f	15 (1973)	1 Form 5 bead	96	Pl. 68a, no. 1
			1 double-bored "button"	100	Pl. 68a, no. 2
		16 (1973)	Single-bored bronze coin	100	Pl. 69b
I.22.065A and B	II.C.4.f	89 (1973)	1 Form 10 glass bead	97-98	cf. Pl. 63b, no. 9
I.22.079	III.L.8.f	63 (1973)	Bronze toe ring	102	Pl. 74c
		64 (1973)	Bronze earring with cloth and 3 Form 7 beads	96-97, 102, 105-6	Pls. 62d, 75a
		67 (1973)	Iron bracelet	104	cf. Pl. 81b
I.22.119	I.F.2.f	236 (1973)	Glass bracelet	103	Pl. 77b
		237 (1973)	Iron ring	101	Pl. 71a
		240 (1973)	8 Form 4 glass beads	95-96	cf. Pl. 61b
		245 (1973)	Fragments of iron bracelets	104	cf. Pl. 80a
		258 (1973)	Fragments of iron bracelets	104	cf. Pl. 81b
I.22.126	II.L.2.f	273 (1973)	1 Form 16 bead	99-100	cf. Pl. 66b, no. 18
I.22.207	II.L.4.h	451 (1973)	Collection of jewelry	91-92	Pl. 58
I.31.026	II.L.0.0	10 (1970)	Iron bracelet fragments	104	cf. Pl. 81b
I.31.049	i.d.	21 (1970)	Glass bracelet	103	cf. Pl. 77a
I.31.051/.053	Burial pit	55 (1970)	Bronze ring	101	cf. Pl. 72b, no. 1
		118 (1970)	Chert blade	109	None
I.31.052	I.C.0.0	27 (1970)	Iron bracelet fragments	104	cf. Pl. 81b
		28 (1970)	Iron bracelet fragments	104	cf. Pl. 81b
		30 (1970)	1 Form 5 glass bead	96	cf. Pl. 63b, no. 6
			1 Form 6 glass bead	96	cf. Pl. 62b, no. 3
			2 Form 8 glass beads	96-97	cf. Pl. 61a
			1 Form 16 carnelian bead	99-100	cf. Pl. 62c, no. 5

Field Data	Burial Type	Nos.	Ob. Reg. Identification	Page(s)	Illustration(s)
I.31.136	I.L.2.0	345 (1971)	Iron bracelet fragments	104	cf. Pl. 81b
I.31.176	II.K.4.f	433 (1971)	Dentalium bead	98	cf. Pl. 67b, nos. 3, 5, 8, 10
		434 (1971)	Glass bracelet fragments	103	cf. Pl. 77a, b
		435 (1971)	Glass bracelet	103	cf. Pl. 77a, b
		436 (1971)	Glass bracelet	103	cf. Pl. 77a, b
		474 (1971)	Glass bracelet fragments	103	cf. Pl. 77a, b
		484 (1971)	Glass bracelet fragments	103	cf. Pl. 77a, b
		487 (1971)	54 Form 4 glass beads	95-96	cf. Pl. 61a, b
		491 (1971)	Glass bracelet fragments	103	cf. Pl. 77a, b
		495 (1971)	2 Form 9 glass beads	97	cf. Pl. 63b
		617 (1971)	1 Form 9 glass bead	97	cf. Pl. 63b
I.32.009	I.C.2.g	33 (1971)	Wood splinter	None	None
I.32.018(?)	II.M.8.0	204 (1973)	Forms 4, 7, 9, and 10 and 4 shell beads	95-98, 100	Pl. 67b
I.32.019A .019B	II.C.8.f II.C.4.f	632 (1971)	1 Form 3 bone bead	95	cf. Pl. 59b, nos. 2, 5
I.32.024A .024B	II.L.2.h II.K.8.g	292 (1971) 481 (1971)	Chert blade Stone grave capper	109 None	None None
I.32.032A .032B	II.C.3.j II.C.2.0	327 (1971) 397 (1971) 428 (1971)	1 Form 4 glass bead 2 Form 12 glass beads 1 Form 11 dentalium bead	95-96 98-99 98-99	cf. Pl. 60b cf. Pl. 67a, no. 2 cf. Pl. 67b, nos. 2, 5, 8, 10
			1 Form 4 glass bead	95-96	cf. Pl. 60b
I.32.037	III.K.6.f	459 (1971) 485 (1971) 493 (1971)	Iron bracelet fragment Iron bracelet fragment Iron bracelet fragment	104 104 104	cf. Pl. 81b cf. Pl. 81b cf. Pl. 81b
I.32.038	III.L.4.h	475 (1971)	Iron bracelet fragments	104	cf. Pl. 81b
I.32.039	III.K.6.0	468 (1971) 502 (1971)	Glass fragment Black pebble	108 109	None None
I.32.046	II.L.7.g	36 (1973) 38 (1973)	Forms 1, 5, 7, 8, 10, 14, and 15 glass beads and mother-of-pearl pendant Bronze and iron ring, fused together	94-100 101-2	Pl. 66a Pl. 72c
I.32.048	III.L.2.0	37 (1973) 40 (1973)	Bronze bracelet Iron bracelet fragments	103-4 104	Pl. 80b cf. Pl. 81b
I.32.049	II.L.4.f	28 (1973) 47 (1973) 66 (1973)	Bronze bracelet with cloth 60 Form 9 bronze beads Iron bracelet fragments	103, 105-6 97 104	Pl. 79a Pl. 63a cf. Pl. 81b
I.32.056	II.L.2.g	48 (1973) 51 (1973) 54 (1973) 55 (1973)	Glass bracelet Iron bracelet fragments Bronze earring? Bronze bracelet fragments	103 104 102 103-4	Pl. 76b Pl. 81b Pl. 75c cf. Pls. 79, 80
I.32.070	II.F.2.f	116 (1973)	Glass fragment	108	None
I.32.094	IV.L.2.f	165 (1973) 176 (1973) 181 (1973)	16 Form 4 glass beads Iron bracelet Numerous Form 4, 5, 9, and 10 glass beads	95-96 104 96-98	Pl. 61b cf. Pl. 81b Pl. 61b
I.32.145	II.L.4.g	320 (1975)	Bronze ring with stone and setting	101-2	Pl. 73b, no. 3

Field Data	Burial Type	Nos.	Ob. Reg. Identification	Page(s)	Illustration(s)
I.41.012	IV.C.8.f	17 (1971)	Iron object	108-9	None
I.41.016	III.F.2.g	210 (1971)	Iron ring	101	Pl. 71a
I.41.019	V.C.0.0	322 (1971)	Glass bracelet fragments	102-3	cf. Pls. 76-78
I.41.035	II.C.8.f	263 (1971)	Form 2 carnelian bead	95	Pl. 60a
I.41.045	i.d.	338 (1971)	Form 5 glass bead	96	cf. Pl. 62a, no. 1
		340 (1971)	Bronze coin pendant	101	cf. Pl. 69b
I.41.048	i.d.	368 (1971)	Iron bracelet fragments	104	cf. Pl. 81b
I.41.050	I.F.4.f	367 (1971)	Form 7 glass bead	96-97	cf. Pl. 61a, no. 11
		376 (1971)	Bronze disc	105	cf. Pl. 80a
I.41.051	III.C.2.a	394 (1971)	Bronze pin with Form 10 bead	97-98, 104	Pl. 64b
		395 (1971)	2 Form 7 glass beads	96-97	cf. Pl. 61a, no. 11
			40 Form 4 glass beads	95-96	cf. Pl. 61a
		407 (1971)	Double-bored mother-of-pearl object	100	Pl. 68c
		449 (1971)	4 Form 4 glass beads	95-96	cf. Pl. 61a
I.41.056	III.F.2.f	500 (1971)	Forms 2, 4, 5, 6, 7, 9, and 12 glass beads	95-99	Pl. 60b
I.41.057	IV.C.4.0	497 (1971)	Glass bracelet fragments	102-3	cf. Pls. 76-78
I.41.058	III.G.2.0	570 (1971)	3 bronze finger rings	101-2	Pl. 72a
		573 (1971)	Bronze bracelet fragments	103-4	cf. Pls. 79, 80
I.41.063(?)	IV.L.8.0	2 (1973)	Forms 7 and 13 glass beads	96-97, 99	Pl. 65b
I.41.064	I.C.2.e	7 (1973)	Bronze toe ring?	102	Pl. 74b
I.41.065	IV.C.2.0	6 (1973)	Glass bracelet	103	Pl. 77a
I.41.076	I.F.2.f	23 (1973)	Bronze bell pendant	101	Pl. 69c
		24 (1973)	Glass bracelet fragments	102-3	cf. Pls. 76-78
		25 (1973)	Forms 7, 10, 11, 14, and 16 glass beads	96-100	Pl. 64a
		26 (1973)	Iron bracelet	104	cf. Pl. 81b
I.41.085A	I.L.2.f	127 (1973)	3 Form 7 glass beads	96-97	Pl. 59b
			2 bone beads	95	Pl. 59b
		207 (1973)	2 Form 4 glass beads	95-96	cf. Pl. 61a
I.41.105	i.d.	82 (1973)	Iron bracelet fragments	104	cf. Pl. 81b
I.41.106	II.L.2.f	87 (1973)	Iron bracelet fragments	104	cf. Pl. 81b
		117 (1973)	Bronze ring	101	cf. Pl. 71b
			Iron fragments	108-9	None
I.41.115	II.C.4.f	121 (1973)	37 Form 4, 7, and 9 beads	95-97	Pl. 61a
I.41.120	I.M.2.0	123 (1973)	Iron ring fragments	101	cf. Pl. 71a
I.41.212	I.C.6.0	253 (1973)	Form 6 beads	96	Pl. 62b
I.41.213	I.C.4.f	256 (1973)	Iron nail or pin	108-9	None
I.41.217B	II.M.0.0	271 (1973)	1 Form 4 glass bead	95-96	cf. Pl. 61a
		272 (1973)	Iron object	108-9	None
I.51.013	I.C.2.e	72 (1973)	Ceramic juglet	108	Pls. 86-88
		106 (1973)	Glass bracelet fragments	102-3	cf. Pls. 76-78

Field Data	Burial Type	Nos.	Ob. Reg. Identification	Page(s)	Illustration(s)
		108 (1973)	Forms 4, 5, 7, and 9 glass beads	95-97	Pl. 61c
		111 (1973)	Bronze coin, bored	101	cf. Pl. 69b
I.51.016	II.C.8.f	142 (1973)	Iron ring fragment	101	cf. Pl. 71a
		198 (1973)	Iron ring fragment	101	cf. Pl. 71a
I.51.028	I.C.8.h	78 (1973)	Double-bored bronze disc	100	Pl. 68b
		80 (1973)	Iron bracelet	104	Pl. 81a
I.51.050	I.C.8.g	168 (1973)	Iron finger ring	101	cf. Pl. 71a
		199 (1973)	Cowrie shell	100	cf. Pl. 67a, nos. 8, 9
I.51.067	II.K.4.g	159 (1973)	Form 14 glass beads	99	Pl. 65c
		160 (1973)	Studded leather band	104	None
		163 (1973)	Combined with 159 (1973)	99	Pl. 65c
I.51.133	II.K.1.g	316 (1975)	Form 4 glass beads	95-96	cf. Pl. 60b, nos. 2-10
I.51.134	I.M.1.b	295 (1975)	Unbored bronze disc	101	Pl. 70
I.51.135	I.M.0.0	297 (1975)	Iron toe ring?	102	Pl. 74a
I.51.136B	I.L.2.g	304 (1975)	Combined with 310 (1975)	94-100	Pl. 59a
		305 (1975)	Combined with 310 (1975)	94-100	Pl. 59a
		310 (1975)	Forms 1, 7, 10, 13, 14, and 16 beads and mother-of-pearl pendant	94-100	Pl. 59a
V.P-1e.005	II.K.0.g	338 (1975)	Handle of glass vessel	108	Pl. 89
VI.P-1a.001	I.C.0.0	384 (1975)	Side-spouted ceramic jug	107-8	Pls. 85, 88b
		388 (1975)	4 Form 5 glass beads	96	cf. Pl. 63b, nos. 5, 6

Bibliography

Abel, F. M.
1933 *Géographie de la Palestine*. Vol. 1. Paris: J. Gabalda.
1938 *Géographie de la Palestine*. Vol. 3. Paris: J. Gabalda.

Amiran, R., and Eitan, A.
1965 "Tel Nagila." *Archaeology* 18: 113-23.

Ashkenazi, T.
1938 *Tribus semi-nomades de la Palestine du Nord*. Études d'ethnographie, de sociologie et d'ethnologie, vol. 2. Paris: Librarie orientaliste Paul Geuthner.

Bennett, W. J., Jr., and Blakely, J. A.
Forthcoming *Tell el Hesi: The Persian Period Remains*. Edited by K. G. O'Connell, S.J. Excavation Reports of the American Schools of Oriental Research: Tell el-Hesi, vol. 3. In preparation.

Berslovsky, A.
1950 *Hayada'at et haAretz*. Vol. 2: *haNegev*. Israel: haKibbutz haMivch.

Bliss, F. J.
1891a "Report on Excavations at Tell el-Hesy during the Spring of 1891." *The Palestine Exploration Fund Quarterly Statement for 1891*, pp. 282-90.
1891b "Excavating from Its Picturesque Side." *The Palestine Exploration Fund Quarterly Statement for 1891*, pp. 291-98.
1894 *A Mound of Many Cities*. London: The Committee of the Palestine Exploration Fund.

Canaan, T.
1924 "Mohammedan Saints and Sanctuaries in Palestine." *Journal of the Palestine Oriental Society* 4: 1-84.

Conder, C. R., and Kitchener, H. H.
1883 *The Survey of Western Palestine III*. London: The Palestine Exploration Fund.

Coogan, M. D.
1975 "The Cemetery from the Persian Period at Tell el-Hesi." *Bulletin of the American Schools of Oriental Research* 220: 37-46. Numbers 220-21 of the *Bulletin* have also appeared as *Essays in Honor of George Ernest Wright*, edited by E. F. Campbell, Jr. and R. G. Boling (Missoula: Scholars Press for the American Schools of Oriental Research.)

Dahlberg, B. T., and O'Connell, K. G., S.J., eds.
Forthcoming *Tell el-Hesi: The Site and the Expedition*. Excavation Reports of the American Schools of Oriental Research: Tell el-Hesi, vol. 4. Winston-Salem: Wake Forest University.

Delury, G. E., ed.
1973 *The World Almanac and Book of Facts*. New York: Newspaper Enterprise Association.

Dever, W. G.; Lance, H. D.; and Wright, G. E.
1970 *Gezer I*. Annual of the Hebrew Union College Biblical and Archaeological School in Jerusalem. Jerusalem: Keter Publishing Company.

Dickson, H. R. P.
1951 *The Arab of the Desert*. 2nd ed. London: Allen & Unwin.

Granqvist, H.
1965 *Muslim Death and Burial*. Helsingfors: Finska vetenskapssocieten.

Guérin, H. V.
1888 *Description géographique, historique, et archaeologique du Palestine*. Vol. 2. Paris: Challamel Aîné.

Hilleson, S.
1938 "Notes on the Bedouin Tribes of Beersheva District, III." *Palestine Exploration Quarterly for 1938*, pp. 117-26.

[Information Canada]
1975 *Canada Yearbook*. Ottawa: Information Canada.

Jaussen, J.-A.
1908 *Coutumes des Arabes au pays de Moab*. Paris: Adrien-Maissoneuve.
1927 *Coutumes Palestiniennes: Naplous et son district*. Paris: Librairie orientaliste Paul Geuthner.

Koucky, F. L.
Forthcoming "The Present and Past Physical Environment of Tell el-Hesi." In *Tell el-Hesi: The Site and the Expedition*, edited by B. T. Dahlberg and K. G. O'Connell, S.J. Excavation Reports of the American Schools of Oriental Research: Tell el-Hesi, vol. 4. Winston-Salem: Wake Forest University.

Kurzman, D.
1970 *Genesis, 1949*. New York: The New American Library.

Lane, E. W.
1860 *An Account of the Manners and Customs of the Modern Egyptians*. New York: Dover Publications.

Lorch, N.
1961 *The Edge of the Sword: Israel's War of Independence, 1947-1949*. Jerusalem: Massada Press.

O'Connell, K. G., S.J.; Rose, D. G.; and Toombs, L. E.
1978 "Tell el-Hesi, 1977." *Palestine Exploration Quarterly* 110: 75-90 and Pls. V-IX.

Ohata, K.
1966 *Tel Zeror I: Preliminary Report of the Excavation. First Season, 1964*. Tokyo: Chiyodaku Press.
1967 *Tel Zeror II: Preliminary Report of the Excavation. Second Season, 1965*. Tokyo: Chiyodaku Press.

Petrie, W. M. F.
1891 *Tell el Hesy (Lachish)*. London: Palestine Exploration Fund.

Plenderleith, H. J., and Warner, A. E. A.
1971 *The Conservation of Antiquities and Works of Art*. London: Oxford University Press.

Robinson, E., and Smith, E.
1856   *Biblical Researches in Palestine: Travels in 1838*. Vol. 2. Boston: Crocker and Brewster.

Rosen, T.
Unpublished MS   "The Hesi *abārīq*."

Snedecor, G. W., and Cochran, W. G.
1967   *Statistical Methods*. 6th ed. Ames, Iowa: Iowa State University Press.

Stern, E.
1978   *Excavations at Tel Mevorakh (1973-1976). Part One: From the Iron Age to the Roman Period*. QEDEM: Monographs of the Institute of Archaeology, The Hebrew University of Jerusalem, vol. 9. Jerusalem: 'Ahva' Press.

Survey of Palestine
1945   *1:20,000 Map Series*. London: 514 C. Field Company, R.E.

Toombs, L. E.
1978   "The Stratigraphy of Caesarea Maritima." In *Archaeology in the Levant: Essays for Kathleen Kenyon*, edited by R. Moorey and P. Parr. Warminster: Aris and Phillips.
Forthcoming   "The Stratigraphy of the Site at the End of Phase One." In *Tell el-Hesi: The Site and the Expedition*, edited by B. T. Dahlberg and K. G. O'Connell, S.J. Excavation Reports of the American Schools of Oriental Research: Tell el-Hesi, vol. 4. Winston-Salem: Wake Forest University.

Volney, M. C.-F.
1848   *Travels through Syria and Egypt*. London: G. G. J. and J. Robinson.

Yeivin, S.
1961   *First Preliminary Report of the Excavations at Tel "Gat" (Tell Sheykh 'Ahmed el 'Areyny): Seasons 1956-1958*. Jerusalem: Siloam Press.

Plates

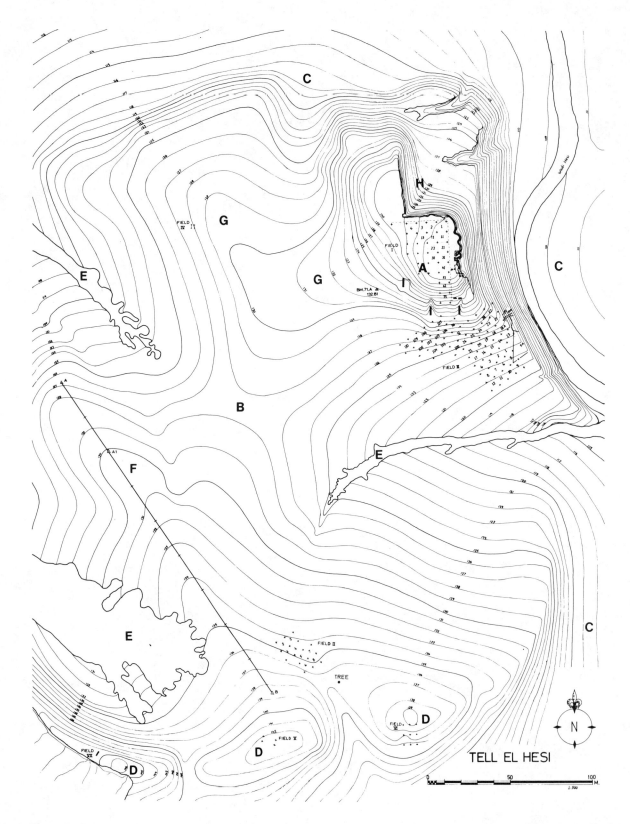

Pl. 1.   Contour map of the site, showing the location and numbering of the fields and areas, and the principal topographical features. Drawn by B. Zoughbi.

158

Pl. 2.   Looking southeast along the military trenching through Areas 21 and 31 of Field I. Photo by T. Rosen.

Pl. 3. Looking northwest along the military trenching through Areas 31, 21, 12, 3, and 4 of Field I. Photo by T. Rosen.

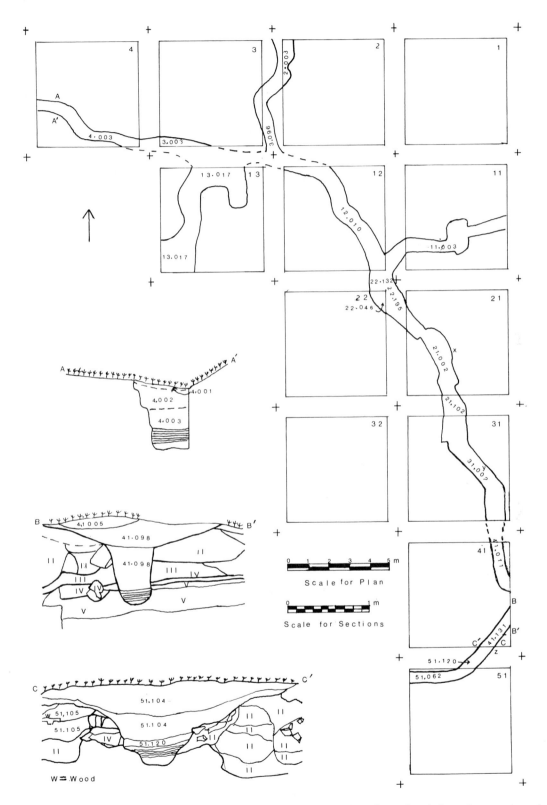

Pl. 4. Plan and sections of the military trenching in Field I. The Roman numerals on the sections indicate the stratum numbers of the layers cut by the trench. x indicates the position of a stone step; y the location of a large metal rectangle; and z the location of a pit which may have been an installation contemporary with the trenching. Drawn by L. E. Toombs from area supervisors' sketches.

161

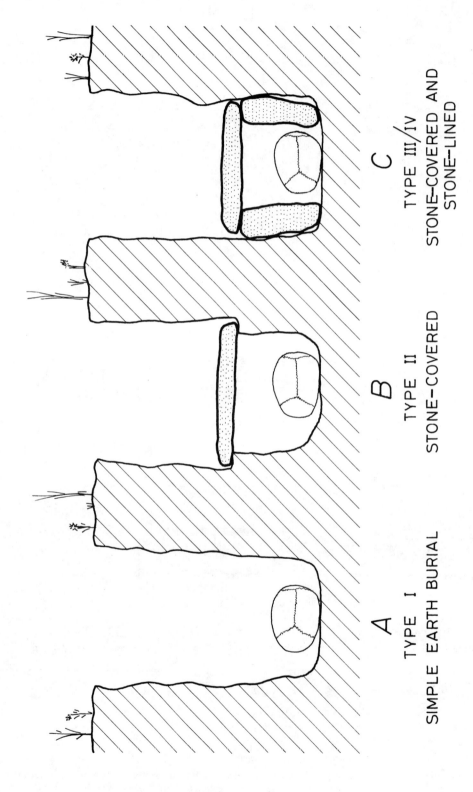

A
TYPE I
SIMPLE EARTH BURIAL

B
TYPE II
STONE-COVERED

C
TYPE III/IV
STONE-COVERED AND
STONE-LINED

Pl. 5. Types of burial chambers found in the Stratum II cemetery: A—simple earth burial (Type I); B—stone-covered but not stone-lined (Type II); C—stone-covered and stone-lined (Type III). In Type IV burials the grave is stone-lined, but the stone covering is absent. Drawn by B. Zoughbi from an original by P. K. H. Jenkins.

162

Pl. 6. Intersecting burials (1). The burial of an adult female in a simple earth grave (I.41.085A; Type I.L.2.f) has cut through an earlier grave (I.41.085B; Type i.d.), the remaining bones of which are seen at the bottom of the photograph. Photo by W. E. Nassau.

163

Pl. 7. Intersecting burials (2). The same area as shown in Pl. 6 after further clearing. The burial of a child (1.41.089; Type I.F.2.e) is seen to have been cut through the abdominal area of the skeleton illustrated in Pl. 6. Photo by W. E. Nassau.

164

Pl. 8. Burial I.21.005A, B, and C. The burial of two infants (Types III.C.8.g and III.C.8.e) and a child (Type III.F.0.0) in a common grave from which the capstones have been removed. Photo by T. Rosen.

165

Pl. 9.   Burial I.22.065A and B (both Type II.C.4.f). Two infants buried in a common grave with the head of the younger resting on the arm of the elder.   Photo by W. E. Nassau.

166

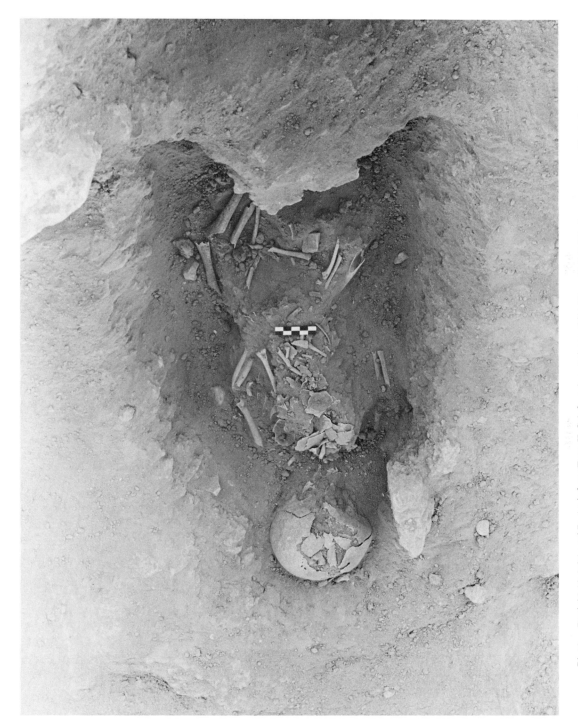

Pl. 10. Burial I.32.012A and B. An infant (Type II.C.2.f) and a newborn child (Type II.C.2.f) in the same grave. The baby rests on the abdomen of the older infant. Only a few bones of the baby survived at the time the photograph was taken. Photo by T. Rosen.

Pl. 11.   Burial I.12.019A. The burial of an adult female (Type IV.L.2.f) in a grave which has a stone lining only on the south side. The burial of an adult male (I.12.019B; Type I.K.8.f), closely associated with this burial, appeared immediately to the north and at a slightly lower level soon after the photograph was taken. Photo by T. Rosen.

168

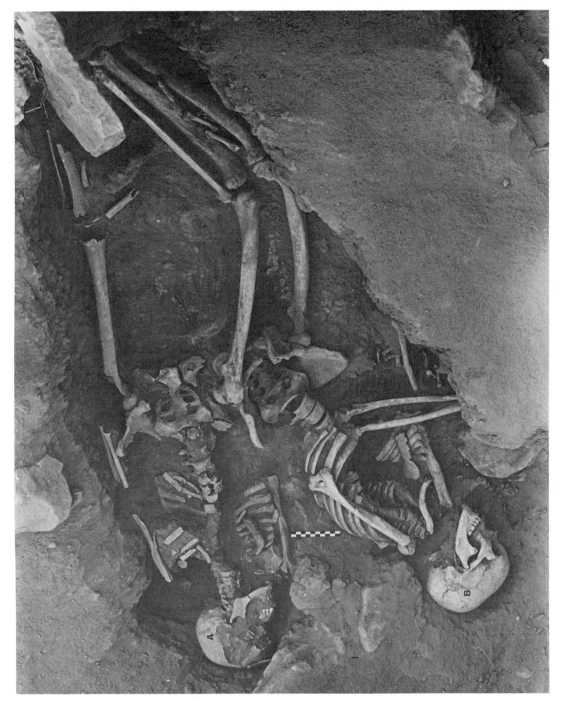

Pl. 12.   Burial I.32.024A and B. The bodies of an adult female (A—Type II.L.2.h) and an adult male (B—Type II.K.8.g) in virtually the same grave. The common set of cappers which covered both bodies has been removed. Photo by T. Rosen.

169

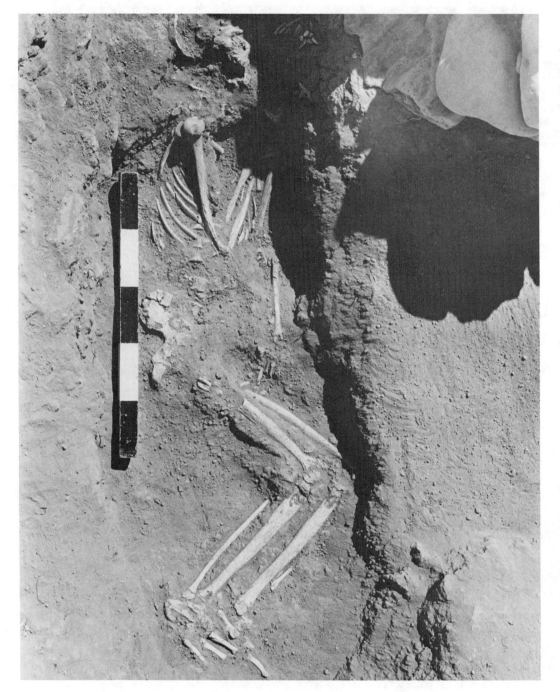

Pl. 13.   Burial I.32.046 (Type II.L.7.g). The body of a young woman found immediately below the capstones shown in Pl. 15 and immediately above the crushed, but still articulated, skeleton shown in Pl. 14. The burial is anomalous in that the head is in the east end of the grave. In order to direct the eyes toward Mecca the body was placed on the *left* side. Photo by W. E. Nassau.

170

Pl. 14. Burial I.32.056 (Type II.L.2.g). The skeleton of a young woman immediately below and crushed by the burial illustrated in Pl. 13. The capstones shown in Pl. 15 covered both burials. Photo by W. E. Nassau.

Pl. 15.   The capstones covering Graves I.32.046 and I.32.056 (see Pls. 13 and 14). Photo by W. E. Nassau.

Pl. 16. Burials I.41.081, .105, and .106. Burials I.41.081 (Type II.K.2.0) and I.41.106 (Type II.L.2.f) shared the same capstones. These burials partially destroyed an earlier grave containing Skeleton I.41.105 (Type i.d.). Photo by W. E. Nassau.

Pl. 17. The grave in which Burials I.41.217A and B were found, shown in relation to the west balk of Area 41. The cappers (A) rest on a ridge of earth (B), left to support them. Below (C) is the ridge of earth which supported the cappers when they were in use with the earlier burial. Photo by W. E. Nassau.

174

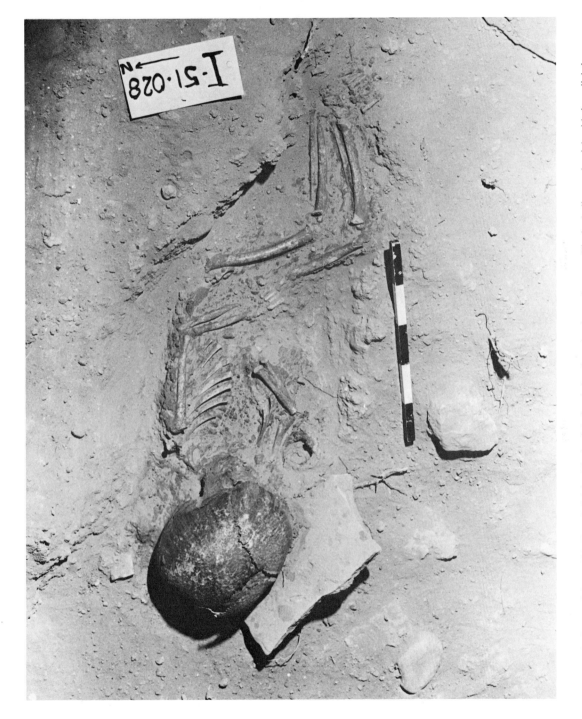

Pl. 18. Burial I.51.028 (Type I.C.8.h). The burial of an infant in a simple earth grave. The body lies on the right side in a slightly flexed position, with a stone pillow under the head. An iron ring lies near the right arm. Photo by W. E. Nassau.

175

Pl. 19.   Burial I.12.037 (Type I.K.4.g). A typical burial of an adult male in a simple earth grave. The only unusual feature is the manner in which the left arm is flexed across the lower chest. Photo by W. E. Nassau.

176

Pl. 20. Cross-section through Grave VI.P-Ia.005. The grave was found with the cappers and skeleton in place, but empty of earth. Photo by J. Whitred.

Pl. 21. Burial I.41.100 (Type III.L.2.g). Although the burial is typical of interments in the cemetery the grave has two unusual features. Most of the capstones have been robbed away, and the lining consists of two rows of small field stones, instead of the usual flat slabs or large stones. Photo by W. E. Nassau.

178

Pl. 22.   Burial I.32.048, the interment of an adult female in a capped and lined grave (Type III.L.2.0). The edges of the lining stones form a platform on which the capstones once rested. Photo by W. E. Nassau.

179

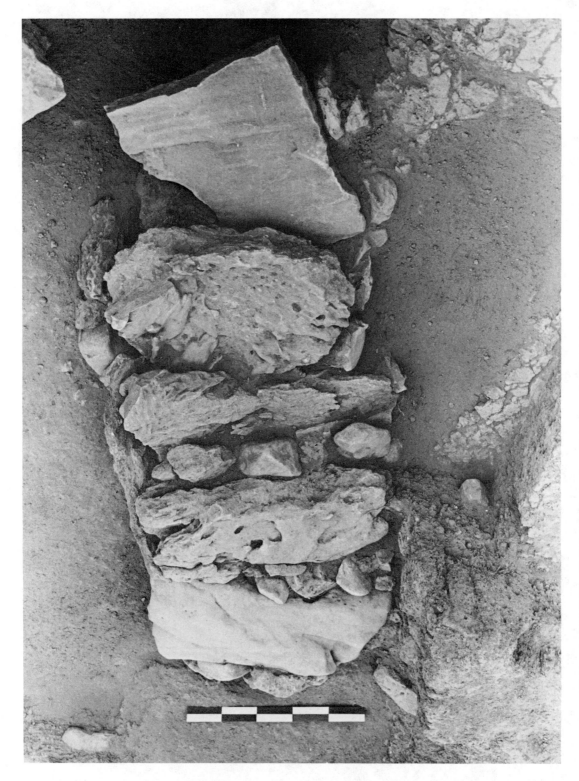

Pl. 23. Burial I.12.017 with the capstones in place. Note the corbel-like structure, and the careful chinking of the joints between the stones. Photo by T. Rosen.

180

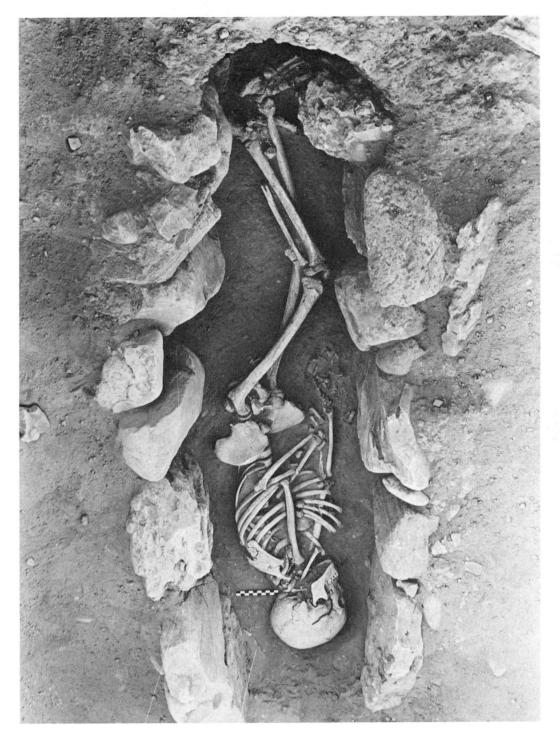

Pl. 24. Burial I.12.017 (Type III.L.8.f). The same burial as Pl. 23 with the capstones removed and the stone lining visible around the skeleton. The lining is absent at the head and foot of the grave. The skeleton is that of an adult female, buried in a typical position, flexed on the right side with the eyes directed to the southeast. Photo by T. Rosen.

Pl. 25. Burial I.32.094 (Type IV.L.2.f). A robbed Type IV grave in which the skeleton of an adult female lies among the remaining stones of the grave lining. The skeleton is extended on the back with the eyes directed to the southeast. Photo by W. E. Nassau.

Pl. 26. Burial I.41.019 (Type V.C.0.0), seen from the southeast. The burial jar contained the remains of an infant, probably newborn. Photo by T. Rosen.

Pl. 27.   Burial I.41.019 (Type V.C.0.0). The same burial as that shown in Pl. 26, viewed from the north. Photo by T. Rosen.

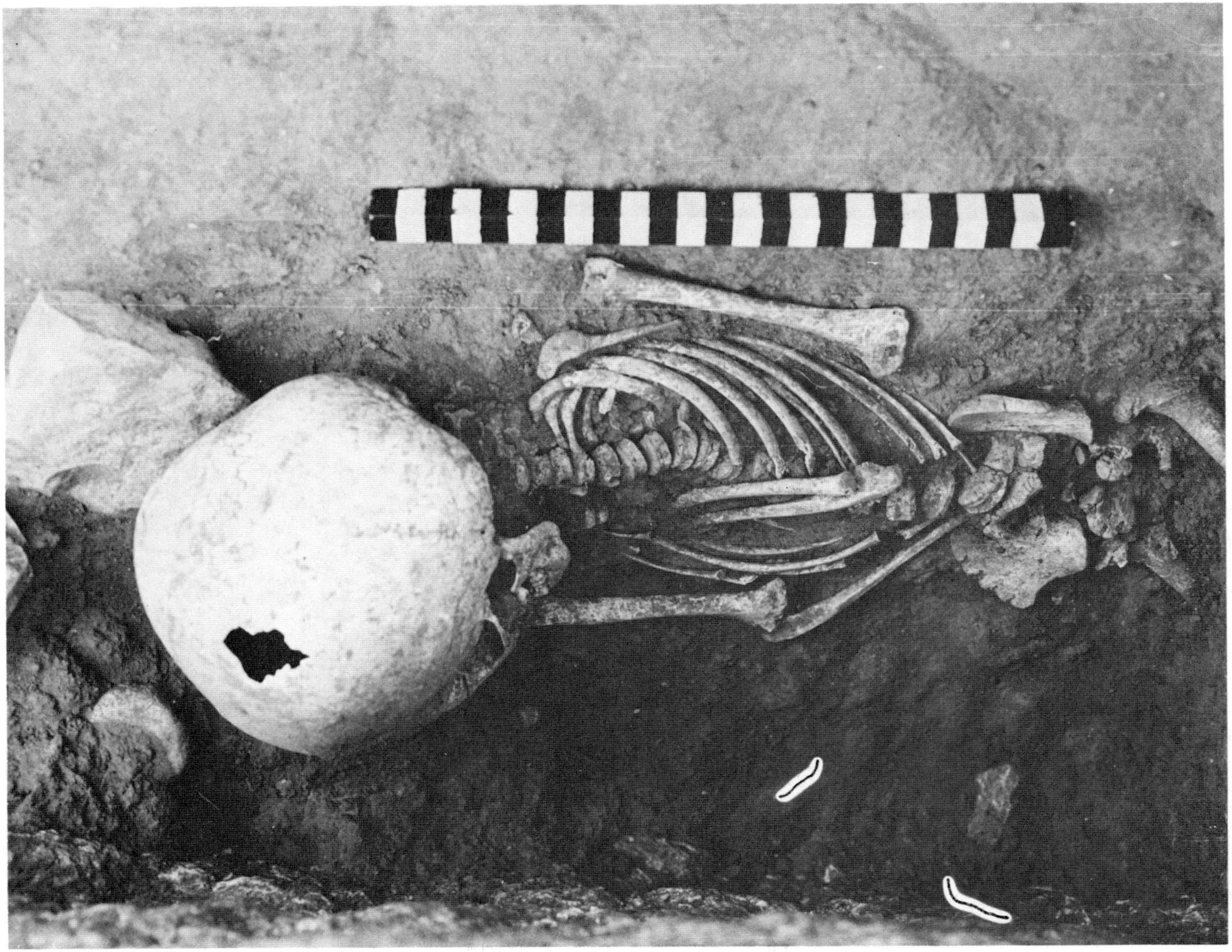

Pl. 28. Burial V.P-1a.006 (Type I.C.2.e). The body of an infant lies in a simple earth grave, extended on the back with the eyes directed to the east. The head rests on a stone pillow. Photo by J. Whitred.

Pl. 29. Burial I.32.039 (Type III.K.6.0). The burial is that of an adult male, slightly flexed on the back. The grave was broken into and many of the lining stones removed. The skull and shoulders were cut away. Photo by T. Rosen.

Pl. 30. Burial I.32.064 (Type II.F.2.f). A burial of a child in an originally capped grave, extended on the back looking to the southeast. The burial was disturbed, the cappers removed, and the skeleton broken by a later grave. Only the skull and upper torso were relatively intact, but enough of the rest of the body was recovered to allow the burial to be typed. Photo by W. E. Nassau.

Pl. 31.   Burial I.32.049 (Type II.L.4.f). The skeleton of an adult female in a capped grave, extended on the right side and looking to the southeast. Most of the skull was removed either by a later grave or by the military trenching. Photo by W. E. Nassau.

Pl. 32.   Burial I.51.024 (Type II.F.2.f). The burial of a child in a capped but unlined grave. The body is extended on the back, and the eyes look southeast. This burial cut off all but the legs and part of the pelvis of Burial I.51.039, seen at the right of the grave cist. Photo by W. E. Nassau.

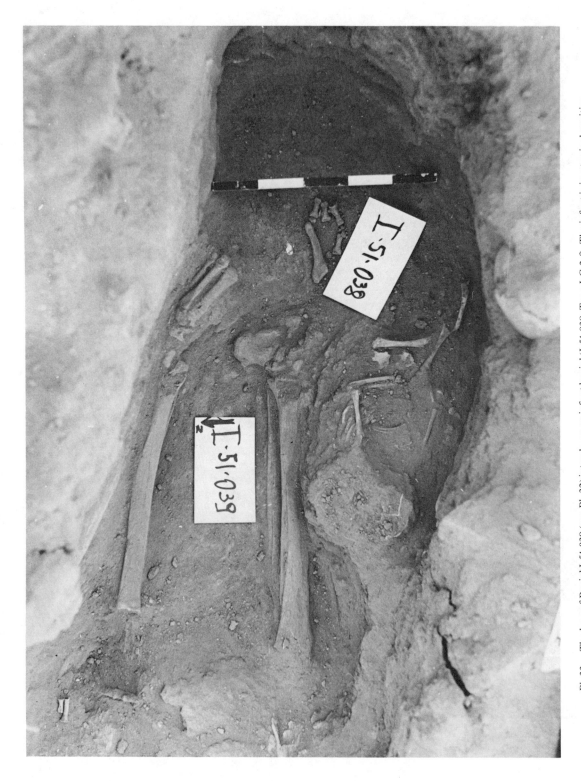

Pl. 33. The legs of Burial I.51.039 (see Pl. 32) intrude on an infant burial (I.51.038; Type I.C.2.f). The infant is in a typical position, extended on the back, looking southeast. Photo by W. E. Nassau.

Pl. 34. The burial of an adult female (A—I.32.038: Type III.L.4.h) extended on the right side, looking southwest, had the lower limbs removed by the burial of an infant (B—I.32.040: Type III.C.2.a), extended on the back and looking up. The cappers and liners of the adult burial had been reused to build the cist of the infant burial. Photo by T. Rosen.

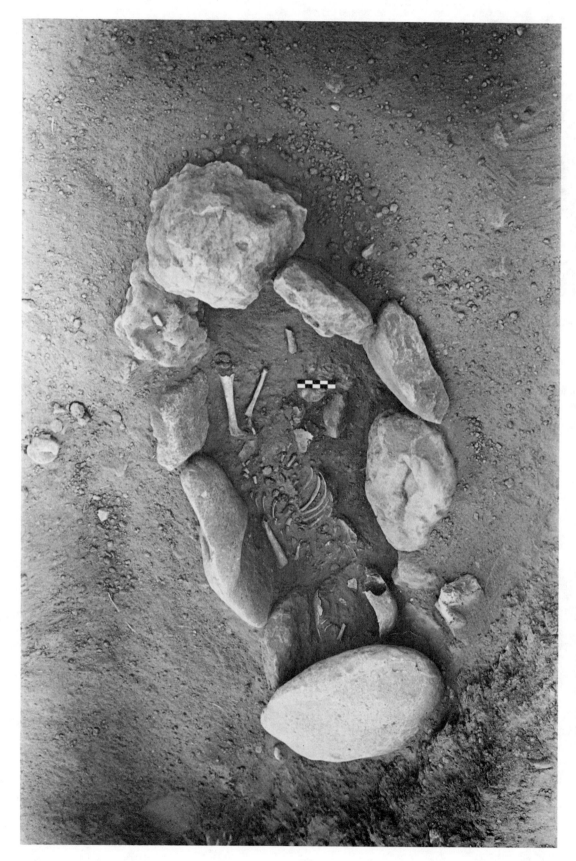

Pl. 35.   Burial 1.41.028 (Type III.C.2.f). The typical burial of an infant in a capped and lined grave. The body rests in the extended position on the back with the eyes directed to the southeast. Photo by T. Rosen.

Pl. 36. Burial V.P-1f.006 (Type I.C.4.g). The typical burial of an infant in the extended position on the right side with the eyes directed to the south. The simple earth grave is dug into the mud brick of an Early Bronze Age wall. The photograph illustrates the difficulty in determining leg position, since most infant burials show a slight flexation of the lower limbs. Photo by J. Whitred.

Pl. 37. Burial I.22.060 (Type II.C.4.f). The typical burial of an infant in the extended position on the right side with the eyes directed to the southeast. The skull has been crushed by the collapse of one of the capstones. The legs are slightly flexed. Photo by W. E. Nassau.

Pl. 38.   Burial I.I2.033 (Type I.C.8.g). The typical burial of an infant in the flexed position on the right side with the eyes directed to the south. The lower part of the skeleton was disturbed by a later grave. Photo by W. E. Nassau.

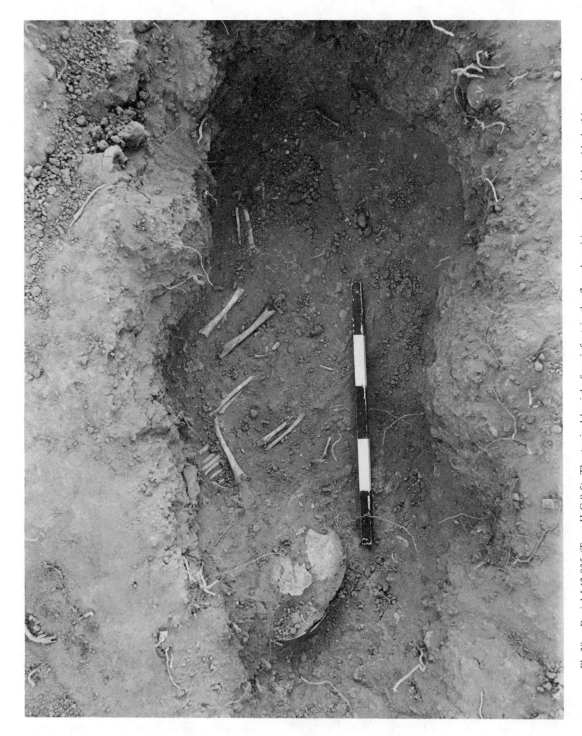

Pl. 39. Burial I.12.035 (Type II.C.8.f). The typical burial of an infant in the flexed position on the right side looking to the southeast. Photo by W. E. Nassau.

Pl. 40.   Burial V.P-Ip.004 (Type I.F.2.f). The typical burial of a child in the extended position on the back looking to the southeast. Note the slight inclination of the body to the right side and the slight flexation of the legs.   Photo by J. Whitred.

Pl. 41. Burial I.32.070 (Type II.F.2.f). The typical burial of a child in the extended position on the back looking to the southeast. The position is fully extended, except for a slight flexation of the right leg. Photo by W. E. Nassau.

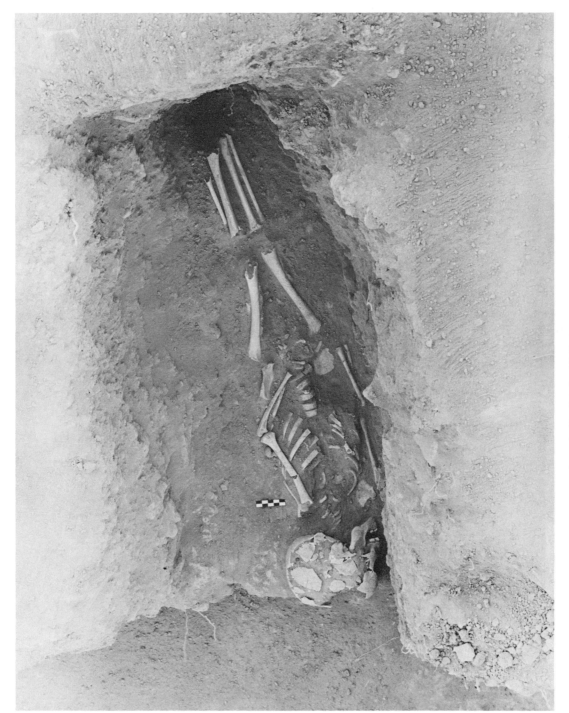

Pl. 42.   Burial I.22.038 (Type II.F.4.g). The typical burial of a child in the extended position on the right side with the eyes directed to the south. Photo by T. Rosen.

199

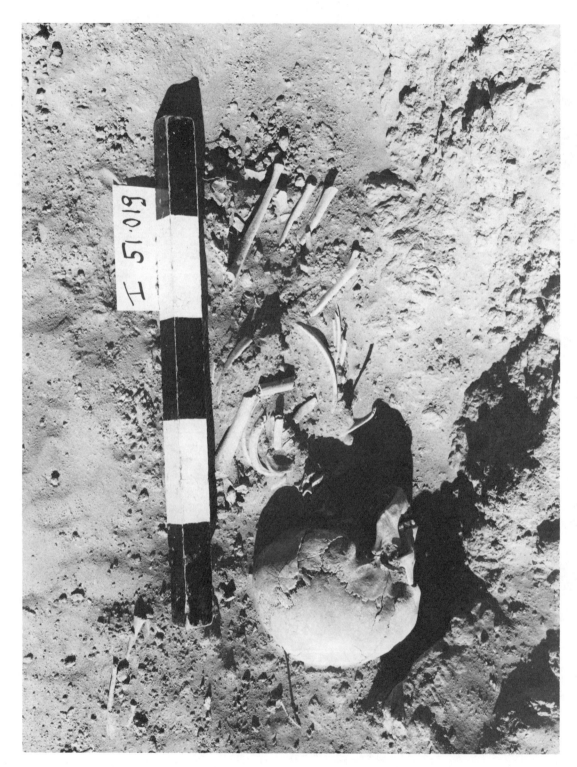

Pl. 43.   Burial I.51.019 (I.J.2.g). The typical burial of a juvenile in an extended position on the back looking to the south. The lower part of the burial was removed by the military trenching. Photo by W. E. Nassau.

Pl. 44. Burial I.4.020 (Type II.K.2.f). The typical burial of an adult male in the extended position on the back with the eyes directed to the southeast. The hands are on the pelvis. The legs are extended with the toes pointing up. Photo by T. Rosen.

Pl. 45. Burial I.12.054 (Type II.K.4.f). The typical burial of an adult male in the extended position on the right side with the eyes directed to the southeast. The right hand is in the pelvis. Photo by W. E. Nassau.

Pl. 46. Burial I.41.218 (Type II.L.4.h). The typical burial of an adult female in the extended position on the right side, looking southwest. Photo by J. Whitred.

Pl. 47. Burial I.12.021 (Type I.L.8.f). The typical burial of an adult female in the flexed position on the right side, looking southeast. The position of the legs is unusual. The grave is too short for the body, and the legs have been flexed in an extreme fashion in order to accommodate the body in the small cist. Photo by T. Rosen.

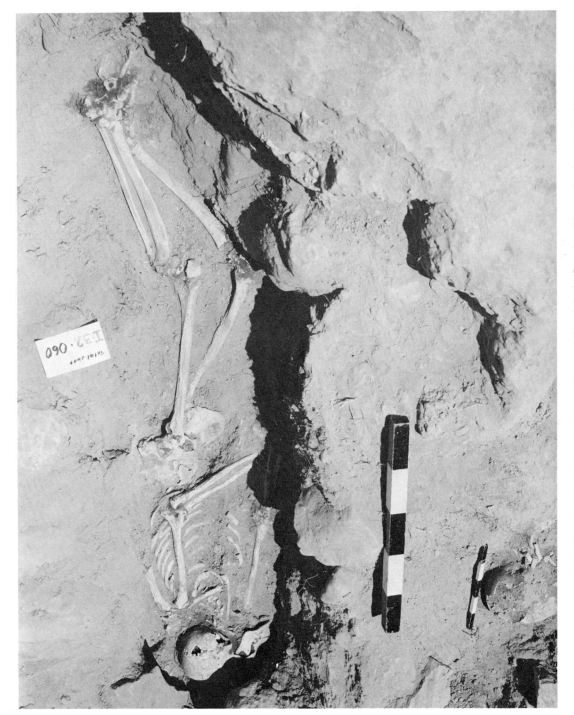

Pl. 48. Burial I.32.060 (Type II.L.8.g). The typical burial of an adult female in the flexed position on the right side, looking south. Photo by W. E. Nassau.

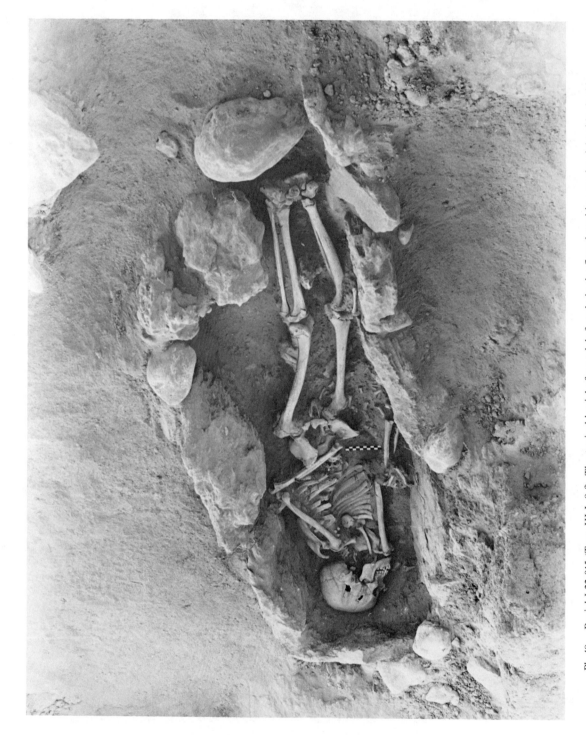

Pl. 49. Burial 1.22.015 (Type III.L.8.f). The typical burial of an adult female in the flexed position on the right side, looking southeast. Photo by T. Rosen.

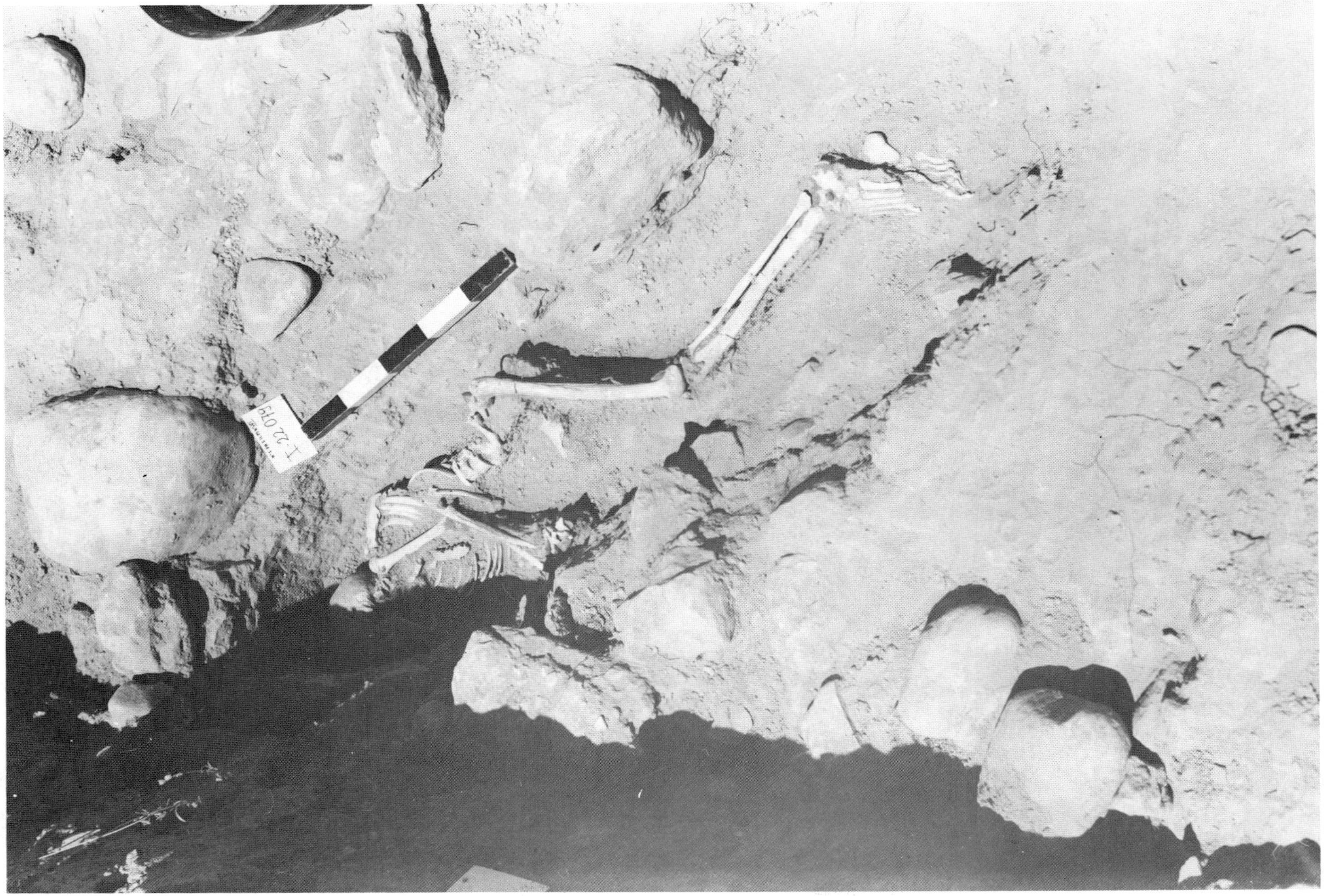

Pl. 50. Burial 1.22.079 (Type III.L.8.f). The typical burial of an adult female in the flexed position on the right side, looking southeast. The left arm lies across the chest. Photo by W. E. Nassau.

207

Pl. 51. Burial I.32.080 (Type II.K.1.h). An anomalous burial in which an adult male is interred on the front with the eyes directed to the southwest. The lower limbs are extended. Photo by W. E. Nassau.

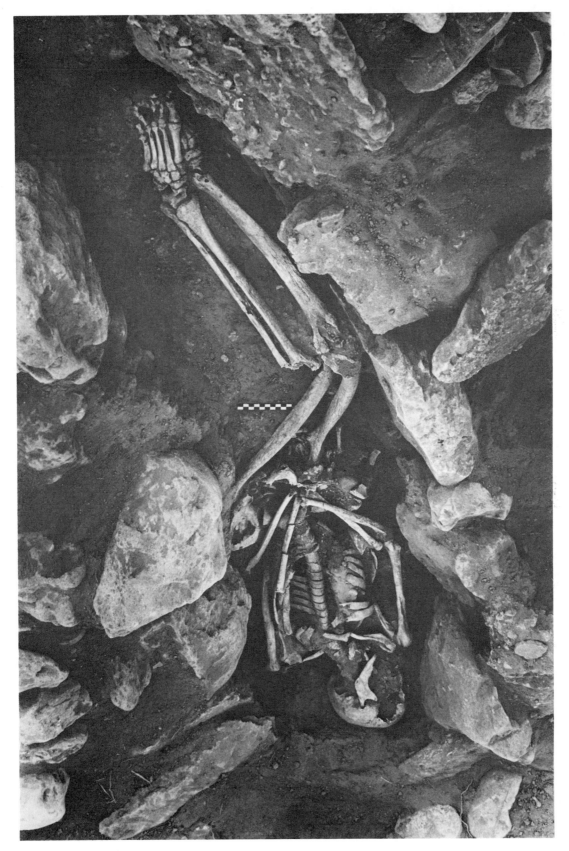

Pl. 52.   Burial I.32.037 (Type III.K.6.f). This burial of an adult male is anomalous in that, while the body is on the back, the legs are flexed. The eyes are oriented in a normal direction (southeast). Photo by T. Rosen.

Pl. 53.   Burial I.12.015 (Type II.C.2.a). The burial is anomalous in that the infant was buried on the back, but with the eyes directed upward. Photo by W. E. Nassau.

Pl. 54. Burial I.22.102 (Type III.K.2.c). An anomalous burial of an adult male extended on the back, but with the eyes directed to the north. Photo by W. E. Nassau.

211

Pl. 55.   Burial I.11.211 (Type I.L.7.c). In this burial of an adult female in a simple earth grave both body position and eye direction are anomalous. The skeleton is in the flexed position on the *left* side and the eyes are directed to the *north*. Photo by W. E. Nassau.

Pl. 56. Burial I.41.058 (Type III.G.2.0). The burial of a male juvenile in a capped and lined grave. The twisting of the torso, the striding position of the legs, and the strained posture of the arms suggest that the individual was buried alive. Photo by T. Rosen.

213

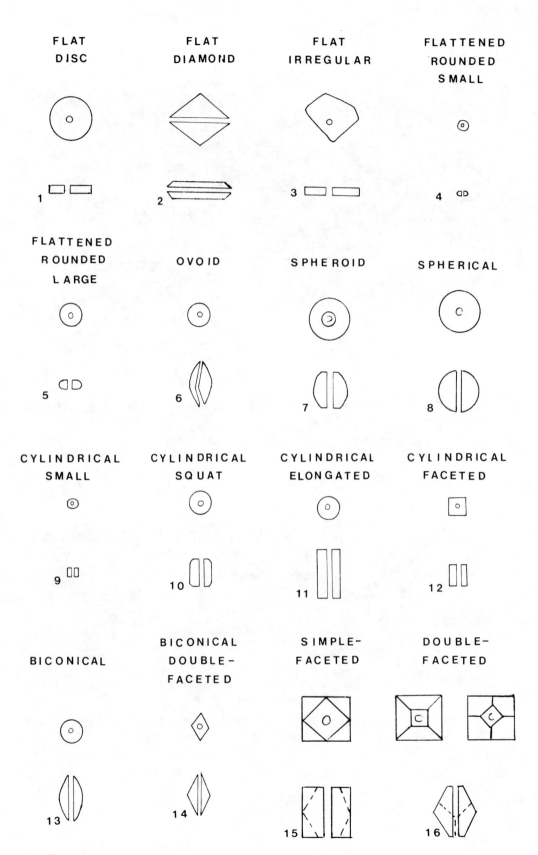

FLAT DISC

FLAT DIAMOND

FLAT IRREGULAR

FLATTENED ROUNDED SMALL

1

2

3

4

FLATTENED ROUNDED LARGE

OVOID

SPHEROID

SPHERICAL

5

6

7

8

CYLINDRICAL SMALL

CYLINDRICAL SQUAT

CYLINDRICAL ELONGATED

CYLINDRICAL FACETED

9

10

11

12

BICONICAL

BICONICAL DOUBLE-FACETED

SIMPLE-FACETED

DOUBLE-FACETED

13

14

15

16

Pl. 57.   An analysis of the bead types found in the Hesi cemetery. Drawings by Ruth Stewart.

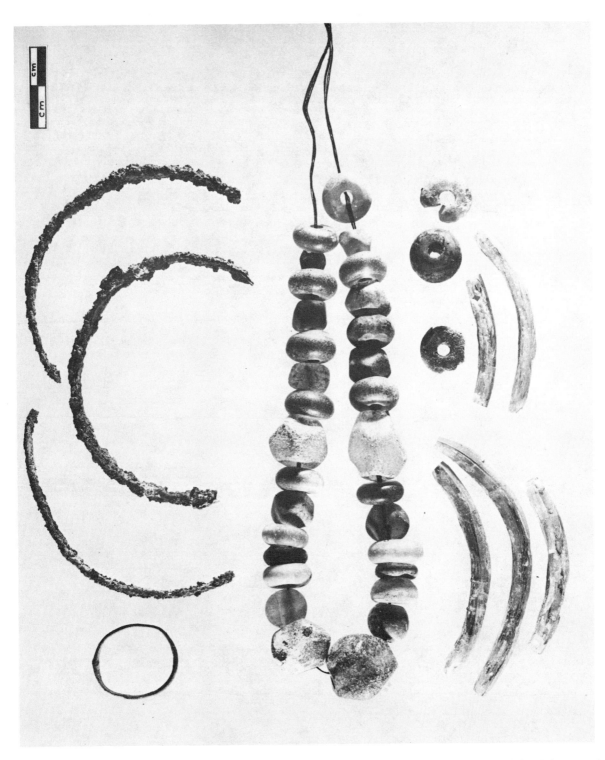

Pl. 58.   A typical collection of jewelry from a single grave. The burial (I.22.207; Type II.L.4.h) is that of an adult female in a capped grave, lying in the extended position on the right side, looking southwest. Photo by E. Nitowski.

215

Pl. 59.   Illustrations of flat beads.

Pl. 59a.   Nos. 2-4, 7-9, 11, 13, 15, 17, 19, 21-23, 25, 27, 29, 31, 33, 35-37, 40-41 illustrate Form 1: flat disc beads. Other forms illustrated are: Forms 7: spheroid beads (10, 12, 14, 16, 18, 20, 24, 26, 28, 30, 32, 34); Form 10: cylindrical, squat beads (1, 5, 42); Form 13: biconical beads (39); Form 14: biconical double-faceted beads (6); and Form 16: double-faceted beads (38). No. 43 is a mother-of-pearl pendant. The collection comes from the burial of an adult female in a simple earth grave, extended on the back, looking south (I.51.136B, Type I.L.2.g). Photo by E. Nitowski.

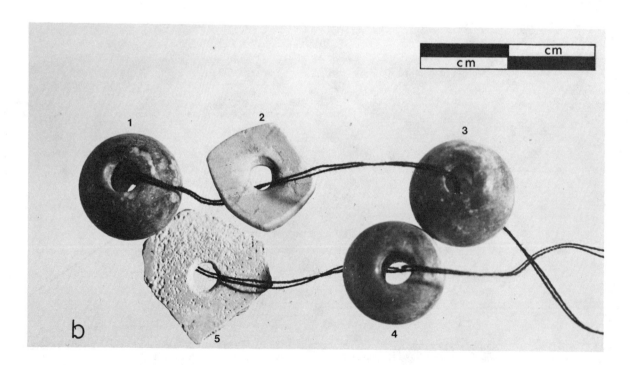

Pl. 59b.   Nos. 2, 5 illustrate Form 3: flat, irregular beads. Also illustrated is Form 7: spheroid beads (1, 3, 4). The collection comes from the burial of an adult female in a simple earth grave, extended on the back, looking southeast (I.41.085A, Type I.L.2.f). Photo by W. E. Nassau.

Pl. 60. Illustrations of Form 2: flat, diamond-shaped beads.

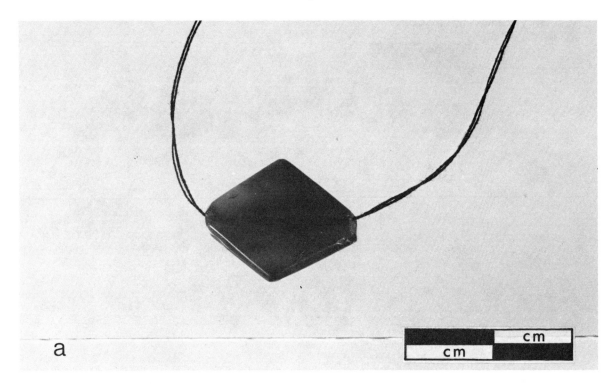

Pl. 60a. A carnelian bead of Form 2 from the burial of an infant in a capped grave, flexed on the right side, looking southeast (I.41.035, Type II.C.8.f). Photo by J. Hertel.

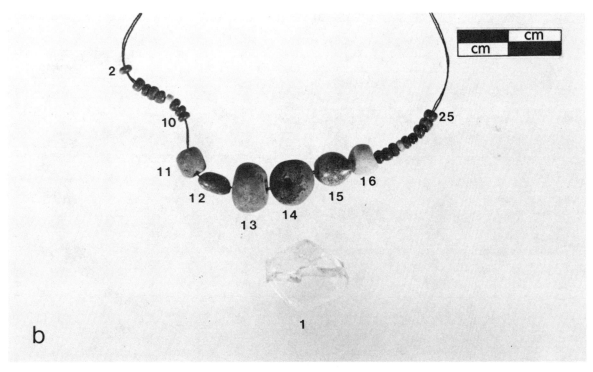

Pl. 60b. No. 1 is a quartz bead of Form 2. Also illustrated are: Form 4: flattened-rounded, small beads (2-6, 8-10, 17-19, 21-25); Form 5: flattened-rounded, large beads (13, 14); Form 6: ovoid beads (12, 15); Form 7: spheroid beads (16); Form 9: cylindrical, small beads (7, 20); Form 12: cylindrical, faceted beads (11). The collection is from the burial of a child in a capped and lined grave, extended on the back, looking southeast (I.41.056, Type III.F.2.f). Photo by J. Hertel.

217

Pl. 61.   Illustrations of Form 4: flattened-rounded, small beads.

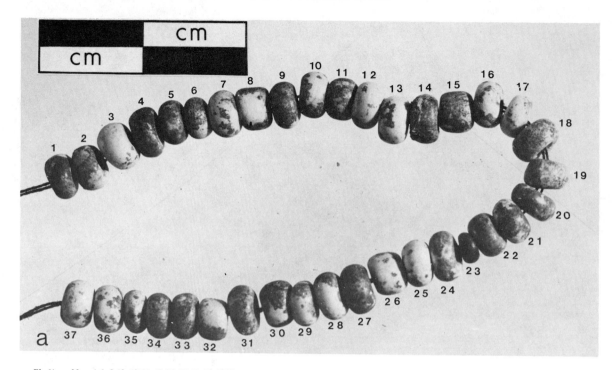

Pl. 61a.   Nos. 1-6, 9-10, 12-14, 17-25, 27-31, 33-37 illustrate Form 4: flattened-rounded, small beads. Also illustrated are: Form 7: spheroid beads (7, 11, 16), and Form 9: cylindrical, small beads (8, 15, 26, 32). The collection is from the burial of an infant in a capped grave, extended on the right side, looking southeast (I.41.115, Type II.C.4.f). Photo by W. E. Nassau.

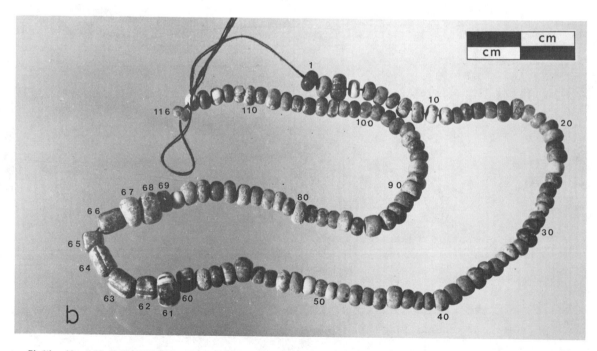

Pl. 61b.   Nos. 1-37, 40-59, 69-85, 87-91, 93-116 illustrate Form 4: flattened-rounded, small beads. Also illustrated are: Form 5: flattened-rounded, large beads (61, 67, 68); Form 9: cylindrical, small beads (38, 39, 86, 92); and Form 10: cylindrical, squat beads (60, 62-66). The collection is from the burial of an adult female in a lined grave without capstones, extended on the back, looking southeast (I.32.094, Type IV.L.2.f). Photo by W. E. Nassau.

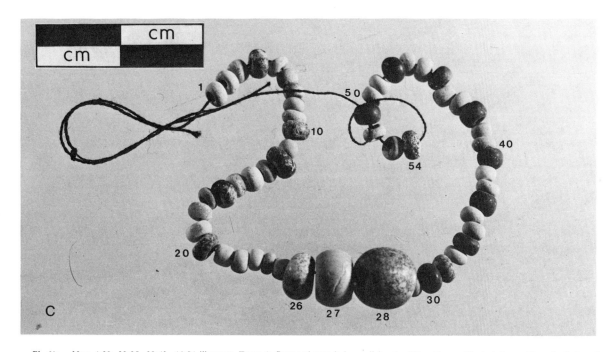

Pl. 61c.   Nos. 1-20, 22-25, 29-42, 46-54 illustrate Form 4: flattened-rounded, small beads. Other Forms illustrated are: Form 5: flattened-rounded, large beads (26, 27); Form 7: spheroid beads (28); and Form 9: cylindrical, small beads (21, 43-45). The collection is from the burial of an infant in a simple earth grave, extended on the back, looking east (I.51.013, Type I.C.2.e). Photo by W. E. Nassau.

Pl. 62.   Illustrations of Forms 5, 6, 7, and 8 beads.

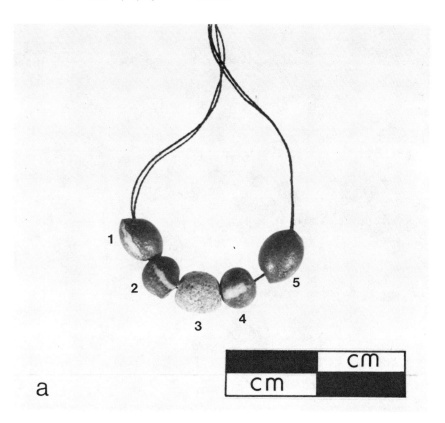

Pl. 62a.   No. 1 illustrates a Form 5: flattened-rounded, large bead. No. 6 is a Form 7: spheroid bead. Nos. 2, 3, and 5 are Form 8: spherical beads. Also illustrated is Form 15: simple-faceted beads (4). The collection is from the burial of an adult male in a capped grave, extended on the right side, looking southeast (I.12.054, Type II.K.4.f). Photo by W. E. Nassau.

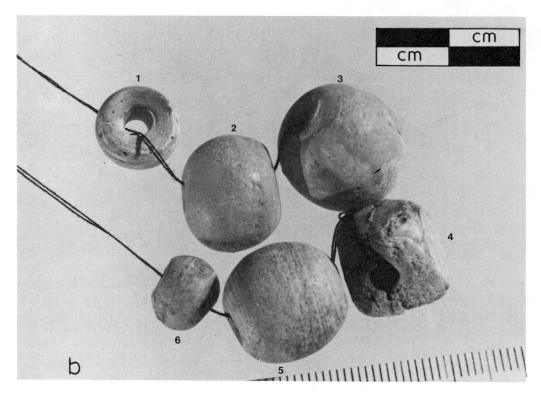

Pl. 62b.   All the beads in the collection are Form 6: ovoid beads. They are from the burial of an infant in a simple earth grave, flexed on the back, eye direction unknown (I.41.212, Type I.C.6.0). Photo by J. Hertel.

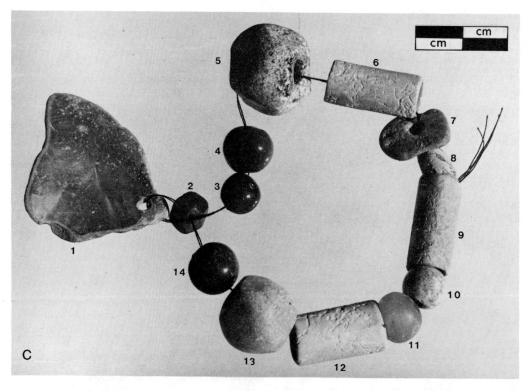

Pl. 62c.   Nos. 10, 11 illustrate Form 7: spheroid beads; nos. 3, 4, 11 illustrate Form 8: spherical beads. Also illustrated are Form 1: flat disc beads (7); Form 10: cylindrical, squat beads (8); Form 11: cylindrical, elongated beads (6, 9, 12); Form 14: biconical, double-faceted beads (2); and Form 16: double-faceted beads (5, 13). No. 1 is a mother-of-pearl pendant. The collection comes from a badly disturbed burial in a simple earth grave (I.12.059, Type I.O.0.f). Photo by W. E. Nassau.

220

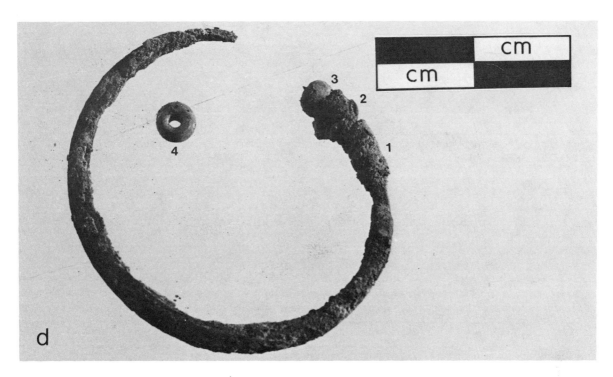

Pl. 62d.   Three Form 7: spheroid beads (nos. 2, 3, 4) associated with a piece of jewelry, probably an earring. The object is from the burial of an adult female in a capped and lined grave, flexed on the right side, looking southeast (I.22.079, Type III.L.8.f). Photo by W. E. Nassau.

Pl. 63.   Illustrations of Forms 9 and 10 beads.

Pl. 63a.   Copper beads of Form 9: cylindrical, small beads from the burial of an adult female in a capped grave, extended on the back, looking southeast (I.32.049, Type II.L.4.f). Photo by W. E. Nassau.

221

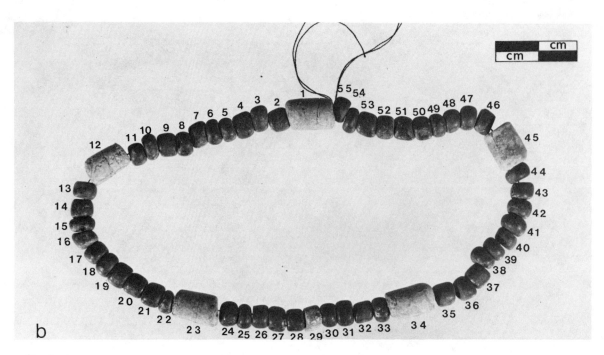

Pl. 63b.   Nos. 2-4, 7, 9, 11, 13-14, 20-21, 26-32, 35-37 illustrate Form 10:cylindrical, squat beads. Other forms illustrated are: Form 5: flattened-rounded, large beads (5-6, 8, 10, 15-16, 22, 24-25, 33, 38-44, 46-55); and Form 11: cylindrical, elongated beads (1, 12, 23, 34, 45). The collection is from the burial of an adult female in a capped grave, extended on the back, looking southeast (I.4.007, Type II.L.2.f). Photo by T. Rosen.

Pl. 64.   Illustrations of Forms 10 and 11 beads.

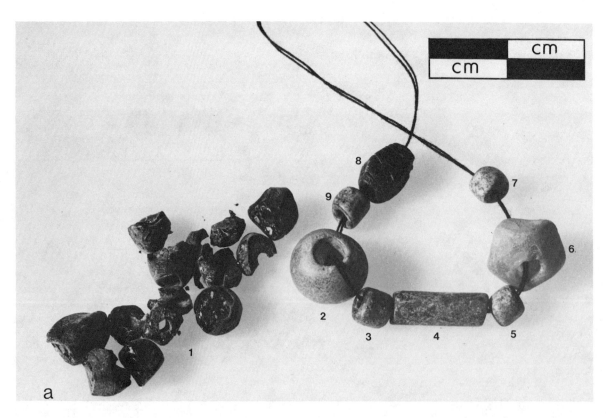

Pl. 64a.   Nos. 3, 5, 7, 9 illustrate Form 10: cylindrical, squat beads. No. 4 illustrates a Form 11: cylindrical, elongated bead. Also illustrated are Form 7: spheroid beads (2); Form 14: biconical double-faceted beads (1, 8) and Form 16: double-faceted beads (6). The collection is from the burial of a child in a simple earth grave, extended on the back, looking southeast (I.41.076, Type I.F.2.f). Photo by W. E. Nassau.

222

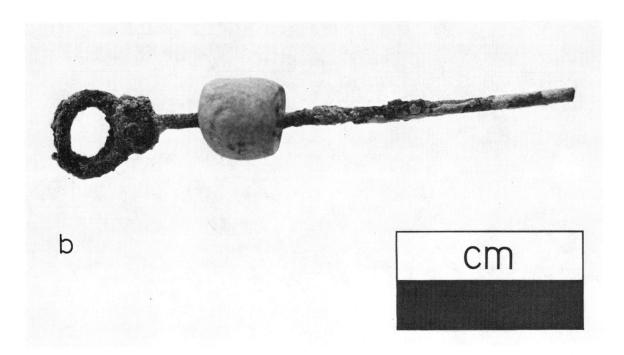

Pl. 64b.   A bronze pin with a Form 10 bead from the burial of an infant in a capped and lined grave, extended on the back, looking up (I.41.051, Type III.C.2.a). Photo by T. Rosen.

Pl. 65.   Illustrations of Forms 13 and 14 beads.

Pl. 65a.   A silver Form 13: biconical bead from the burial of an infant in a simple earth grave, flexed on the right side, looking south (I.12.033, Type I.C.8.g). Photo by W. E. Nassau.

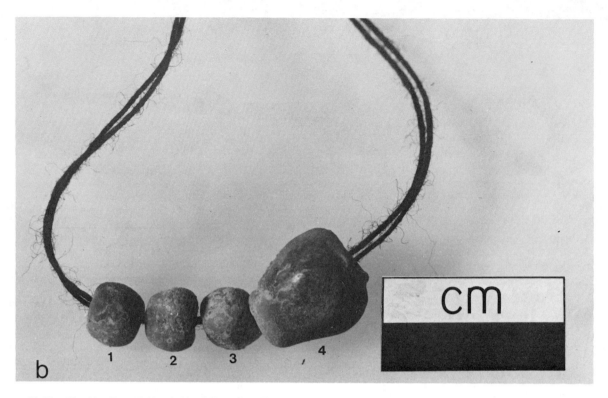

Pl. 65b.   No. 4 is a Form 13: biconical bead. Nos. 1-3 are Form 7: spheroid beads. The collection is probably from the throw-out from Burial I.41.063. Photo by W. E. Nassau.

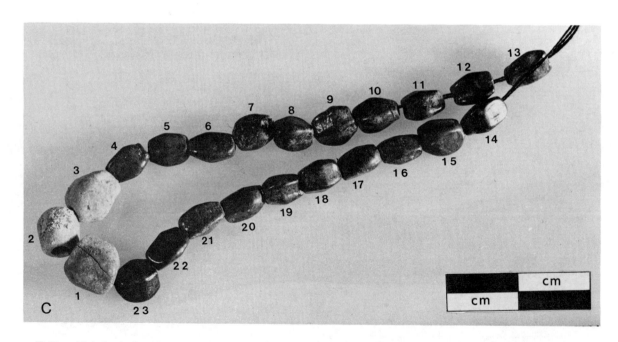

Pl. 65c.   All the beads shown belong to Form 14: biconical, double-faceted beads. The collection is from the burial of an adult male in a capped grave, extended on the right side, looking south (I.51.067, Type II.K.4.g). Photo by W. E. Nassau.

Pl. 66.   Illustrations of Forms 15 and 16 beads.

Pl. 66a.   No. 24 is a Form 15: simple-faceted bead. Also illustrated are Form 1: flat disc beads (7, 14, 21, 22); Form 5: flattened-rounded, large beads (2, 11); Form 7: spheroid beads (1, 4, 8, 12); Form 8: spherical beads (9); Form 10: cylindrical, squat beads (5-6, 10, 13, 15, 20); and Form 14: biconical, double-faceted beads (3, 16-19). No. 23 is a mother-of-pearl pendant. The collection is from the burial of an adult female in a capped grave, flexed on the left side, looking south (I.32.046, Type II.L.7.g). Photo by W. E. Nassau.

Pl. 66b.   Nos. 2-4, 6, 9-11, 15-18 are Form 16: double-faceted beads. Also illustrated are Form 1: flat disc beads (8); Form 7: spheroid beads (5, 7, 13); Form 8: spherical beads (12); Form 13: biconical beads (19); and Form 14: biconical double-faceted beads (1). No. 14 is a carnelian chip bored as a bead. The collection is from the burial of an adult female in a capped and lined grave, flexed on the right side, looking southeast (I.22.015, Type III.L.8.f). Photo by J. Hertel.

Pl. 67.   Illustrations of shell beads.

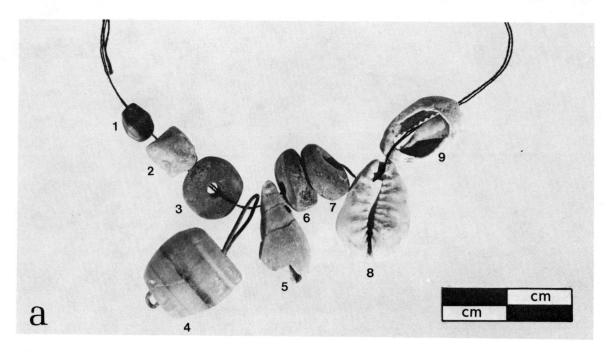

Pl. 67a.   A snail shell (5) and two cowrie shells (8, 9), used as beads. Also illustrated are Form 1: flat disc beads (6, 7); Form 5: flattened-rounded, large beads (3); Form 10: cylindrical, squat beads (4); Form 12: cylindrical, faceted beads (2); and Form 14: biconical double-faceted beads (1). The collection is from the burial of an adult female in a capped grave, looking south (I.11.022, Type II.L.0.g). Photo by J. Hertel.

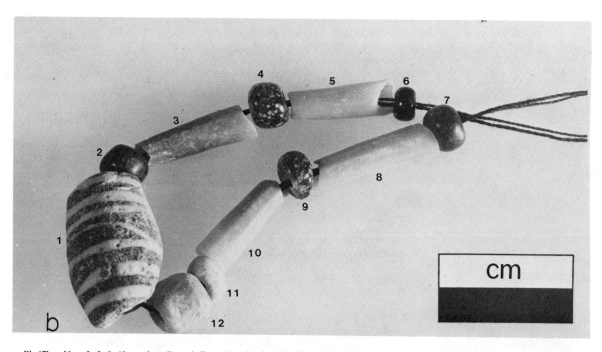

Pl. 67b.   Nos. 3, 5, 8, 10 are dentalium shells used as beads. Also illustrated are Form 4: flattened-rounded, small beads (6, 9, 11); Form 7: spheroid beads (4, 7); Form 9: cylindrical, small beads (2); and Form 10: cylindrical, squat beads (1). The beads are from the throw-out from Burial I.32.018. Photo by W. E. Nassau.

Pl. 68.   Illustrations of double-bored objects.

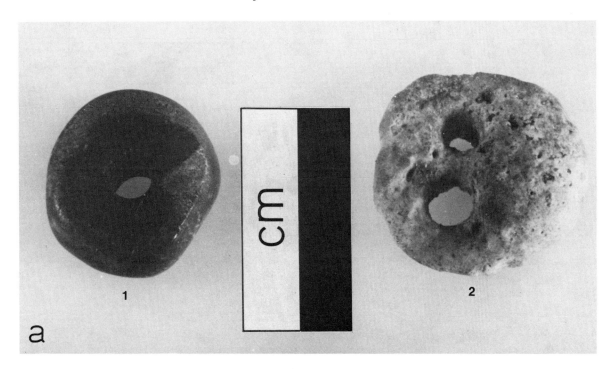

Pl. 68a.   No. 2 is a double-bored, button-like frit object. No. 1 is a Form 5: flattened-rounded, large bead. Both objects come from the burial of an infant in a capped grave, extended on the right side, looking southeast (I.22.060, Type II.C.4.f). Photo by W. E. Nassau.

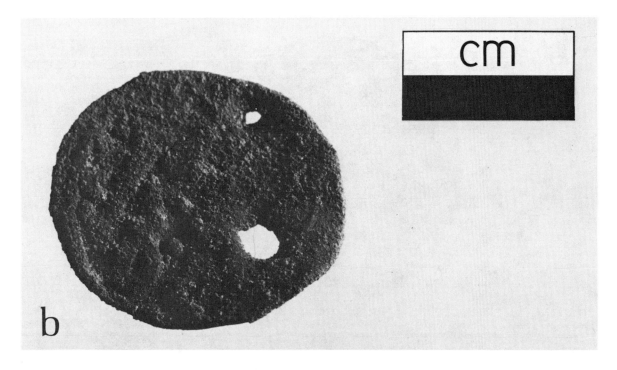

Pl. 68b.   Double-bored copper/bronze coin from the burial of an infant in a simple earth grave, flexed on the right side, looking southwest (I.51.028, Type I.C.8.h). Photo by W. E. Nassau.

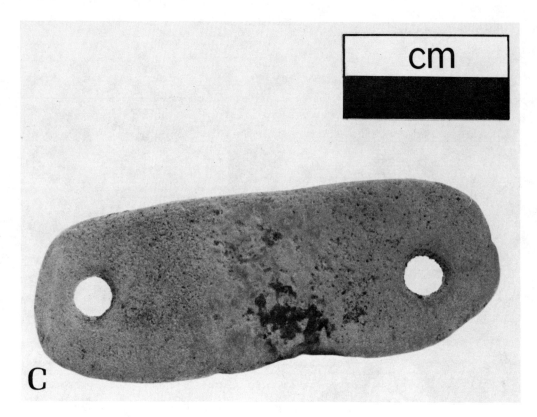

Pl. 68c.   Double-bored mother-of-pearl object from the burial of an infant in a capped and lined grave, extended on the back, looking up (I.41.051, Type III.C.2.a). Photo by T. Rosen.

Pl. 69.   Pendants.

Pl. 69a.   Single-bored silver coin from the burial of an adult in a capped grave (I.21.015, Type II.M.0.0). Photo by T. Rosen.

228

b

Pl. 69b.   Single-bored copper/bronze coin from the burial of an infant in a capped grave, extended on the right side, looking southeast (I.22.060, Type II.C.4.f). Photo by W. E. Nassau.

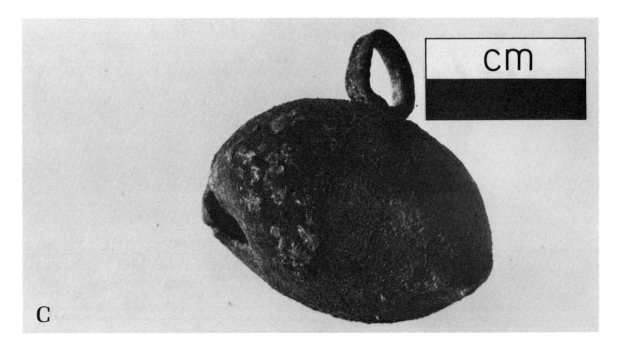

c

Pl. 69c.   Copper/bronze bell-shaped pendant from the burial of a child in a simple earth grave, extended on the right side, looking southeast (I.41.076, Type I.F.2.f). Photo by W. E. Nassau.

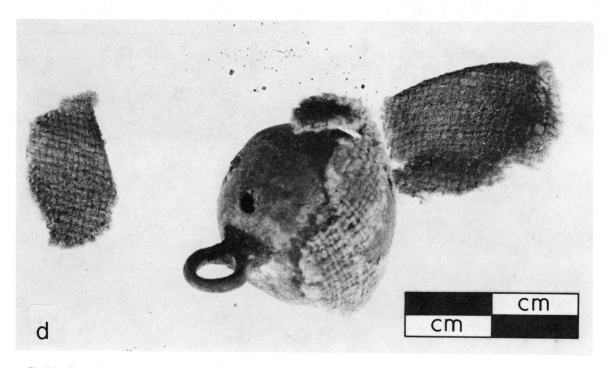

Pl. 69d. Copper/bronze bell-shaped pendant with cloth adhering from the burial of an adult female in a capped grave, looking south (I.11.022, Type II.L.0.g). Photo by T. Rosen.

Pl. 70. Unbored copper/bronze disc from the burial of an adult in a simple earth grave, extended on the front, looking down (I.51.134, Type I.M.1.b). Photo by E. Nitowski.

230

Pl. 71. Simple band rings.

Pl. 71a. Simple band ring in iron from the burial of a child in a capped and lined grave, extended on the back, looking south (I.41.016, III.F.2.g). Photo by T. Rosen.

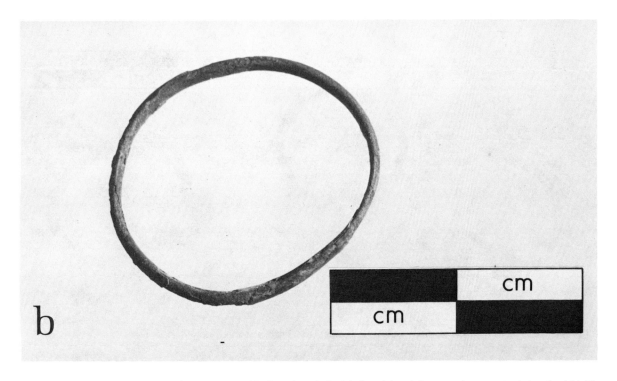

Pl. 71b. Simple band ring in copper/bronze, plated with silver, from the burial of an adult male in a capped grave, extended on the right side, looking southeast (I.12.054, Type II.K.4.f). Photo by W. E. Nassau.

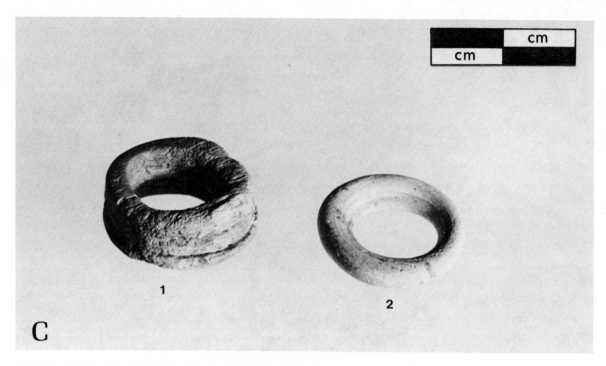

Pl. 71c.   Two simple band rings in bone from the burial of an adult female in a capped grave, looking south (I.11.022, Type II.L.0.g). Photo by J. Hertel.

Pl. 72.   Center-disc rings.

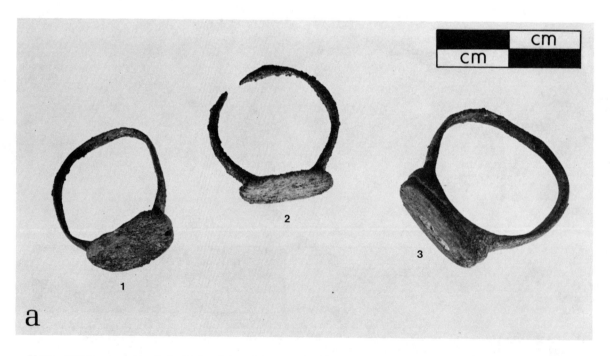

Pl. 72a.   Three specimens from the burial of a male juvenile in a capped and lined grave, extended on the back (I.41.058, Type III.G.2.0). Photo by J. Hertel.

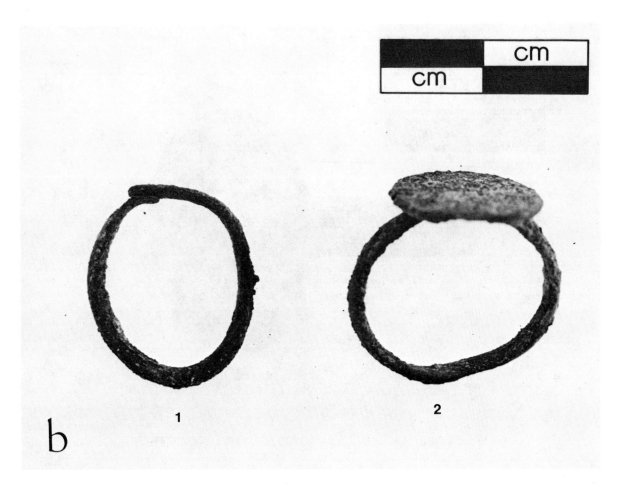

Pl. 72b.   No. 2 is from the burial of an adult female in a simple earth grave, looking south (I.11.026A, Type I.L.0.g). No. 1 is a simple band ring in copper/bronze. Photo by T. Rosen.

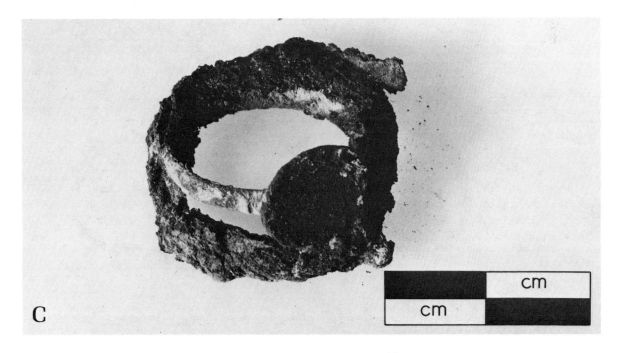

Pl. 72c.   Iron ring and copper/bronze ring fused together, from the burial of an adult female in a capped grave, flexed on the left side, looking south (I.32.046, Type II.L.7.g). Photo by W. E. Nassau.

233

Pl. 73. Center-disc rings.

Pl. 73a. A copper/bronze ring from the burial of an adult in a capped grave (I.21.013, Type II.M.0.0). Photo by T. Rosen.

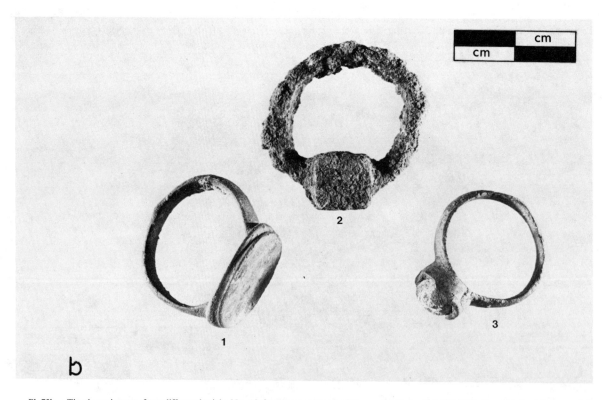

Pl. 73b. The three rings are from different burials. No. 1 is from a cut on the wadi face east of Area 51 (I.51A.002). Since this burial was not fully recorded, it does not appear in the indices. No. 2 is from I.31.300, the throw-out from gravedigging. It cannot be assigned to a specific burial. No. 3 is from the burial of an adult female in a capped grave, extended on the right side, looking south (I.32.145, Type II.L.4.g). Photo by E. Nitowski.

Pl. 74.   Toe rings.

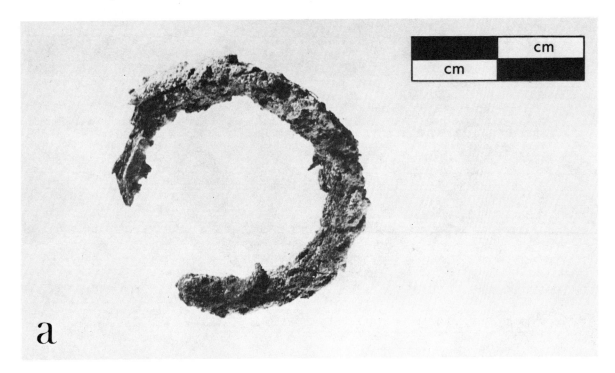

Pl. 74a.   An iron ring from the burial of an adult in a simple earth grave (I.51.135, Type I.M.0.0). Photo by E. Nitowski.

Pl. 74b.   A copper/bronze ring from the burial of an infant in a simple earth grave, extended on the back, looking east (I.41.064, Type I.C.2.e). Photo by W. E. Nassau.

c

Pl. 74c.   A copper/bronze ring from the burial of an adult female in a capped and lined grave, flexed on the right side, looking southeast (I.22.079, Type III.L.8.f). Photo by W. E. Nassau.

Pl. 75.   Earrings.

a

Pl. 75a.   A ring with cloth fragments and a bead from the burial of an adult female in a capped and lined grave, flexed on the right side, looking southeast (I.22.079, Type III.L.8.f). Photo by W. E. Nassau.

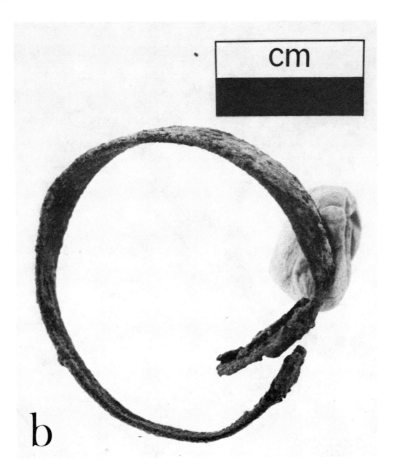

Pl. 75b.   A copper/bronze ring from I.32.005, the throw-out from gravedigging. The object cannot be assigned to a specific burial. Photo by
T. Rosen.

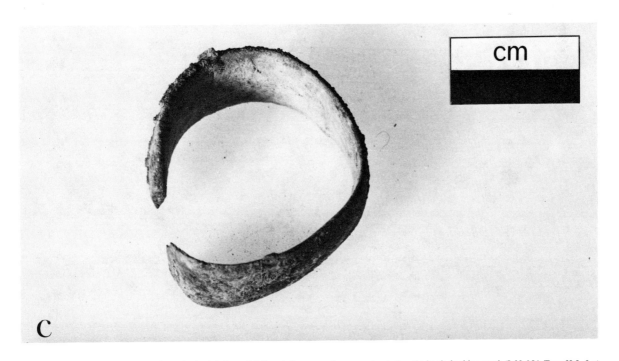

Pl. 75c.   A copper/bronze ring from the burial of an adult female in a capped grave, extended on the back, looking south (I.32.056, Type II.L.2.g).
Photo by W. E. Nassau.

237

Pl. 76. Undecorated glass bracelets.

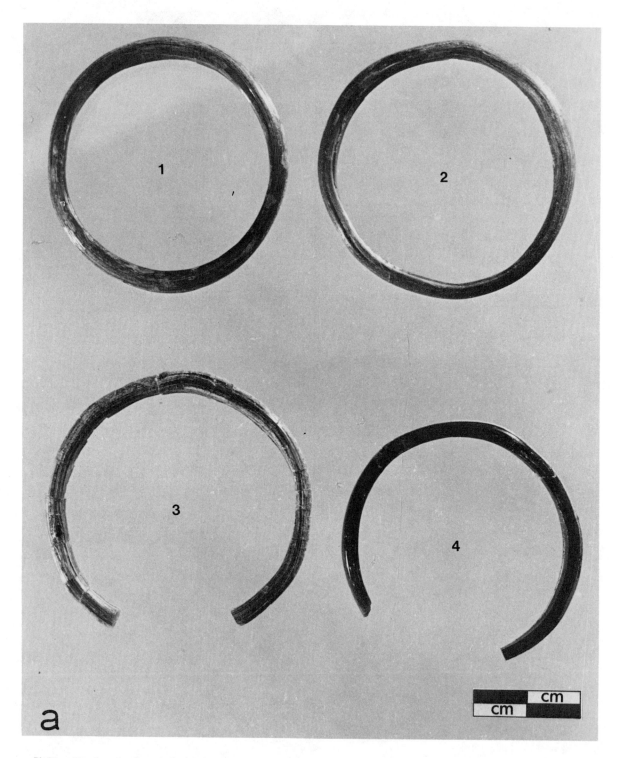

Pl. 76a. Four bracelets from the burial of an infant in a capped grave, extended on the back, looking up (I.12.127, Type II.C.2.a). Photo by E. Nitowski.

238

Pl. 76b.   Bracelet from the burial of an adult female in a capped grave, extended on the back, looking south (I.32.056, Type II.L.2.g). Photo by W. E. Nassau.

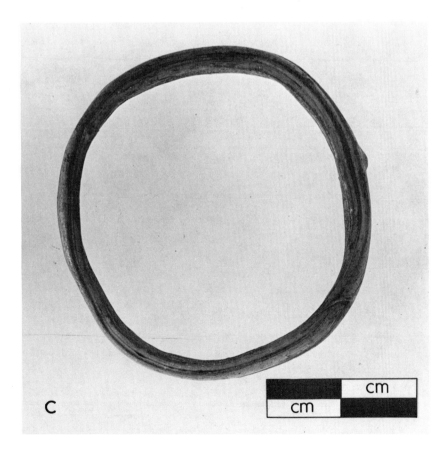

Pl. 76c.   Bracelet from the burial of an adult in a capped and lined grave (I.21.026A, Type III.M.0.0). Photo by T. Rosen.

239

Pl. 77.   Decorated glass bracelets.

Pl. 77a.   Bracelet from the burial of an infant in a lined but uncapped grave, extended on the back (I.41.065, IV.C.2.0). Photo by W. E. Nassau.

Pl. 77b.   Bracelet from the burial of a child in a simple earth grave, extended on the back, looking southeast (I.22.119; Type I.F.2.f). Photo by W. E. Nassau.

240

Pl. 78.   Copper/bronze bracelet of the continuous band type, from I.21.077, throw-out from gravedigging. The bracelet cannot be assigned to a specific burial. Photo by T. Rosen.

Pl. 79.   Copper/bronze bracelets of the simple open type.

a

Pl. 79a.   Wide thin band with cloth adhering from the burial of an adult female in a capped grave, extended on the right side, looking southeast (I.32.049, Type II.L.4.f). Photo by W. E. Nassau.

241

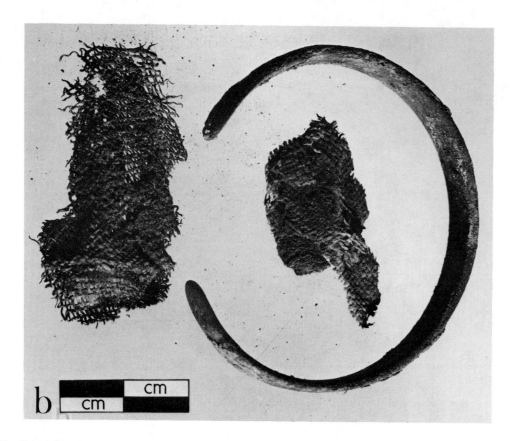

Pl. 79b.   Rounded band with detached cloth from the burial of an adult male in a capped grave, extended on the right side, looking southeast (I.12.054, Type II.K.4.f). Photo by W. E. Nassau.

Pl. 80.   Copper/bronze bracelets of the open, snake-decorated type.

Pl. 80a.   Snake bracelet with cloth, bones, and copper/bronze discs from the burial of a child in a simple earth grave, looking west (I.21.017A, I.F.0.i). Photo by T. Rosen.

Pl. 80b.   Twisted snake bracelet from the burial of an adult female in a capped and lined grave, extended on the back (I.32.048, Type III.L.2.0). Photo by W. E. Nassau.

Pl. 81.   Iron bracelets.

Pl. 81a.   Heavy continuous band from the burial of an infant in a simple earth grave, flexed on the right side, looking southwest (I.51.028, I.C.8.h). Photo by W. E. Nassau.

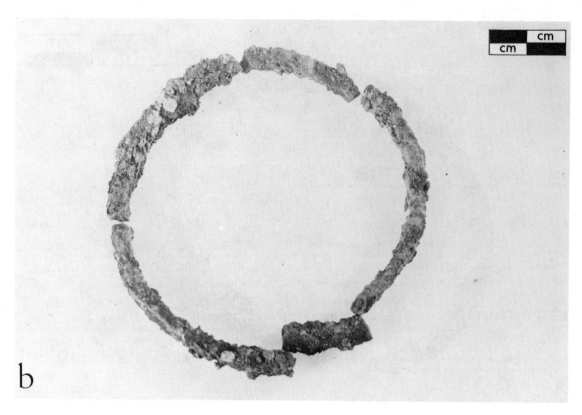

b

Pl. 81b.   Thin continuous band from the burial of an adult female in a capped grave, extended on the back, looking south (I.32.056, II.L.2.g). Photo by W. E. Nassau.

c

Pl. 81c.   Apparently open band from the burial of an adult male in a capped grave, extended on the right side, looking southeast (I.12.054, Type II.K.4.f). Photo by W. E. Nassau.

Pl. 82.   Three *abārīq in situ* in the shaft of Burial I.4.020, just above the capstones. A and B are cappers; C, D, and E are the *abārīq*. The burial is that of an adult male in a capped grave, extended on the back, looking southeast (II.K.2.f). Photo by T. Rosen.

Pl. 83.   The six *abārīq* from Burial I.4.020. Photos by R. Doermann.

Pl. 83—Continued. The six *abārīq* from Burial I.4.020. Photos by R. Doermann.

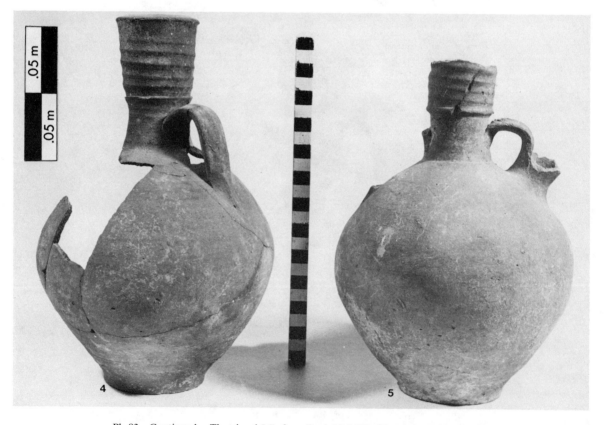

Pl. 83—Continued. The six *abārīq* from Burial I.4.020. Photos by R. Doermann.

Pl. 83—Continued. The six *abārīq* from Burial I.4.020. Photos by R. Doermann.

Pl. 84. The jar which contained Burial I.41.019, an infant newly or prematurely born. Photo by R. Doermann.

247

Pl. 85. Side-spouted jar from Burial VI.P-1a.001, the interment of an infant in a simple earth grave (I.C.0.0). Photo by E. Nitowski.

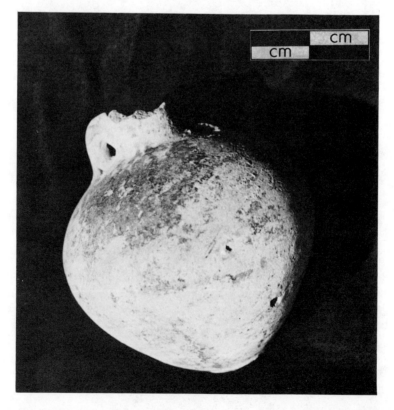

Pl. 86. Piriform juglet from the burial of an infant in a simple earth grave, extended on the back, looking east (I.51.013, Type I.C.2.e). Photo by W. E. Nassau.

248

Pl. 87.   Piriform juglet *in situ* in the east end of Burial I.51.013. The skeleton has already been removed. Photo by W. E. Nassau.

249

Pl. 88.   Drawings of (a) the piriform juglet of Pl. 86 and (b) the side-spouted vessel of Pl. 85. Drawings by J. Hammond.

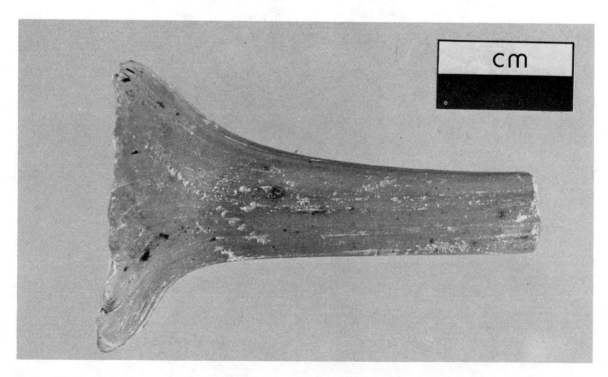

Pl. 89.   The handle of a glass vessel from the burial of an adult male in a capped grave, looking south (V.P-1e.005, Type II.K.0.g).
Photo by E. Nitowski.

250